Basic Knowledge of Computer and ICT

Basic Knowledge of Computer and ICT

Edited by
Dr. G. VISVANATHAN
Professor, Department of Education,
Annamalai University, Tamil Nadu
and
Dr.S.K.PANNEER SELVAM
Assistant Professor, Department of Education
Bharathidasan University, Tamil Nadu

RANDOM
RANDOM PUBLICATIONS
NEW DELHI (INDIA)

Basic Knowledge of Computer and ICT

ISBN 978-93-5111-313-3

Published in 2014 in India by

RANDOM PUBLICATIONS

4376-A/4B, Gali Murari Lal, Ansari Road

NewDelhi-110 002

Phone : +9111-43580356, 011-23289044

e-mail : sales@randompublications.com

info@randompublications.com

Reprinted 2025

Type Setting by : Shah Computer Graphics, Delhi-110094

Digitally Printed at: Replika Press Pvt. Ltd.

Contents

1

ICT in Education

INTRODUCTION

Globalization and technological change processes that have accelerated in tandem over the past fifteen years have created a new global economy "powered by technology, fueled by information and driven by knowledge." The emergence of this new global economy has serious implications for the nature and purpose of educational institutions. As the half-life of information continues to shrink and access to information continues to grow exponentially, schools cannot remain mere venues for the transmission of a prescribed set of information from teacher to student over a fixed period of time. Rather, schools must promote "learning to learn," i.e., the acquisition of knowledge and skills that make possible continuous learning over the lifetime. "The illiterate of the 21st century," according to futurist Alvin Toffler, "will not be those who cannot read and write, but those who cannot learn, unlearn, and relearn."

Education is one of the main keys to economic development and improvements in human welfare. As global economic competition grows sharper, education becomes an important source of competitive advantage, closely linked to economic growth, and a way for countries to attract jobs and investment. In addition, education appears to be one of the key determinants of lifetime earnings. Countries therefore frequently see raising educational attainment as a way of tackling poverty and deprivation. In developing countries, education is also linked to a whole batch of indicators of human development. Education of women influences the health of children and family size. The experience of Asian economies in particular in the past two decades has demonstrated the benefits that public investment in education can bring. To eradicate all the social problems in the society, it is only possible through education in general and quality education in particular. More educational reforms are necessary to attain our goals.

Information and communication technologies (ICTs) which include radio and television, as well as newer digital technologies such as computers and the Internet have been touted as potentially powerful enabling tools for educational change and reform.

ICT – ORIGIN & DEFINITION

Information and communications technology, usually called ICT, is often used as a synonym for information technology (IT) but is usually a more general term that stresses the role of communications (telephone lines and wireless signals) in modern information technology. ICT consists of all technical means used to handle information and aid communication, including computer and network hardware as well as necessary software. In other words, ICT consists of IT as well as telephony, broadcast media, and all types of audio and video processing and transmission. The expression was first used in 1997 in a report by Dennis Stevenson to the UK government and promoted by the new National Curriculum documents for the UK in 2000.

ICT is often used in the context of "ICT roadmap" to indicate the path that an organization will take with their ICT needs. The term ICT is now also used to refer to the merging (convergence) of telephone networks with computer networks through a single cabling or link system. There are large economic incentives (huge cost savings due to elimination of the telephone network) to merge the telephone network with the computer network system.

IMPORTANCE OF ICT IN EDUCATION

In developing countries, there is frequently a shortage of qualified school teachers. People may live in scattered communities in rural areas. Money for books and teaching materials may be scarce. In wealthier countries, money is also a problem: in particular, the cost of university education has risen sharply, and students are increasingly expected to meet all or part of the cost directly. But, at the level of higher education and training, the problem is often also one of time. Students who are already in full-time employment find it hard to take part in a university course offered at conventional times of day. Finally, employers, keen to train staff, are often acutely conscious of the costs of taking people away from their main job in order to attend training courses. They are therefore eager for more efficient and flexible ways to deliver information to employees.

All these factors have encouraged an interest in the use of information and communications technologies (ICT) to deliver education and training. Computers began to appear in school and university classrooms in the more advanced countries around the early 1980s. Broadband connections to schools and universities became commonplace in wealthier countries in the second half of the 1990s. In developing countries, experience is more limited. This is not necessarily a bad thing, as it should allow those countries to learn from the investments of richer countries.

Initially, educators saw the use of ICTs in the classroom mainly as a way to teach computer literacy. Most now see a broader role: that of delivering many kinds of learning at lower cost and with higher quality than traditional methods of teaching allow. In addition, schools and universities increasingly use ICTs, as do other large organizations, to reduce the costs and improve the efficiency of administration.

ICTS IN EDUCATION

In recent years there has been a groundswell of interest in how computers and the Internet can best be harnessed to improve the efficiency and effectiveness of education at all levels and in both formal and non-formal settings. But ICTs are more than just these technologies; older technologies such as the telephone, radio and television, although now given less attention, have a longer and richer history as instructional tools. For instance, radio and television have for over forty years been used for open and distance learning, although print remains the cheapest, most accessible and therefore most dominant delivery mechanism in both developed and developing countries. The use of computers and the Internet is still in its infancy in developing countries, if these are used at all, due to limited infrastructure and the attendant high costs of access.

Moreover, different technologies are typically used in combination rather than as the sole delivery mechanism. For instance, the Kothmale Community Radio Internet uses both radio broadcasts and computer and Internet technologies to facilitate the sharing of information and provide educational opportunities in a rural community in Sri Lanka. The Open University of the United Kingdom (UKOU), established in 1969 as the first educational institution in the world wholly dedicated to open and distance learning, still relies heavily on print-based materials supplemented by radio, television and, in recent years, online programming. Similarly, the Indira Gandhi National Open University in India combines the use of print, recorded audio and video, broadcast radio and television, and audio conferencing technologies.

Education policymakers and planners must first of all be clear about what educational outcomes (as discussed above) are being targeted. These broad goals should guide the choice of technologies to be used and their modalities of use. The potential of each technology varies according to how it is used. Haddad and Draxler identify at least five levels of technology use in education: presentation, demonstration, drill and practice, interaction, and collaboration. Each of the different ICTs print, audio/video cassettes, radio and TV broadcasts, computers or the Internet may be used for presentation and demonstration, the most basic of the five levels. Except for video technologies, drill and practice may likewise be performed using the whole range of technologies. On the other hand, networked computers and the Internet are the ICTs that enable interactive and collaborative learning best; their full potential as educational tools will remain unrealized if they are used merely for presentation or demonstration.

In general there are many tools used by teachers and students in educational institutions. The popular technologies used in educational institutions are given below:

Radio and Television

Radio and television have been used widely as educational tools since the 1920s and the 1950s, respectively. There are three general approaches to the use of radio and TV broadcasting in education:

- o Direct class teaching, where broadcast programming substitutes for teachers on a temporary basis;
- o School broadcasting, where broadcast programming provides complementary teaching and learning resources not otherwise available; and
- o General educational programming over community, national and international stations which provide general and informal educational opportunities.

Teleconferencing

Teleconferencing refers to "interactive electronic communication among people located at two or more different places". There are four types of teleconferencing based on the nature and extent of interactivity and the sophistication of the technology: 1) audio conferencing; 2) audio-graphic conferencing, 3) videoconferencing; and 4) Web-based conferencing. *Audio conferencing* involves the live (real-time) exchange of voice messages over a telephone network. When low-bandwidth text and still images such as graphs, diagrams or pictures can also be exchanged along with voice messages, then this type of conferencing is called audio graphic. Non-moving visuals are added using a computer keyboard or by drawing/writing on a graphics tablet or whiteboard. *Video-conferencing* allows the exchange not just of voice and graphics but also of moving images. Videoconferencing technology does not use telephone lines but either a satellite link or television network (broadcast/cable). *Web-based conferencing*, as the name implies, involves the transmission of text, and graphic, audio and visual media via the Internet; it requires the use of a computer with a browser and communication can be both synchronous and asynchronous.

Teleconferencing is used in both formal and non-formal learning contexts to facilitate teacher-learner and learner-learner discussions, as well as to access experts and other resource persons remotely. In open and distance learning, teleconferencing is a useful tool for providing direct instruction and learner support, minimizing learner isolation. For instance, an audio graphic teleconferencing network between Tianjin Medical University in China and four outlying Tianjin municipalities was piloted in 1999 as part of a multi-year collaboration between Tianjin Medical University and the University of Ottawa School of Nursing funded by the Canadian International Development Agency. The audio graphic teleconferencing network aims to provide continuing education and academic upgrading to nurses in parts of Tianjin municipality where access to nursing education has been extremely limited. Other higher education institutions using teleconferencing in their online learning programs include the Open University of the United Kingdom, Unitar (University Tun Abdul Ruzak) in Malaysia, Open University of Hong Kong, and Indira Gandhi National Open University.

Computer and Internet

There are three general approaches to the instructional use of computers and the Internet, namely:

1) Learning about computers and the Internet, in which technological literacy is the end goal;

2) Learning with computers and the Internet, in which the technology facilitates learning across the curriculum; and
3) Learning through computers and the Internet, integrating technological skills development with curriculum applications

Learning with the technology means focusing on how the technology can be the means to learning ends across the curriculum. It includes:

- Presentation, demonstration, and the manipulation of data using productivity tools
- Use of curriculum-specific applications types such as educational games, drill and practice, simulations, tutorials, virtual laboratories, visualizations and graphical representations of abstract concepts, musical composition, and expert systems
- Use of information and resources on CD-ROM or online such as encyclopedia, interactive maps and atlases, electronic journals and other references

Technological literacy is required for learning with technologies to be possible, implying a two-step process in which students learn about the technologies before they can actually use them to learn. However, there have been attempts to integrate the two approaches.

Learning through computers and the Internet combines learning about them with learning with them. It involves learning the technological skills "just-in-time" or when the learner needs to learn them as he or she engages in a curriculum-related activity. For example, secondary school students who must present a report on the impact on their community of an increase in the price of oil for an Economics class may start doing research online, using spreadsheet and database programs to help organize and analyze the data they have collected, as well using a word processing application to prepare their written report.

Telecollaboration

Online learning involving students logging in to formal courses online is perhaps the most commonly thought of application of the Internet in education. However, it is by no means the only application. Web-based collaboration tools, such as email, list serves, message boards, real-time chat, and Web-based conferencing, connect learners to other learners, teachers, educators, scholars and researchers, scientists and artists, industry leaders and politicians in short, to any individual with access to the Internet who can enrich the learning process.

The organized use of Web resources and collaboration tools for curriculum appropriate purposes is called telecollaboration. Judi Harris defines *telecollaboration* as "an educational endeavor that involves people in different locations using Internet tools and resources to work together. Much educational telecollaboration is curriculum-based, teacher-designed, and teacher-coordinated. Most use e-mail to help participants communicate with each other. Many telecollaborative activities and projects have Web sites to support them." The best telecollaborative projects are those that are fully integrated into the curriculum and not just extra-curricular activities, those in which technology use enables activities that would not have been possible without it, and those that empower students to become active, collaborative, creative, integrative, and evaluative learners. There are currently hundreds of telecollaborative projects being implemented worldwide and many more that have either been completed or are in development.

One example is the Voices of Youth project developed by UNICEF. It encourages students to share their views on global issues, such as HIV/AIDS and child labour, with other youth and adults around the world through an electronic discussion forum. The Voices of Youth website also provides background information on the different discussion topics as well as resource materials to help teachers integrate the Voice of Youth discussions in their other classroom activities.

The International Telementor Program (ITP) links students with mentor-experts through email and discussion forums. Founded in 1995 with support from Hewlett Packard, ITP provides project-based online mentoring support to 5th to 12th grade and university students, especially from at-risk communities. The ITP telementor typically meets online with the student at least once every two weeks to answer questions, discuss key issues, recommend useful resources, and comment on student output. The teacher's role, on the other hand, is to provide support to both student and tele-mentor, monitor the telementoring process, and track the student's progress.

COMPONENTS OF ICT IN EDUCATION

Actual components of ICT in Education:

- Deployment
- Curriculum Development
- Content Availability
- Training and Usage Support
- Educational Management
- Maintenance and Technical Support

ACCESS & USES OF ICT IN EDUCATION

ICTs are a potentially powerful tool for extending educational opportunities, both formal and non-formal, scattered and rural populations, groups traditionally excluded from education due to cultural or social reasons such as ethnic minorities, girls and women, persons with disabilities, and the elderly, as well as all others who for reasons of cost or because of time constraints are unable to enroll on campus.

• **Anytime, anywhere.** One defining feature of ICTs is their ability to transcend time and space. ICTs make possible asynchronous learning, or learning characterized by a time lag between the delivery of instruction and its reception by learners. Online course materials, for example, may be accessed 24 hours a day, 7 days a week. ICT-based educational delivery (e.g., educational programming broadcast over radio or television) also dispenses with the need for all learners and the instructor to be in one physical location. Additionally, certain types of ICTs, such as teleconferencing technologies, enable instruction to be received simultaneously by multiple, geographically dispersed learners (i.e., synchronous learning).

• **Access to remote learning resources.** Teachers and learners no longer have to rely solely on printed books and other materials in physical media housed in libraries (and available in limited quantities) for their educational needs. With the Internet and the World Wide Web, a wealth of learning materials in almost every subject and in a variety of media can now be accessed from anywhere at any time of the day and by an unlimited number of people. This is particularly significant for many schools in developing countries, and even some in developed countries, that have limited and outdated library resources. ICTs also facilitate access to resource persons, mentors, experts, researchers, professionals, business leaders, and peers all over the world.

CONCLUSION

The development of any nation depends mainly on the standards of its educational institutions. Quality of education is important. So many innovative methods are using in education for effective teaching and learning. Information and communication technology is a boost not only for students but also for teachers for effective learning. The impact of ICT is very much on the students. We are living in the highly globalized and technological society. We are using advanced scientific applications. Lifelong learning is very easy with the help of ICT. We are getting any type of information within seconds throughout world. ICT in education is more important in the present scenario. ICT based curriculum is important. It is our duty to move from chalk & talk to ICT based education.

REFERENCES

1. MHRD, Govt. of India, New Delhi.
2. NCTE, New Curriculum Framework for Teacher Education, New Delhi.
3. Scholte, Jan Aart (2000), "Globalization: A Critical Introduction" (New York: St. Martin's).
4. SSA, Govt. of India, New Delhi.
5. UNESCO & MHRD, 'A Study of ICT Usage in 1000 Schools of India'.
6. Usha Vyasulu Reddi & Vineeta Sinha, 'UNESCO Meta-survey on the Use of Technologies in Education'.
7. Victoria L. Tinio, 'ICT in Education'.

2

ICT in Distance Education

DISTANCE EDUCATION IN INDIA

"The most important and urgent reform needed in education is to transform it, to endeavor to relate it to the life, needs and aspirations of the people and thereby make it the powerful instrument of social, economic and cultural transformation necessary for the realization of the national goals. For this purpose, education should be developed so as to increase productivity, achieve social and national integration, accelerate the process of modernization and cultivate social, moral and spiritual values."

The distance education system is a crucial vehicle in the sustained development of a knowledge society. Its potential for flexible education delivery, scope for self and life-long learning and cost effectiveness make it instrumental in meeting the needs of individual and communities at this juncture-in the rapid transition being made from the industrial to the information age.

However, as India prepares to face the knowledge challenges of the 21st century, higher education presents a rather dismal picture. According to the Ministry of Human Resource

Development, India, only about 10% of the population in the relevant age-group is enrolled in higher education, and a mere 5% graduate with degrees. With the rapid growth of the service, knowledge and associated sectors in the economy, it is imperative that the populace is equipped to contribute to and benefit from these developments. This requires a radical overhaul of the higher education system, with regard to access, enrolment and most importantly, quality. Failure to address this need and foster more inclusive growth will adversely affect India's future economic prospects and the welfare of its citizens.

Independent India has witnessed an upsurge in the growth of higher education. Yet from an international perspective, we are relatively slow, despite being steady in registering advancements in learning. Today India has the second largest education system in the world, next only to the USA. Yet, the total number of students represents hardly six percent of the relevant age group, i.e. 18-23 years, which is much below the average of developed countries which is about 47 percent. The gap is glaring. Hence the phenomenal challenge. The journey from being 'Good' to being 'Great' appears to be long and arduous. According to UGC-2006, there are 20 central universities, 217 state universities, 106 deemed universities and 10 private universities are working. 17625 colleges were established in India. The only way to increase the number of students in higher education is distance education. Now almost all universities in India are offering courses in distance mode. The cost of distance education is cheap when compared to education in regular mode.

IMPORTANCE OF 'ICT' IN DISTANCE EDUCATION

Globalization and technological changes have accelerated during the last fifteen years and have created a new global economy. One of the challenges facing the developing countries is preparing their governments and their people to participate in the globalization process as well as in the communication and information revolution. Alongside, there is a growing concern among policy makers, planners, business executives to make their societies competitive in the emergent global economy. Education is one of the main keys to economic development and improvements in human welfare. As global economic competition grows sharper, education becomes an important source of competitive advantage, closely linked to economic growth, and a way for countries to attract jobs and investment. In addition, education appears to be one of the key determinants of lifetime earnings. Countries therefore frequently see raising educational attainment as a way of tackling poverty and deprivation.

In developing countries, education is also linked to a whole batch of indicators of human development. Education of women influences the health of children and family size. The experience of Asian economies in particular in the past two decades has demonstrated the benefits that public investment in education can bring. In richer countries, education is seen as important not just in the early years, but also in later life. As the pace of technological change quickens and as the workforce in many rich countries grows older, education offers a way to improve and update the skills and capabilities of the workforce. There are, however, many constraints on delivering education to the right people at the right time.

In developing countries, there is frequently a shortage of qualified school teachers. People may live in scattered communities in rural areas. Money for books and teaching materials may be scarce. In wealthier countries, money is also a problem: in particular, the cost of university education has risen sharply, and students are increasingly expected to meet all or part of the cost directly. But, at the level of higher education and training, the problem is often also one of time. Students who are already in full-time employment find it hard to take part in a university course offered at conventional times of day. Finally, employers, keen to train staff, are often acutely conscious of the costs of taking people away from their main job in order to attend training courses. They are therefore eager for more efficient and flexible ways to deliver information to employees.

All these factors have encouraged an interest in the use of information and communications technologies (ICT) to deliver education and training. Computers began to appear in school and university classrooms in the more advanced countries around the early 1980s. Broadband connections to schools and universities became commonplace in wealthier countries in the second half of the 1990s. In developing countries, experience is more limited. This is not necessarily a bad thing, as it should allow those countries to learn from the investments of richer countries.

Initially, educators saw the use of ICTs in the classroom mainly as a way to teach computer literacy. Most now see a broader role: that of delivering many kinds of learning at lower cost and with higher quality than traditional methods of teaching allow. In addition, schools and universities increasingly use ICTs, as do other large organizations, to reduce the costs and improve the efficiency of administration.

ICT enabled linkages - propelled by broadband and satellite networks-are of a new, unprecedented kind, with special implications in a globalised world. They give rise to the 'A-3' scenario, where Anyone, Anytime, Anywhere can be connected to others through networks and access devices in a virtual space. This facilitates new forms of organizations and communities, often constituted by the users themselves, and manifested in myriad ways – for example through wiki, blogs, social networks, open resource movements, virtual institutes etc. In working together, these groups and organizations create new resources and ways of empowerment in virtual and real spaces.

By far the largest investments so far in ICTs have been in the United States. The United States' budget for the use of technology in schools is enormous: since 1989, the US Department of Education has invested almost US$1 billion in the use of technology in public education. Not surprisingly, most of the work relating to developing educational ICTs and their most widespread applications are in the United States. And, as a result, many of the evaluations of ICTs have been carried out in the United States. Some lessons from American experience will be universal. Others will be peculiar to that country's education system, which at the higher level involves more private money and enterprise than higher education in most other countries.

In examining the development of ICTs in schools, universities and training, an important distinction should be made. In the case of schools, teachers primarily use ICTs in the school as an instructional device. "Distance" learning is rarely part of school teaching. In the case of higher education and training, students are more likely to use ICTs partly to learn at a distance from the instructor. Different teaching techniques are thus probably required in the two areas of education.

ICTs are sometimes seen as a way to widen the opportunities regarding education. If ICTs can be used effectively to improve the delivery of education, they offer worthwhile prizes: in particular, lower costs and wider access. But policy-makers increasingly want to see value for money and clear evidence that educational investments will deliver commensurate benefits. And some of the early enthusiasts for ICTs in education have become more cautious, or even downright skeptical.

DISTANCE EDUCATION IN THE 21st CENTURY

The open and distance education system of the 21st century must be based on personalized and cooperative learning and teaching processes enabled by the above. About 10% of the relevant age-group in India is currently enrolled in higher education, whereas in developed countries corresponding figures stand between 30%-50% of the relevant population. Out of this 10%, the DE system in India accounts for about 20% of the total enrolment.

ICT must be suitably integrated into the DE system, not only to ensure wider outreach and delivery but also to make the pedagogical process more relevant, user-friendly, accessible and updatable. Pedagogical delivery in the DE system must discard its heavy reliance on textual material and content-based evaluation and move towards skill, competency and capability development suited to the life and work situation of the learner. At the same time, the learner must have the freedom to choose any pedagogical mode of one's convenience from the present modes of pedagogical transaction, be it print, audio-visual or internet based.

To develop an open and distance education system for an educated, value-oriented, ever developing and dynamic Indian society, that meets global as well as local and individual needs of the knowledge age, it must be predicated on the following principles

1. Quantity- access to large numbers
2. Quality – standards and relevance.
3. Equality – affordability and inclusiveness
4. Speed of operations
5. Core values and principles
6. Governance

These issues can be addressed simultaneously through ICT enabled education that is designed and developed to best utilize the new processes of the information age.

New Processes:

IT Generated:

- Digitization,
- Virtualization
- Mass-personalization and mass-customization.

Network Generated:

- Global standards for communicating and working together,
- Self-organisation (Blogs)
- Mass collaborations (Wiki -processes for creating free resources)
- Open resource development
- Meta-databases.

DISTANCE EDUCATION FOR ALL THROUGH 'ICT'

The biggest challenge faced in distance education, therefore, is the provision of *quality education* to the greatest number, at the lowest possible cost to the learner. And this is where ICT enabled distance education has significant advantages. Using ICT effectively for distance education can bridge the distance between the learner, instructor and the market by transcending barriers of space and time. Seamless access, flexible schedules, quality content and inclusive delivery mechanisms have enormous potential to increase the scale of access and, in that process, bring down the cost of education for the individual learner. Despite the physical absence of a 'real' teacher (which often causes ICT enabled education to be perceived as restricted in its social context and pedagogical rigour), ICT based modes foster the engagement of the learner with instructional content as well as work-place applications, to enable one to assess and apply strategies of personal development in meaningful and measurable ways. Most importantly, ICT has the potential to foster greater inclusiveness and overcome spatial isolation by effectively bridging geographical and social divides, especially the rural urban imbalance.

CONCLUSION

Undoubtedly, ICTs are potentially a useful tool both for managing education and for teaching in distance mode. Use in managing educational institutions should be encouraged, as should use by instructors to gain access to educational materials. And, by teaching computer skills to youngsters, they may influence inward investment. But getting the best from ICTs depends on several variables, including the appropriate design of software and hardware; the training and attitude of instructors; and the realization that different students have different requirements. It also requires a willingness to experiment. Effective use of ICTs in distance education and training is likely to require quite different pedagogical techniques from traditional classroom teaching. These will probably take a long time to devise and disseminate. Moreover, the new emphasis on cost-effectiveness may discourage innovation. Well-designed ICTs can allow educators to reach new groups (distance mode) of potential students, particularly mature students, lifelong learners, students with physical disabilities, students in employment and students who are far from education centers. Most of these groups are composed mainly of older and well-motivated students.

REFERENCES

1. Blurton, C. (1999): "*New Directions of ICT-Use in Education*", UNESCO's World Communication and Information Report.

2. Dighe, A. "*Use of ICTs in Non-Formal Education and Life Long Learning*"
3. Dighe, A. & Reddi U. V. (2006): "*Women's literacy and Information and Communication Technologies: Lessons that experience has taught us*", New Delhi, Commonwealth Educational Media Centre for Asia (CEMCA) & Commonwealth of Learning (COL).
4. Dighe A., Hakeem H. A. and Shaeffer S. (2009) "*ICTs in Non-Formal Education in Asia Pacific' in Digital Review of Asia Pacific*", 2009-2010, ed. Shahid Akhtar and Patricia Arinto, Sage, New Delhi.
5. Frances Cairncross. "*ICTs for education and building human capital*". http://www.itu.int/visions.
6. NCTE, New Curriculum Framework for Teacher Education, New Delhi.
7. National Knowledge Commission of India, Government of India, New Delhi.
8. Report of Ministry of HRD, Government of India, New Delhi.

3

Role of Information Technology in Teacher Education

INTRODUCTION

Now we are living in the modern world. A lot of change is occurring in every day. With the help of science and technology we have developed all the fields like Education, Banking Industry, Agriculture, Insurance, Transport and Medicine etc. With the help of technology now it is easy to know any type of information within seconds throughout the world.

Radio, Television, Phone, Mobile, Computer and Internet have changed the human life. Through education we can learn anything easily with the help of these instruments. According to Mahatma Gandhi, the father of Indian Nation, by giving good education to each and every one we can remove poverty and develop good character.

India is a developing country. Now we have very much demand in the IT field. The development of IT is a wonder. Now lacks of student are entering in to the IT field. Our central and state governments are also giving more importance for Information Technology.

There is a separate department for Information Technology under the Ministry of Communication and Information Technology.

DEFINITION OF INFORMATION TECHNOLOGY

Information Technology (IT): The science and activity of using computers and other electronic equipment to store and send information.

Information Technology is also defined as "The technology involved with the transmission and storage of information, especially the development, installation, implementation, and management of computer systems within companies, universities" and other organizations".

GOALS AND OBJECTIVES OF INFORMATION TECHNOLOGY

1. To provide in-service training to teachers and teacher educators on computers and IT.
2. To incorporate all the IT facilities into teacher education model.
3. To extend internet, e-mail facilities to all teachers and students in teacher education.
4. To provide network how to operate computers and internet to all the student teachers.
5. To provide network to teacher education centres all over India.
6. To extend distance mode of teacher education online and also include a live interactive practical teaching.
7. To restructure teacher education curriculum.
8. To incorporate use of IT in special education.
9. To use IT in teacher education research.
10. To create a virtual teacher education centre.
11. To incorporate good hidden curriculum strategies to restore the humanistic tendencies required for a teacher.
12. Ensure the protection and security of data.
13. Minimize duplication of effort, services and resources.
14. Eliminate inefficient and costly redundancies.
15. Define what services, if any, should be restructured or eliminated.
16. Eliminate non-compatible standards and architectures.

17. Identify obstacles for departments wanting to move computing operations to the Division of Information Technology.
18. Recommend a strategy for evaluating the university-wide impacts of major information technology purchases including analysis of total cost of ownership.
19. Evaluate the complexity and risks of managing a complex distributed computing environment, including system security, exposure to data loss and virus protection.
20. Identify issues and trends in technology that may affect the university's technology infrastructure and long-term architecture.
21. Recommend the most effective balance of central and distributed technology services, staffing and resources. Detail any logical alternatives. Recommendations will include background, advice and alternatives that address the following:

- Create a cost efficient blend of centralization and decentralization of information technology resources - properly aligning the university's information technology infrastructure to best meet the needs of its teaching, research and outreach missions.
- Create a coherent campus-wide information technology computing architecture and a solid foundation for the university's information technology infrastructure.
- Develop a long-term organizational process and structure to ensure the best utilization of the university's information technology resources for the future.
- Estimate the costs of infrastructure and support, including personnel and training, in the current distributed environment and to estimate the same costs for the alternatives proposed.

NEED OF INFORMATION TECHNOLOGY IN TEACHER EDUCATION

It is well known fact that IT and Cyber age have brought a revolutionary transformation and drifted the whole life style of people. No area left untouched with it. We have arrived at global village concept with all virtual realities on our desktops. But is it the teacher education, which has remained untouched in this direction.

We have a lot of educational institutions in the field of Information Technology like 'Indian Institute of Information Technology (IIIT), 'International Institute of Information Technology, 'Tata Institute of Information Technology' and 'Deerubai Ambani Institute of Information Technology'. There are so many Information Technology departments in the universities at state and central level. The impact of Information Technology is very much on human life. It is necessary to use Information Technology in teacher education system. There is a separate subject for trainee teachers 'Educational Technology'. With the help of Information Technology it is possible to give quality and effective education for trainee teachers.

A nation's development potential depends upon its ability to continuously educate its population and its ability to create armies of skilled manpower. In particular, use of Information Technology (IT) in acquiring knowledge and skill has become an essential element in education and training. These IT elements in the educational process have magical effects.

Higher education without the support of IT makes the lives of learner and teachers equally difficult. A nation's intellectual strength depends on IT support. The use of computing and communication technology to enhance the efficacy of transaction and productivity is the driving force in this new era of social and economic transformation in the new society called Information Society.

A strong IT infrastructure can give an institution a competitive advantage for the best students and faculty and an advantage in competition for absorbing external research grants to execute studies, research etc. in a short time and with great resolution. The quality of an institution's environment for digital information storage and retrieval has, for any disciplines, become more important than the institution's conventional, library resources in print media.

Virtually every economic sector that is labour intensive has managed to improve productivity through the use of technology except education. Faculty/student ratios in higher education have changed significantly in more than 50 years. The most advanced technology in common use in the classroom today in our country is the overhead projector, and it took nearly three decades to migrate from the national level training institute to the classroom. Institutions like UGC, IGNOU, and CIET have begun to transact curriculum on DD 1 but the ETV programmes are mostly of enrichment type and not as per the demand of the students. It is unlikely that IT will have a major impact on teaching and learning if the current paradigm for instruction changes.

Generally majority trainee teachers have no knowledge about usage of technology. Because their lower classes curriculum is separate. It is necessary to change curriculum at school level and implement Information Technology at school level also. 'Today's children are tomorrow's citizens', so it is necessary to take care about school curriculum. It is government duty to provide Information Technology labs for all type of Educational Institutions in the country.

USES OF INFORMATION TECHNOLOGY

Now we are using Information Technology in all the fields like education agriculture, banking, transport, medicine, research and manufacturing and in social service mode.

Specific Uses of Information Technology

- o Animation for simulation of urban environments and video for assembling and disseminating results of the analysis and design work.
- o Graphic Information System (GIS) for the study of housing and development patterns.
- o Computer Aided Design (CAD) for geometric modeling: Digital image archival systems for compiling data about the built environment.

ROLE OF INFORMATION TECHNOLOGY IN TEACHER EDUCATION

In-service Training

There is a need to provide in-service training to all the teachers and teacher educators with updated computer operation skills and provide with IT know how. To utilize the facilities to access updated information and solutions to their problems in their areas of specialization, it can be provide on-line.

Teacher Education Training Programmes through IT Facilities

A virtual teacher education centre can be created. All the necessary skills and training can be provided in different modes on the network. It should incorporate all the available facilities like, tele-education, teleconferencing, floppy diskettes and CD-ROMs in teacher education. Networks like ERNET, INTERNET and futuristic concept of bringing satellite channels directly to homes by DTS (Direct to Home) service and expert talks through virtual classrooms can also be made available.

Distance Mode of Education

The present practice of TV and other media in distance mode of education can be substituted by multimedia systems which have an extra advantage of intractability through GUI (Graphics User Interface) which controls the response of information transfer process according to the learners pace. It helps in using screen as an instructor for self-learning.

IT in Special Education

IT is providing solutions for the education of physically challenged people as well. As reported by BBC web-site (web-site at BBC news, science), the Germans have developed a technology and associated software for which people, where computer will sense the signals from the head of a paralyzed person through two attached electrodes, and thereby, allow him to surf the net like a normal person. These facilities will transform the lives of the physically challenged and IT can be used even for diagnosing.

Research and INTERNET

Internet facilities should be made available to research students, teacher educators. All the departments should have internet connectivity. It helps in accessing information about the ongoing research in their respective fields and it also avoids overlapping.

Restructuring Curricula of Teacher Education

1. Teacher education curriculum needs drastic changes by incorporating all facilities available through IT. Primarily IT can be used to keep on par with the existing knowledge structure. It can be thoroughly incorporated into methodologies of teacher education.
2. There should not be exclusive theoretical orientation in curriculum. It shall have more practically demonstrable skill and strategies in the curriculum.
3. All possible attempts should be made to train teachers apart from virtual classrooms, to incorporate the necessary live interactive experiences to understand the significance of physical interaction with the child in the classroom.
4. Humanistic and affective hidden curriculum and an effective training to acquire all traits and qualities required in teacher to handle human society should also be included in the curriculum.

CONCLUSION

Information Technology has a prominent role in the field of teacher education. With the help of information technology it is easy to know any type of information within seconds throughout the world. The advanced knowledge of information technology is much helpful for research in all the fields of education. With the help of Information Technology it is easy to educate trainee teachers. By knowing the usage of technology they have a chance to share their opinions with other teacher throughout the world. Information Technology motivates the teacher to learn lot of things in their subject area.

Now we are happy that our State and Central Governments are taking good steps to introduce online education in the educational institutions. There are separate subjects in D.Ed., and B.Ed., like Computer Education and Educational Technology. Now teachers are using computers and internet in the educational institutions. But the percentage is very less. It is more important to give equal importance to theory and practical in the computer education and educational technology subjects. It is the main duty of Government to establish Computer and Educational technology labs for each and every teacher education institution in the country.

Now NCTE, CIET, NUEPA, NCERT, SCERT and other educational departments have recognized the advantages of Information Technology in the field of education in general and teacher education in particular. They are conducting national seminars, workshops, and conferences about Information Technology. Teachers must be given excellent training in setting, grading papers and preparing assignment, etc. These can be used in teacher training network. Excellent stimulated models can be made available to access on network.

REFERENCES

1. Promotion of Quality of Teacher Education for 21st Century, Dr. N. Ramanath Kishan, Editor, Ashoka Krishna Offset Printers, Warangal.
2. http://www.ciet.nic.in/
3. http://www.aponline.gov.in/

4

Importance of 'ICT' Pedagogy Integration in Teacher Education

"The illiterate of the 21st century will not be those who cannot read and write but those who cannot learn, unlearn and relearn".

...Alvin Toffler

INTRODUCTION

ICT has great potential for enhancing teaching and learning outcomes. The realization of this potential depends much on how the teacher uses the technology. This would in turn depend, among other things, on the kind of training that the teacher has undergone.

Information and communication technologies (ICTs) have the potential to enhance access, quality, and effectiveness in education in general and to enable the development of more and better teachers in particular. As computer hardware becomes available to an increasing number of schools, more attention needs to be given to the capacity building of the key transformers in this process, namely, teachers.

ICTs are one of the major contemporary factors shaping the global economy and producing rapid changes in society. They have fundamentally changed the way people learn, communicate, and do business. They can transform the nature of education – where and how learning takes place and the roles of students and teachers in the learning process.

ICT – ORIGIN & DEFINITION

Information and communications technology, usually called ICT, is often used as a synonym for information technology (IT) but is usually a more general term that stresses the role of communications (telephone lines and wireless signals) in modern information technology. ICT consists of all technical means used to handle information and aid communication, including computer and network hardware as well as necessary software. In other words, ICT consists of IT as well as telephony, broadcast media, and all types of audio and video processing and transmission. The expression was first used in 1997 in a report by Dennis Stevenson to the UK government and promoted by the new National Curriculum documents for the UK in 2000.

ICT is often used in the context of "ICT roadmap" to indicate the path that an organization will take with their ICT needs. The term ICT is now also used to refer to the merging (convergence) of telephone networks with computer networks through a single cabling or link system. There are large economic incentives (huge cost savings due to elimination of the telephone network) to merge the telephone network with the computer network system.

IMPORTANCE OF 'ICT' IN TEACHER EDUCATION

The development of any nation depends mainly on the standards of its educational institutions. Teacher has a pivotal role in the process of development. According to Dr. Sarvepalli Radhakrishnan, Mahatma Gandhi and Vivekananda teacher has a prominent role in character building, quality education, value oriented education and health promotion through their teaching. In the 21st century, education in general and quality education in particular has a dominant role in the process of development.

Today's trainee teachers are tomorrow's real teachers. It is important and necessary to take care about present teacher education system. In the scientific and technological world ICT has a crucial role in the process of teaching and learning.

Globalization and technological changes have accelerated during the last fifteen years and have created a new global economy. Education is one of the main keys to economic development and improvements in human welfare. Teaching is becoming one of the most challenging professions in our society where knowledge is expanding rapidly and much of it is available to students as well as teachers at the same time. In today's world teachers need to be equipped not only with subject-specific expertise and effective teaching methodologies, but with the capacity to assist students to meet the demands of the emerging knowledge-based society. Teachers therefore require familiarity with new forms of information and communication technology (ICT) and need to have the ability to use that technology to enhance the quality of teaching and learning. Many countries including India have realized the need for providing teachers with training in ICT and have launched various professional development initiatives. However, many of the training activities to date have been one-off, crash courses which focus on computer literacy and do not enable teachers to integrate ICT in their day-to-day teaching activities and master the use of ICT as an effective tool to improve teaching and learning. The EFA Global Monitoring Report also confirms the central role of teachers in any education system, emphasizing that the quality of education is directly linked to how well teachers are prepared for teaching.

TABLE-1 Process of Learning and Memory

LEARNING THROUGH	WE REMEMBER
Taste 1.0%	20% of what hear
Touch 1.5%	30% of what we see
Hearing 11.0%	50% of what we see and hear
Smell 3.5%	80% of what we say
Sight 83.0%	90% of what we say and do

The given below table gives full information about learning and memory. ICT is a multi-dimensional tool. The impact of ICT is very much when compare to any other. More learning and memory takes place through ICT.

Thus, the very basis of learning is sense experience, and the very psychology of teaching aids is as follows:

I hear – I forget
I see – I remember
I do – I learn/understand

Information and communication technologies (ICTs) which include radio and television, as well as newer digital technologies such as computers and the Internet have been touted as potentially powerful enabling tools for educational change and reform.

'ICT' PEDAGOGY INTEGRATION IN TEACHER EDUCATION

One of the essential aims of teacher education is to enable student teachers to develop their knowledge and understanding of subject matter, children, teaching strategies, and the school curriculum, and to help them draw upon this knowledge in the shaping of their classroom practice. Typically, through lectures and seminars on teaching methods, child psychology, classroom processes, and subject matter, through classroom observation and teaching experience, through discussions with tutors and teachers about classroom practice, and through the encouragement to reflect upon and analyze their own teaching, it is expected that student teachers will build a coherent, enlightened, integrated body of knowledge that will inform, and in turn be informed by, classroom practice.

The picture depicted by Calderhead and Robson describes how teachers' professional journeys start and continue throughout their teacher preparation. One of the key features of the profession of teaching is that teacher learning does not stop with teacher preparation in teacher education institutions. Classroom practice continues to inform teachers' classroom instruction. Teachers' classroom instruction has been studied for decades. Numerous studies have analyzed teaching and how and why teachers act and teach in particular ways. In studying what teachers do in classrooms, social science research has also focused on teachers' thought processes and what they believe about their work.

Teachers think about a variety of issues during the planning and the implementation of teaching; they constantly make decisions. In reviewing the teacher thinking research, Clark and Peterson explain that teachers have theories and belief systems that influence their perceptions, plans, and actions. Teachers' teaching and the thought that precedes and follows it produce teaching preferences. A teacher's preferred way of teaching is based on the teacher's values or ideal teaching style and on the teacher's abilities and skills.

In the scientific, technological, modern and globalized world Information and Communication Technologies (ICTs) have pivotal role in the process of teaching and learning. ICT helps the students and the teachers to learn effectively with in the period. It affects the multi-senses of the individuals. It is necessary to integrate ICT methodology in Teacher Education curriculum for the best learning of the trainee-teachers.

Components of ICT in Teacher Education

Actual components of ICT in Teacher Education:

- Deployment
- Curriculum Development
- Content Availability
- Training and Usage Support
- Educational Management
- Maintenance and Technical Support

Teacher Training Approaches

Research indicates that ICT can change the way teachers teach and that it is especially useful in supporting more student-centered approaches to instruction and in developing the higher order skills and promoting collaborative activities (Haddad, 2003). Recognizing the importance of ICT in teaching and learning, a majority of the countries in the world including India have provided ICT teacher training in a variety of forms and degrees. Even though many teachers report that they have not had adequate training to prepare themselves to use technology effectively in teaching and learning, there seem to be several efforts around the world in which countries are effectively using technology to train teachers, and/or are training teachers to use technology as tools for enhancing teaching and learning.

ICT teacher training can take many forms. Teachers can be trained to learn how to use ICT or teachers can be trained via ICT. ICT can be used as a core or a complementary means to the teacher training process (Collis & Jung, 2003).

ICT Use as Part of Teaching Methods

This approach integrates ICT into teacher training to facilitate some aspects of training. Two cases below show how a variety of ICT are adopted as part of effective training methods. In these cases, teachers are provided with examples of ICT-pedagogy integration in their training process.

Captured Wisdom is a resource developed by the federally-funded (USA) North Central Technology in Education Consortium for K-12 teachers, school administrators and extended to adult literacy educators. It uses videotape and CD-ROM to help US teachers to see how technology can be integrated into their work. The Captured Wisdom (tm) CD-ROM Library is made up of stories about teachers who are making meaningful and creative uses of technology in their instruction. These CD-ROMs contain video descriptions and demonstrations of how technology is used in teachers' classrooms. They provide "examples of real educators and learners using successful practices of technology to support instruction and learning in their classrooms. Video sequences are viewed by teachers' focus groups who then discuss the strategies and techniques of classroom management, assessment, etc. In this specific case, teachers learn how to use ICT in their classrooms by actually being engaged in the process of ICT-integrated training.

Another example of this approach can be found in the School Administrators' Technology Integration Resource project. It is a bilingual Canadian initiative which provides tools and resources to help school administrators successfully integrate ICT into curriculum in their school. It includes the National Center for Technology Planning clearinghouse of school district ICT plans, advice on how to provide technology, successful practices in introducing ICT, perspectives on staff development, a beginners' guide to the Internet, etc. The focus of this project is not on the basic skill development but on the development of ICT pedagogy integration skills of educators by sharing successful cases and practical ideas.

UNICEF's Teachers talking about learning also illustrates the application of this approach to ICT teacher training. It is designed for international collaboration between teachers in developing countries using the Internet and television. It provides access to teacher training materials and useful links and promotes discussions among teachers.

All the cases discussed above use ICT as part of training methods and promote teachers' ICT-pedagogy integration in the classroom by demonstrating examples and allowing discussions among teachers throughout the whole training process. Participants of the training are asked to actually use ICT to learn about ICT skills and develop ICT-integrated pedagogies. These training strategies seem to be supported by other research that argues that teachers are likely to benefit by actively experiencing ICT skills as a learner (Jung, 2003).

ICT pedagogy approach

Emphasis is on integrating ICT skills in a respective subject. Drawing on the principles of constructivism, pre-service teachers design lessons and activities that center on the use of ICT tools that will foster the attainment of learning outcomes. This approach is useful to the extent that the skills enhance ICT literacy skills and the underlying pedagogy allows students to further develop and maintain these skills in the context of designing classroom-based resources.

UNESCO planning guide for ICT in teacher-education cites three key principles for effective ICT development in Teacher Education that were put forward by the *Society for Information Technology and Teacher Education.*

1) That technology should be infused into the entire teacher education programme, implying that ICT should not be restricted to a single course but needs to permeate in all courses in the programmes.
2) That Technology should be introduced in context. Accordingly, ICT application like word-processing, databases, spread-sheet and telecommunications should not be taught as separate topics rather encountered as the need arises in all courses of Teacher-Education programmes.
3) That students should experience innovative technology supported learning environment in Teacher-Education programmes. This requires that students should see their lecturers engaging in technology to present their subjects utilizing power point or simulations in lectures and demonstrations. Students should also have the opportunity to use such applications in practical classes, seminars and assignments.

The application of these three principles will be a mile stone towards effectively integrating ICT in Teacher-Education.

TEACHER AND TECHNOLOGY

Teacher has a prominent role in the process of teaching and learning. First of all it is necessary to give training for teachers for effective use of technology.

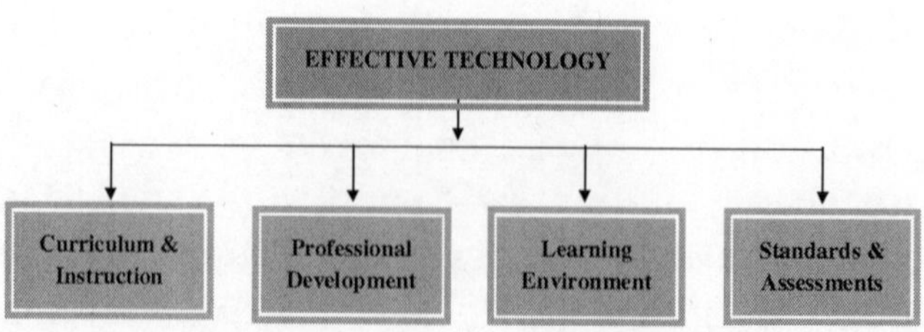

Fig-2: *Teacher and Technology*

Changing Role of Teacher

Under the changing scenario, there is a need to redefine the role of a teacher-educator. The National Council of Teacher Education, Jaipur (NCTE), based on a thorough job analysis, has come out with three areas in which a teacher-educator needs to acquire mastery. These are i) five performance areas; ii) ten competency areas; and iii) five commitment areas (NCTE, 1998). For the successful integration of ICT in teacher education, the teacher in addition to taking up the role responsibilities mentioned in these areas, must shoulder the additional, rather survival responsibilities outlined below :-

- Act as a role model for pre-service trainees and in-service teachers, demonstrating the use of technology across the curriculum.
- Encourage technology integration among the trainees, colleagues, teachers and parents.
- Be involved in planning and implementing ICT professional development training.
- Be up-to-date with the latest technological developments and advise the institutions concerning technology advancements and upgradation.
- Interact through e-mail/forum/communities/blogging with trainees, participating schools and parents.
- Aid in the implementation of technology plans of the institutions.
- Plan, design and demonstrate the use of multimedia applications for instructional use through multimedia projects.
- Examine a variety of evaluation and assessment tools including electronic portfolio assessment.
- Become active, competent online users of telecommunication services and act as model in the use of internet as an instructional tool.
- Direct trainees and teachers to digital resources that will be able to answer their questions.
- Address issues related to acceptable user policies, student safety, ethics, security, copyright, etc.

- o Be involved in marketing the best practices of technology integration.
- o Manage the available resources more productively to face the ever increasing financial crunch.
- o Use information literacy to access, evaluate, and use information from a variety of sources.
- o Have the competencies in software evaluations and advise the institutions in making the right choices.

Globalization and advancements in technology are driving changes in the social, technological, economical, environmental and political landscapes at such a pace and magnitude that is too great, and too multiple to ignore. As society changes, the skills that students need to be successful in life also change.

Teacher has a prominent role to teach all type of skills to the students. It is the duty of institute of teacher education to develop all the skills in the trainee teachers. Teacher has a multiple role in the process of teaching and learning. All of you know about the value of teacher in our Indian tradition. He acts as a guide, philosopher, friend and parent. Among these roles a role model and effective teacher has the above mentioned skills i.e., 21st century skills. ICT helps the teacher to teach and learn these skills effectively.

CONCLUSION

Several paradoxes could be recognized in the research literature considering the use of Information and Communication Technologies (ICT) at school as well as in teacher education. Students have rich experiences of use of technology outside of school, but do not use technology for learning at school. Teachers are skilled technology users, but they are unable to take advantage of their competence and to apply it to the way they teach in school. Today's trainee teachers are tomorrow's real teacher. It is necessary and important to take care about trainee teachers. Integration of ICT in pedagogy of teacher education is important. ICT helps both in teaching and learning process. The impact of ICT is very much on the student community. It is the time to change the attitude of teachers and students towards use of ICT in teaching and learning process.

REFERENCES

1. Amareswaran, N., & Sheela Reddy, C. (2009): "*Importance of 'ICT' in Distance Education*", Published by Acharya Nagarjuna University, Guntur, Andhra Pradesh.
2. Anjali Khirwadkar. "*Integration of ICT in Education: Pedagogical Issues*".
3. Jung, I. (2005): "*ICT-Pedagogy Integration in Teacher Training: Application Cases Worldwide. Educational Technology & Society*", International Forum of Educational Technology & Society (IFETS).
4. Mike Aston, et.al (2002): "*Elementary ICT Curriculum for Teacher Training*", UNESCO Institute for Information Technologies in Education (IITE), Moscow.
5. Priscilla G. Cabanatan. "*ICT Trends in Teacher Curricula: An Asia-Pacific Perspective*".
6. Ramachandra Reddy, B. (1995): "*Educational Technology*", S.V. University Press, Sri Venkateswara University, Tirupati, Andhra Pradesh.
7. Veijo Meisalo., et. al (2010): "*New Millennium Learners- ICT in Initial Teacher Training: Country Report Finland*", School of Applied Education and Teacher Education, University of Eastern Finland.
8. Victoria L. Tinio. "*ICT in Education*", United Nations Development Programme, Bureau for Development Policy, New York.
9. Amareswaran, N. & Ramachandra Reddy, B. "Educational *Technology for Teachers in the 21st Century*", unpublished book.

5

ICT for Rural Women: Poverty Alleviation and Improving Quality of Life

"The new information and communications technologies are among the driving forces of globalization. They are bringing people together, and bringing decision makers unprecedented new tools for development. At the same time, however, the gap between information 'haves' and 'have-nots' is widening, and there is a real danger that the world's poor will be excluded from the emerging knowledge-based global economy". **...***Kofi Annan "By the end of 2008, an important milestone in the ICT development race was achieved: over 4 billion mobile cellular subscriptions worldwide, translating into a penetration rate of 61 per cent. At the same time, ITU estimates that the world had 1.3 billion fixed telephone lines – or 19 per 100 inhabitants – and that almost a quarter of the world's 6.7 billion people were using the Internet"*....ITU (2009)

INTRODUCTION

The impact of science and technology is very much on all human beings in the society. We are living in the high-tech, modernized, industrialized, scientific and globalized world. It is possible to get any type of information within seconds. The living standard of human being is increasing. At the same time women in general and rural women in particular are facing so many problems in the community. The situation of women at rural is changing. Some more welfare programmes are important including ICT for rural women empowerment.

Article 19 of the 1948 Universal Declaration of Human Rights states that, '*everyone has the right to seek, receive and impart information and ideas through any media*'. When Article 19 was formulated, the mass media was print and, to a lesser extent, radio. Televisions and telephones were not yet popularized. Computers and satellites were objects of science fiction. In less than half a century since 1948, all of these technologies have become a part of everyday life for millions of people around the world. Humankind is in the midst of an information revolution empowered by Information and Communication Technology (ICT). Over the last few decades, vast resources have been invested to extend the reach and application of ICTs. Many hope that ICTs will have a very positive impact for poverty reduction. These technoevangelists proclaim ICTs as 'engines for growth' and 'powerful tools' for poverty reduction. In some parts of the world, this is true; in other parts, the rhetoric is way ahead of reality. Furthermore, some commentators have expressed concern that the rapid emergence of ICTs is just as likely to widen the gap between rich and poor. The task of making access to ICTs a practical reality for all, including the poor, is becoming more urgent every day.

WOMEN IN RURAL INDIA

In rural India, the Indian population is 48.1% women and 51.9% men and female illiteracy is 62% whereas the male illiteracy rate is 34%. The labour force participation rate of women is 22.7%, less than half of the men's rate of 51.6%.In rural India, agriculture and allied industrial sectors employ as much as 89.5% of the total female labour. Women have extensive workloads with dual responsibility for farm and household production. Women's work is getting harder and more time-consuming due to ecological degradation and changing agricultural technologies and practices. Women have an active role and extensive involvement in livestock production, forest resource use and fishery processing. Women spend up to six hours per day bringing water from distant sources to their homes.

Women contribute considerably to household income through farm and nonfarm activities as well as through work as landless agricultural labourers. Women's work as family labour is underestimated. There are high degrees of inter-state and intra-state variations in gender roles in agriculture, environment and rural production.

Indian women are extensively involved in agricultural activities. The mode of female participation in agricultural production varies with the land-owning status of farm house holds. In overall farm production, women's average contribution is estimated at 55% to 66% of the total labour. Rural Indian women's interface with the forests is varying - gathering, wage employment, production in farm forestry and management of afforested areas in the community plantation. Nature and extent of women's participation in fishery varies across the states. Fish drying/curing, marketing and hand braiding and net-mending are the main areas of women's involvement in Tamil Nadu, Andhra Pradesh and Orissa.

In rural areas, women make basket, broom, rope making, tasar silk cocoon rearing, oil extraction, and bamboo works, etc. Women constitute 51% of the total employed in forest-based small-scale enterprises. Women who receive training at the Institute are encouraged to return to their communities and share what they have learned, whether reading and writing, health and hygiene techniques, or, even, how to make better decisions as a group.

Issues of rural poverty and health have traditionally been the concern of governments. In the past and even today, most programs designed to benefit rural India are funded and managed exclusively by the government.

Now a days, the internet is beginning to have a revolutionary effect on the 700 million people who live in villages in India - and the charge is being led by women. A project set up by one of India's leading technology institutes has put women in charge of forging the way across the digital divide as the proprietors of a fast-growing number of internet cafes or kiosks around the sub-continent. In total 80% of these new kiosks are run by women, many of whom have had very little or no acquaintance with technology before.

POVERTY IN RURAL INDIA

Before examining how ICTs might be used to alleviate poverty, it is appropriate to consider what is actually meant by poverty. The World Bank reports that of the world's six billion people, 2.8 billion, almost half, live on less than US$2 a day, and 1.2 billion, a fifth, live on less than US$1 a day, with 44 percent of them living in South Asia. The Millennium Development Goals set for 2015 by international development agencies include reducing by half the proportion of people living in extreme income poverty, or those living on less than US$1 a day.

According to a recent Indian government committee constituted to estimate poverty, nearly 38% of India's population (380 million) is poor. This report is based on new methodology and the figure is 10% higher than the present poverty estimate of 28.5%.

The committee was headed by SD Tendulkar has used a different methodology to reach at the current figure. It has taken into consideration indicators for heath, education, sanitation, nutrition and income as per National Sample Survey Organization survey of 2004-05. This new methodology is a complex scientific basis aimed at addressing the concern raised over the current poverty estimation.

Since 1972 poverty has been defined on basis of the money required to buy food worth 2100 calories in urban areas and 2400 calories in rural areas. In June this year a government committee headed by NC Saxena committee estimated 50% Indians were poor as against Planning Commission's 2006 figure of 28.5%.

Poverty is one of the main problems which have attracted attention of sociologists and economists. It indicates a condition in which a person fails to maintain a living standard adequate for his physical and mental efficiency. It is a situation people want to escape. It gives rise to a feeling of a discrepancy between what one has and what one should have. The term poverty is a relative concept. It is very difficult to draw a demarcation line between affluence and poverty. According to Adam Smith - Man is rich or poor according to the degree in which he can afford to enjoy the necessaries, the conveniences and the amusements of human life.

Even after more than 50 years of Independence India still has the world's largest number of poor people in a single country. Of its nearly 1 billion inhabitants, an estimated 260.3 million are below the poverty line, of which 193.2 million are in the rural areas and 67.1 million are in urban areas. More than 75% of poor people reside in villages. Poverty level is not uniform across India. The poverty level is below 10% in states like Delhi, Goa, and Punjab etc whereas it is below 50% in Bihar (43) and Orissa (47). It is between 30-40% in Northeastern states of Assam, Tripura, and Mehgalaya and in Southern states of Tamil Nadu and Uttar Pradesh.

Poverty has many dimensions changing from place to place and across time. There are two inter-related aspects of poverty - Urban and rural poverty. The causes of rural poverty are manifold including inadequate and ineffective implementation of anti-poverty programmes.The overdependence on monsoon with non-availability of irrigational facilities often result in crop-failure and low agricultural productivity forcing farmers in the debt-traps. The rural communities tend to spend large percentage of annual earnings on social ceremonies like marriage; feast etc. Our economic development since Independence has been lopsided .There has been increase in unemployment creating poverty like situations for many. Population is growing at an alarming rate. The size of the Indian family is relatively bigger averaging at 4.2.The other causes include dominance of caste system which forces the individual to stick to the traditional and hereditary occupations.

Women in general are the most disadvantaged people in Indian society, though their status varies significantly according to their social and ethnic backgrounds. Women are particularly vulnerable to the spread of HIV/AIDS from urban to rural areas. In 2005 an estimated 5.7 million men, women and children in India were living with HIV/AIDS. Most of them are in the 15-49 age group and almost 40 per cent of them, or 2.4 million in 2008, are women (National AIDS Control Organization).

ICT FOR RURAL WOMEN – POVERTY ALLEVIATION

Access to Information and Communication Technologies (ICTs) can have dramatic impact on poverty alleviation for rural women and for achieving socio-economic development goals. Rural women need to treat ICTs as an empowerment tool and a means to a living. The use of mobile communication devices and internet are changing the way agricultural activities are managed by farmers nowadays. Rural women's lack of mobility and less hands-on computer experience might hinder women's welfare and empowerment. Research says that 80 per cent of women are working in the agricultural sector, but among them only 1-10 per cent women are land owners. Literacy rate of women is also poor when compared to men. There is a large gap between rural and urban women in education, employment and health status. There is a huge difference in socio-economic and political status of women in the Africa, the America, the Europe and The Asia. The quality of life depends on socio-economic status of women. Education is a key factor to upgrade the quality of life of women in general and rural women in particular. ICT has a prominent role in the process of empowerment of rural women not only in India, but also other parts of the world. In this paper an attempt has been made to analyze the role of ICT in the process of poverty alleviation and improving the quality of life of rural women.

The World Development Report 2000-01: Attacking Poverty identifies three priority areas for reducing poverty: increasing opportunity, enhancing empowerment, and improving security. Opportunity makes markets work for the poor and expands poor people's assets. Empowerment makes state institutions work better for poor people and removes social barriers. Security helps poor people manage risk. In light of current experiences in rural India and elsewhere in the developing world, it is apparent that ICT -defined as the set of activities that facilitates the capturing, storage, processing, transmission and display of information by electronic means - can be utilized to support poverty reduction strategies. The use of ICT applications can enhance poor people's opportunities by improving their access to markets, health, and education. Furthermore, ICT can empower the poor by expanding the use of government services, and reduce risks by widening access to microfinance.

The Gyandoot project in Madhya Pradesh State of India is an intranet in the district of Dhar that connects rural cyber cafes catering to the everyday needs of the masses. It provides the following services:

- o Commodity marketing information system
- o Income certificate
- o Domicile certificate
- o Caste certificate
- o Landholder's passbook of land rights and loans
- o Rural Hindi e-mail
- o Advisory module
- o Public grievance redressal
- o Forms of various govern-ment schemes.
- o Below-Poverty-Line FamilyList
- o Employment news
- o Rural matrimonial
- o Rural market
- o Rural newspaper
- o E-education

In Gujarat, computerized milk collection centres using embedded chip technology are helping ensure fair prices for small farmers (women) who sell milk to dairy cooperatives. The fat content of milk used to be calculated hours after the milk was received; farmers were paid every 10 days and had to trust the manual calculations of milk quality and quantity made by the staff of cooperatives. Farmers often claimed that the old system resulted in malfeasance and underpayments, but such charges were difficult to prove. Computerized milk collection now increases transparency, expedites processing, and provides immediate payments to farmers (World Bank, 2002).

Indeed, small-scale entrepreneurs in developing countries, especially women, have shown the ability to harness ICTs for developing their enterprises. For example, a group of ladies in Kizhur village, Pondicherry decided that they wanted to start a small business enterprise manufacturing incense sticks. They began as sub-contractors but their confidence and enterprise grew from utilizing the local telecentre. As a result of some searches by the telecentre operators, they were able to develop the necessary skills for packaging and marketing their own brand name incense. The ladies were quickly able to develop local outlets for their products and they are confidently using the telecentre to seek out more distant customers.

ICT and e-commerce are attractive to women entrepreneurs (who in many developing countries account for the majority of small and medium-size enterprise owners), as it allows them to save time and money while trying to reach out to new clients in domestic and foreign markets. There are many success stories in business-to-consumer (B2C) retailing or e-tailing from all developing-country regions, demonstrating how women have used the Internet to expand their customer base in foreign markets while at the same time being able to combine family responsibilities with lucrative work. However, in spite of the publicity given to e-tailing, its scope and spread in the poorer parts of the world have remained small, and women working in micro-enterprises and the informal sector are far from being in a position to access and make use of the new technologies. Moreover, B2C e-commerce is small compared to business-to-business (B2B) e-commerce and thus benefits only a small number of women (UNCTAD, 2002).

The 220,000 women members of India's Self-Employed Women's Association (SEWA) who earn a living through their own labour or through small businesses have started using telecommunications as a tool for capacity building among the rural population. SEWA uses a combination of landline and satellite communication to conduct educational programs on community development by distance learning. The community development themes covered in the education programs delivered include organizing, leadership building, forestry, water conservation, health education, child development, the Panchayati Raj System and financial services.

The ILO notes that some developing countries have been able to create employment for thousands of women and men through community-access points and telecentres. One common option is to purchase a mobile phone through a micro credit program and to earn income by providing low cost phone calls to others (Curtain, 2001). Telecentres can also offer use of ICT facilities for business purposes to small and micro-enterprises that do not have their own private facilities.

Despite the recognized potentials of ICTs for alleviating poverty, still they are not equally accessible, leaving the poorest people behind (von Braun, 2010). There is a set of interrelated and continually unfolding factors influencing the field of ICT and its role in development (Chambers, 2010):

1. Change in the dimensions that define ICT and development has accelerated, not only in communication technologies and the expansion of 'web 2.0' (the read/write web) but also in the awareness and aspirations of those living in poverty
2. Following on from the relatively open and participatory approaches in the aid sector during the 1990s, an emphasis on control, accountability and impact assessment has developed in recent years
3. Paradoxically, at the same time there has been a multiplication and diversification of participatory methodologies in the development field
4. Evolving theoretical understandings of the nature of complexity and of technology have afforded additional conceptual tools for the theory and practice of development
5. There is an increased acknowledgement of the significance of power relations in development.

Many organizations in the women's movement recognize this potential and have projects that provide support for ICT to be used as an advocacy tool. ICTs can also enable certain individuals, especially early adopters, to spark catalytic change in their communities. For example, one very resourceful lady in a small

Mongolian town who single-handedly runs an NGO supporting women's micro-enterprises used the local telecentre to contact a donor agency in the UK and received an award of US$10,000, a huge sum in that context, to help her in her work.

In some countries in the region, telecentres are being set up through public and private initiatives in telephone shops, schools, libraries, community centres, police stations and clinics. Sharing the expense of equipment, skills and access among an ever-increasing number of users also helps to cut costs and make these services viable in remote areas. India, for example, has seen rapid growth in cyber kiosks that provide access to social communication as well as business support services for underprivileged groups. The kiosks are often upgraded Subscriber Trunk Dialling booths that are widely found in all parts of the countryside in India. These are small street shops, offering access to public phones for long distance calls. They number about 300,000 and have generated more than 600,000 jobs among them majority are women. Youth unemployment constitutes over 30% of total unemployment in Asia Pacific and young people are particularly well placed to take advantage of such growth areas.

ICT FOR BETTER LIFE

Gender empowerment and economic development go hand in hand. United Nations former Secretary-General Kofi Annan (2005) called the empowerment of women 'the most effective development tool'. Research says that 'societies that discriminate by gender pay a high price in terms of their ability to develop and to reduce poverty'. Indeed, the annual UNDP Human Development reports of 2003, 2004, 2005 and 2007 consistently show a direct correlation between the level of gender empowerment in a society, measured on the basis of women's literacy and education rates, access to healthcare, capital, means of production, and degree of women's participation in public and professional life and that country's level of economic, social and political development. The reason is clear: countries that effectively exclude women from learning, healthcare and the public sphere 'deprive themselves of the creativity and productivity of half its citizens . . .' and will find it nearly impossible to close the economic gap with advanced developed nations. ICTs have been identified as one of the most effective tools to bring about gender and economic development almost simultaneously. IT has been dubbed 'the great equalizer'. ICT ... opens up a direct window for women to the outside world. Information flows to them without distortion or any form of censoring, and they have access to the same information as their counterparts. This leads to broadening of perspectives, building up of greater understanding of their current situation and causes of poverty, and initiation of interactive processes for information exchange. Furthermore, such forms of networking open up alternate forms of communication.

ICTs in the form of multimedia community centres/telecentres, especially at the rural level can act as a nodal point for community connectivity, local capacity building, content development and communications, and serve as hubs for applications, such as distance education, telemedicine, support to small, medium sized and micro-credit enterprises, promotion of electronic commerce, environmental management, and empowerment of women and youth. Where such services have a pro-ultra-poor strategy, then the benefits of ICTs can be directed to them.

Capacity building also relates to the accumulation of social capital, which refers to those features of social organization such as networks, norms and social trust that facilitate coordination and cooperation for mutual benefit. The establishment of networks for mutual benefit can be nurtured and extended through the use of ICTs. ICTs can help create and sustain on-line and off-line networks that introduce and interconnect people who are working toward similar goals.

People with appropriate skills, possibly obtained from ICT-based learning facilities, may gain employment as a result of the growth in remote ICT processing facilities that are located outside high-income countries. The facilities provide a range of services, including help lines, technical support, reservations handling, sales, data conversion, as well as voice and data transcription. Other remote processing services are payroll accounting, internal auditing and credit appraisals. High-end remote processing includes creating digitized maps of townships, utilities, roads and other facilities. It is claimed that back office functions that are likely to grow in importance are settling insurance claims and summarizing legal documents, such as witness depositions.

The use of ICT in Education and Health is increasing day by day. With the help of ICT people in general and women in particular are getting more benefits. Women are getting more jobs than men at data entry centre, reception centre, administration centre, call centre and medical labs. They are getting information within seconds. Research says that, there is a positive correlation between use of ICT and life status of women in the society.

CONCLUSIONS

Information and Communication Technology is the road, which must be brought to the doorsteps of the poor be it rural or urban regions. The poor should be given the equal opportunity to master the skills to use this technology to their advantage. We must have to design the information technology in such a way that a totally unprepared poor person can immediately get hang of it without feeling threatened and convert acquired knowledge for his wealth creation. Using ICT for the empowerment of poor and lead them to the road of prosperity. Government policy should be poor-oriented rather than corporate-oriented that prevents many poor people from making use of ICT for their empowerment. While there is recognition of the potential of ICT as a tool for the promotion of gender equality and the empowerment of women, a “gender divide” has also been identified, reflected in the lower numbers of women accessing and using ICT compared with men. It is the duty of government to provide ICT for all rural women to improve their quality of life.

REFERENCES

1. Charru Malhotra, Chariar V.M., Das L.K., and Ilavarasan. “*ICT for Rural Development: An Inclusive Framework for e-Governance*”, Computer Society of India.
2. Conference of ‘*Women Scientists and Technologist: Role in National Development*’, Government of India, New Delhi, March 8th – 9th, 2002.

3. International Workshop on '*Empowerment of Women through Science and Technology Interventions*' Tehran, Iran, December 14th -16th, 2008.
4. Kalesanwo, O.O., &. Bilesanmi-Awoderu, J.B., (2009): *Women Entrepreneurship in Science and Technology: Impetus for Female participation in National Development in Nigeria,* Academic Leadership, Online Journal, Volume 7, Issue 3.
5. Ministry of Science & Technology, Government of India, New Delhi.
6. Praveen Dalal. "*Use of ICT for Women Empowerment in India*", Economic and Social Commission for Asia & the Pacific, UN.
7. Simone Cecchini and Christopher Scott (2003): "*Can Information and Communications Technology Applications contribute to Poverty Reduction? Lessons from Rural India*", ECLAC, United Nations, Casilla 179-D, Santiago, Chile.

6

ICT for Women Empowerment - A Case Study of sri Venkateswara University

ICT AND DEVELOPMENT

The role of Information and Communication Technologies (ICT) as a tool for development has attracted the sustained attention of the United Nations over recent years. Strategic partnerships have been developed with donors, the private sector and civil society, and working groups and task forces have been established to enhance interagency collaboration throughout the United Nations system.

In 2000, the Economic and Social Council adopted a Ministerial Declaration on the role of information technology in the context of a knowledge based economy. In 2001, the Secretary-General established a high level Information and Communication Technologies Task Force to provide overall leadership to the United Nations on the formulation of strategies to put ICT at the service of development. The Millennium Declaration adopted in 2000 underscored the urgency of ensuring that the benefits of new technologies, especially ICT, are made available to all. To achieve this goal, a United Nations World Summit on the Information Society (WSIS) was planned in two phases. The first phase, the Geneva Summit in December 2003, aimed to develop political will and to establish the foundations for an Information Society for all. In total, 175 Governments endorsed the Declaration of Principles and Plan of Action at the first phase. The second phase of WSIS was held in the month of November 2005 in Tunis.

Information and Communication Technologies comprise a complex and heterogeneous set of goods, applications and services used to produce, process, distribute and transform information. The ICT sector consists of segments as diverse as telecommunications, television and radio broadcasting, computer hardware, software and services and electronic media (for example, the Internet and electronic mail). Information and communication needs can be met by more traditional means, such as print media and fixed telephone lines, or by satellite technology, mobile phones and the Internet. Traditional technologies continue to be important for large numbers of people around the world, particularly in rural areas.

However, new technologies have a vast potential for empowerment which needs to be fully exploited. The term ICT has been used to encompass technological innovation and convergence in information and communication leading to the development of so-called information or knowledge societies, with resulting changes in social interaction, economic and business practices, political engagement, education, health, leisure and entertainment. Over the past decade, there has been a growing understanding that these technologies can be powerful instruments for advancing economic and social development through the creation of new types of economic activity, employment opportunities, improvements in health-care delivery and other services, and the enhancement of networking, participation and advocacy within society. ICT also have the potential to improve interaction between Governments and citizens, fostering transparency and accountability in governance. While the potential of ICT for stimulating economic growth, socioeconomic development and effective governance is well recognized, the benefits of ICT have been unevenly distributed within and between countries.

The term “digital divide” refers to the differences in resources and capabilities to access and effectively utilize ICT for development that exist within and between countries, regions, sectors and socio-economic groups.

The digital divide is often characterized by low levels of access to technologies. Poverty, illiteracy, lack of computer literacy and language barriers are among the factors impeding access to ICT infrastructure, especially in developing countries. Internet usage figures collected by the International Telecommunications Union (ITU) in 2003 illustrate this gap in access. For instance, in 2003, the United States reported 5,558 Internet users per 10,000 persons, compared with 690 users per 10,000 persons in Asia and 156 users per 10,000 persons in Africa. The enthusiasm over the rapid growth of ICT and their applications have generated a variety of initiatives to foster the use of ICT for development, including research, projects, workshops and other activities. Many of these initiatives are directed at addressing the growing digital divide. Increased attention is being paid to reviewing and evaluating the impact of these initiatives. Early findings point to mixed results about the impact of 10 years of experience in ICT for development.

An InfoDev report published in 2003 suggests that despite the vast amounts of resources that have been invested in efforts to increase access to ICT in developing countries and among the poor, these technologies have not proven as transformative as expected. The InfoDev report indicates that to harness ICT more effectively for development and poverty reduction, ICT must be mainstreamed as tools for broader strategies and programmes for building opportunity and empowering the poor. The report further states that the ICT for development agenda should identify the broader changes required in developing countries, the role ICT can have in effecting these changes, and to be more selective and strategic about the attention and resources devoted to the dissemination of these technologies.

GENDER EQUALITY AND ICT

The so-called digital divide is actually several gaps in one. There is a technological divide—great gaps in infrastructure. There is a content divide. A lot of web-based information is simply not relevant to the real needs of people. And nearly 70 per cent of the world's websites are in English, at times crowding out local voices and views. There is a gender divide, with women and girls enjoying less access to information technology than men and boys. This can be true of rich and poor countries alike".

While there is recognition of the potential of ICT as a tool for the promotion of gender equality and the empowerment of women, a "gender divide" has also been identified, reflected in the lower numbers of women accessing and using ICT compared with men. Unless this gender divide is specifically addressed, there is a risk that ICT may exacerbate existing inequalities between women and men and create new forms of inequality.

If, however, the gender dimensions of ICT—in terms of access and use, capacity-building opportunities, employment and potential for empowerment—are explicitly identified and addressed, ICT can be a powerful catalyst for political and social empowerment of women, and the promotion of gender equality.

A "Canon on Gender Partnerships and ICT Development", developed primarily by women participants at the first international conference on ICT, the Global Knowledge Partnership Conference in 1997 outlined key principles for the development and design of ICT, prioritizing equal participation and gender-aware assessments and evaluations of ICT projects and programmes. At the second Global Knowledge Partnership Conference held three years later, a specific Women's Forum developed a comprehensive set of recommendations. The major recommendations included:

- Mainstreaming and monitoring of a gender perspective in all ICT initiatives;
- Collecting sex disaggregated data on the use of ICT and women's participation in policy-making as well as developing

targets, indicators and benchmarks to track the progress of women's and girl's access to the benefits of ICT;

- Identifying and promoting good practices and lessons learned on the ways women and girls are using ICT;
- Capacity-building towards gender equality in education and employment;
- Enhancing democracy and women's participation through electronic connectivity; and
- Developing research and policies on health and environmental hazards of ICT industries.

ACCESS AND EFFECTIVE USE OF ICT FOR WOMEN EMPOWERMENT

In addition to physical access to the technology and the ability to utilize it, access also refers to the ability to make use of the information and the resources provided. The factors identified as constraints to access and use, i.e. poverty, illiteracy, including computer illiteracy, and language barriers are particularly acute for women. Women are, for example, less likely to own communication assets, such as radios, mobile phones and computers. In addition, women's access to and use of ICT is constrained by factors that go beyond issues of technological infrastructure.

Socially constructed gender roles and relationships play a key role in determining the capacity of women and men to participate on equal terms in the information society. A UNESCO report on "Gender Issues in the Information Society" points out that the capability of women to effectively use information obtained through ICT is clearly dependent on many social factors, including literacy and education, geographic location, mobility and social class. Women are in the minority of users in almost all developed and developing countries. The trend for differentiation in use starts early, as seen in the United States where boys are five times more likely than girls to use home computers and parents spend twice as much on ICT products for their sons as they do for their daughters. The development of infrastructure includes many decisions about the location of facilities, the type of technology, and issues of costs and pricing. Decisions which do not explicitly consider access for rural areas and poor and marginalized social groups, but favour urban areas with high-end and expensive communication services and technologies, can negatively influence access to and use of ICT by women.

Use of Radio Networking in Brazil

CEMINA (Communication, Education, and Information on Gender) is a Brazilian organization with the mission of improving education on gender equality, health and environment issues and strengthening poor women's rights and citizenship through the use of radio. In 1995, a group of women's radio programmes founded the Women's Radio Network, which includes 400 women's radio programmes distributed across Brazil reaching thousands of listeners located in the poorest communities. CEMINA is committed to integrating the Internet into a more traditional media that people are already familiar with in order to address cultural barriers which constitute a major challenge to overcoming the gender digital divide. CEMINA aims to empower women communicators by providing them access to the Internet through the creation of community radio telecentres and a defined space on the Internet with gender content.

Mobile Phones for Rural Women in Senegal

The Senegalese telephone company Sonatel, and Manobi, a French company, provided cell phones with Web Access Protocol (WAP) to rural women agricultural producers in Senegal, thereby extending their access to the Internet. This technology helped women obtain information about market prices of the inputs for their food processing activities and for the sale of their produce. The women preferred cell phones to computers because of the ease of transport. Women in the project appreciated the economic benefits of the technology, and other women were interested in becoming part of the project.

Impact of Women's use of Telecentres in South Asia

In 2002, UNESCO explored the potential of ICT to contribute to poverty reduction in nine locations within five countries in South

Asia. Access to ICT represented real and symbolic access to modernity, the future, education and knowledge. ICT centres constituted a space in which people could develop a sense of change and possibility. The study showed that gender perspectives played a significant part in determining both the barriers as well as the positive effects of ICT for empowerment. Social and economic exclusion due to gender-based restrictions on mobility was found in many households, with most women's interaction generally restricted to their immediate family, a few neighbours and some extended family. The restrictions resulted in narrowing women's access to the information and resources that ICT centres provided.

Benefits for Women of an ICT Centre in India

As women became involved in the Baduria ICT Centre in West Bengal, India, they reported that they gained more respect in their local communities as a result of the ICT skills acquired at the centre—learning to use a computer and accessing and distributing information to local people. This resulted in greater respect at both the family and community levels. Younger women felt they were able to approach the job market with greater confidence. There was also an emergence of solidarity; since women learned to use computers together at the ICT Centre, they often discussed their problems, creating a sense of unity among them and bringing forth leadership qualities.

Functional Literacy through ICT in Ghana

A project in Ghana uses radio to develop functional literacy and to provide information in local languages on a wide range of topics. The topics include HIV/AIDS, teenage pregnancy, nutrition, community empowerment, income generating activities, food preservation, animal husbandry, child labour, and energy-saving. Radio is also used to support literacy teaching with more detailed information that could not be provided in the classroom. Although faced with problems such as poor radio infrastructure and inadequate airtime to offer literacy in 15 local languages, the project illustrated that the use of radio strengthened the coverage of the functional and development themes of the literacy programme, changing people's attitudes towards family planning and contributing to the establishment of income-generating ventures.

ICT for Education in African Countries

World Links, an organization that promotes international tele-collaboration among secondary school teachers and students in developing countries, commissioned a gender assessment study in 2001. The research focused on male and female students in four African countries: Ghana, Mauritania, Senegal and Uganda. The evaluation found that despite efforts to make the programme gender sensitive, gender inequalities in access persisted. In some schools in Ghana and Uganda, girls do not enjoy equitable access to the computer labs. High student-to computer ratios and first come, first-served policies do not favour girls who are typically heavily outnumbered by boys at the secondary level. Girls have earlier curfew hours and domestic responsibilities that limit their access time. Proposed measures to correct this gender bias include encouraging schools to develop "fair use" policies in computer labs, conducting gender sensitivity sessions and advocating for reducing after-school duties of girls to give them more time.

ICT in Support of Women's Health in Uganda

The United Nations Population Fund (UNFPA), in collaboration with Uganda's Ministry of Health and Population Secretariat and Uganda district authorities, initiated the project, RESCUER, with the objective of reducing Uganda's high maternal mortality rate (506 per 100,000) by improving local care and referral systems. The project combined communications, transport and quality health services. High frequency (VHF) radios were installed at base stations, health units, referral hospital ambulances and District Medical Officer's vehicles. Birth attendants were equipped with walkie-talkies which improved the image of the birth attendants and built confidence in their patients, allowing them to help more women. Rural health personnel are now able to call and give practical advice even when there is no transport available.

The RESCUER project is being replicated in three districts and there are plans to extend it to 30 more.

ICT FOR WOMEN EMPOWERMENT - SRI VENKATESWARA UNIVESITY

Profile of Sri Venkateswara University

Established on September 2nd, 1954 as the brain-child of visionary luminaries Sri Prakasam Pantulu, Sri Neelam Sanjeeva Reddy and others, Sri Venkateswara University has been catering to the higher educational needs and aspirations of the people of Rayalaseema. Christened after the Lord of the Seven Hills, the University was launched with generous help from the Tirumala Tirupati Devastanams which donated 1200 acres of sprawling campus along with the then existing college buildings, besides a munificent annual grant of 10 lakhs which has been increased to one crore from the financial year 2008-09.

Efficiently nurtured by committed Vice-chancellors starting from Prof. S. Govindarajulu to the present Vice-Chancellor Prof. N. Prabhakar Rao, the University has grown from strength to strength, emerging as a premiere institution of learning, teaching, research, extension and consultancy.

The university has four constituent campus colleges, S.V.U. College of Arts, S.V.U. College of Sciences, S.V.U. College of Management Studies and S.V.U. College of Engineering, with 60 Departments offering 73 Post-Graduate Courses, 7 Engineering Under-Graduate Colleges spread over Chittoor, Kadapa and Nellore districts.

Affiliated to the University are 37 PG Colleges, 2 Engineering colleges, 23 MBA/MCA Colleges, 6 Law Colleges, 76 College of Education, 2 Physical Education Colleges, 3 Oriental Colleges, 1 College of Music and Dance, 166 Under-Graduate Colleges spread over Chittoor, Kadapa and Nellore districts.

The selection to all PG and Research programs is through entrance tests conducted by the Directorate of Admissions, EAMCET, ICET, Ed.CET, LAWCET etc.

The constituent colleges in the University campus and the Post-Graduate at Kavali together have 5000 students and 600 well qualified faculty members in various disciplines. The faculties have achieved national and international repute for their research output, quality teaching, and have been awarded several national and international fellowships in their respective fields.

ICT FOR WOMEN EMPOWERMENT

There are so many departments viz., Adult & Continuing Education, Computer Science, Extension Studies, Gandhian Studies, Instrumentation Centre, Population Studies, Social Work, Sociology, Women Studies and other Science departments have conducting many programmes for the empowerment of women. There is a separate state resource centre for women to give training and awareness programmes of science and technology. Well established computer lab and other information and communication technology are also available for women to strengthen their educational and economic status. The university is giving training for usage of ICT for unemployed women. Short term and long term courses are running. Some of them are... computer basic knowledge, Photostat, online-business, online-data entry, scanning (earn and learn program) and simple electrical and electronics course. Rajiv Knowledge Centre was established in the university to give computer training for women in general and rural women in particular. There are number of UGC science projects going on in the university. The given below departments are doing a lot of work towards women empowerment.

Recently the university has organized Andhra Pradesh Science Congress in the university campus to motivate students towards science and technology.

1. Adult & Continuing Education

The Adult & Continuing Education Department is organizing so many programmes for women welfare. Those are 'Short term and long term Computer training programme; Photoshop, Xerox, Internet usage, online-booking and online-data entry'. Every year more than nearly 400 women are getting employment through training given by the department. The main aim of department is to achieve 100 per cent female literacy and employment.

2. Computer Science

The Department of Computer Science is offering M.Sc. Computer Science and Master of Computer Application. The department have well established computer lab. The department is regularly organizing seminars/workshops on ICT. So many multinational companies are conducting campus interviews for both M.Sc., and MCA students. Every year more than 30 students are getting placements. Among them majority are female students.

3. Engineering

The College of Engineering is one of the prestigious institutions in India. The old students of this institution are well settled in all over the world. Every year more than 300 students (7 undergraduate engineering courses) are getting placements. All departments are conducting innovative programmes. There is a separate well established women hostel for engineering students. Jawahar Knowledge Centre was established in the campus of engineering. The students of engineering are getting part-time jobs also for packet money.

4. Home Science

The Department of Home Science is doing good job to improve the health status of people in general and women in particular. The department is giving training programme for women towards preparation of nutritional foods by the help of well established scientific lab. It organizes so many programmes to inculcate nutritional food values for women at children's day, Women's Day and Mothers' Day etc.

5. Women Studies

The Department of Women Studies is successfully running so many programmes for women empowerment. The department has taken some villages to conduct case studies. The department is giving computer and internet training programmes for rural intermediate students without collecting any fee. It is providing guest lecturers twice in every month to improve students' skills.

6. University Computer Centre

The University Computer Centre providing internet facility for all students and faculties in the university. High-speed 1Gbps internet facility is available in the university. There is a separate lab for women students and scholars at their hostel. The centre is providing 24 hours free internet facility. The centre is also conducting so many programs on ICT.

CONCLUSIONS

Attention to gender perspectives in existing capacity-building activities and development of specific training for women's groups and networks, including national machineries for the advancement of women, is critical to successfully incorporating gender perspectives in all areas of ICT development. Training is needed at national, regional and local levels. Government bodies could support the development of, and fully utilize the training capacity of, NGOs or civil society organizations involved in ICT. The empowerment of women is possible through education in general and quality education in particular. It is the correct time to think about the curriculum of universities at state and central level. Science and technology oriented quality education is necessary for female students at school, college and university levels. Sri Venkateswara University, Tirupati is taking good steps towards women empowerment.

REFERENCES

1. Academic Reports of S.V.Univesity-2009, Tirupati.
2. Ghosh, Jayati (2004). '*Globalization and the economic empowerment of women*'. Paper presented to the United Nations Economic and Social Commission for Asia and the Pacific (ESCAP) High Level Intergovernmental Meeting to Review the Implementation of the Beijing Platform for Action and its Regional and Global Outcomes, Bangkok, Thailand, 7-10 September 2004.
3. Gonzales, Rosa M. (2004). '*Role of media and communication: new possibilities for local content distribution*'.
4. Gurumurthy, Anita (2004). '*Gender and ICTs: Overview Report*'. Brighton, United Kingdom: Bridge.
5. International Labour Organization (ILO) (2001).

6. Kripalani, Manjeet, Pete Engardio and Steve Hamm (2003). *'The rise of India'*, Business Week Online. 8th December 2003.
7. Marcelle, Gillian M. (2002). *'Information and Communication Technologies (ICT) and their impact on and use as an instrument for the advancement and empowerment of women'*. Report from the online conference hosted by the United Nations Division for the Advancement of Women.
8. Marcelle, Gillian M. (2000). *'Transforming Information and Communications Technologies for gender equality'*. Gender in Development Monograph Series, No. 9.
9. United Nations Economic and Social Council, 2000.
10. United Nations Information and Communication Technologies (UN ICT) Task Force, 2002.
11. World Employment Report 2001.
12. www.svuniversity.in

7

Computer Fundamentals

COMPUTER

1. A computer is an electronic device which takes input and processes that data and outputs information in a desired manner.
2. Computer is a programmable machine.

HARDWARE & SOFTWARE

Modern computers are electronic and digital. The actual machinery — wires, transistors, and circuits — is called **hardware**; the instructions and data are called **software**. All general-purpose computers require the following hardware components:

1. **Memory :** Enables a computer to store, at least temporarily, data and programs.
2. **Mass storage device:** Allows a computer to permanently retain large amounts of data. Common mass storage devices include disk drives and tape drives.
3. **Input device:** Usually a keyboard and mouse, the input device is the conduit through which data and instructions enter a computer.

4. **Output device:** A display screen (monitor), printer, or other device that lets you see what the computer has accomplished.
5. **Central Processing Unit (CPU):** The heart of the computer, this is the component that actually executes instructions.

HISTORY OF COMPUTERS

Webster's Dictionary defines "computer" as any programmable electronic device that can store, retrieve, and process data. The basic idea of computing develops in the 1200's when a Moslem cleric proposes solving problems with a series of written procedures.

As early as the 1640's mechanical calculators are manufactured for sale. Records exist of earlier machines, but Blaise Pascal invents the first commercial calculator, a hand powered adding machine. Although attempts to multiply mechanically were made by Gottfried Liebnitz in the 1670s the first true multiplying calculator appears in Germany shortly before the American Revolution.

In 1801 a Frenchman, Joseph-Marie Jacquard builds a loom that weaves by reading punched holes stored on small sheets of hardwood. These plates are then inserted into the loom which reads (retrieves) the pattern and creates (process) the weave. Powered by water, this "machine" came 140 years before the development of the modern computer.

Shortly after the first mass-produced calculator (1820), Charles Babbage begins his lifelong quest for a programmable machine. Although Babbage was a poor communicator and record-keeper, his difference engine is sufficiently developed by 1842 that Ada Lovelace uses it to mechanically translate a short written work. She is generally regarded as the first programmer. Twelve years later George Boole, while professor of Mathematics at Cork University, writes An Investigation of the Laws of Thought (1854), and is generally recognized as the father of computer science.

The 1890 census is tabulated on punch cards similar to the ones used 90 years earlier to create weaves. Developed by Herman

Hollerith of MIT, the system uses electric power (non-mechanical). The Hollerith Tabulating Company is a forerunner of today's IBM.

Just prior to the introduction of Hollerith's machine the first printing calculator is introduced. In 1892 William Burroughs, a sickly ex-teller, introduces a commercially successful printing calculator. Although hand-powered, Burroughs quickly introduces an electronic model.

In 1925, unaware of the work of Charles Babbage, Vannevar Bush of MIT builds a machine he calls the differential analyzer. Using a set of gears and shafts, much like Babbage, the machine can handle simple calculus problems, but accuracy is a problem.

The period from 1935 through 1952 gets murky with claims and counterclaims of who invents what and when. Part of the problem lies in the international situation that makes much of the research secret. Other problems include poor record-keeping, deception and lack of definition.

In 1935, Konrad Zuse, a German construction engineer, builds a mechanical calculator to handle the math involved in his profession. Shortly after completion, Zuse starts on a programmable electronic device which he completes in 1938.

John Vincent Atanasoff begins work on a digital computer in 1936 in the basement of the Physics building on the campus of Iowa State. A graduate student, Clifford (John) Berry assists. The "ABC" is designed to solve linear equations common in physics. It displays some early features of later computers including electronic calculations. He shows it to others in 1939 and leaves the patent application with attorneys for the school when he leaves for a job in Washington during World War II. Unimpressed, the school never files and ABC is cannibalized by students.

The Enigma, a complex mechanical encoder is used by the Germans and they believe it to be unbreakable. Several people involved, most notably Alan Turing, conceive machines to handle the problem, but none are technically feasible. Turing proposes a "Universal Machine" capable of "computing" any algorithm in 1937. That same year George Steblitz creates his Model K (itchen), a conglomeration of otherwise useless and leftover material, to solve complex calculations. He improves the design while working at Bell Labs and on September 11, 1940, Steblitz uses a teletype machine at Dartmouth College in New Hampshire to transmit a problem to his Complex Number Calculator in New York and receives the results. It is the first example of a network.

First in Poland, and later in Great Britain and the United States, the Enigma code is broken. Information gained by this shortens the war. To break the code, the British, led by Touring, build the Colossus Mark I. The existence of this machine is a closely guarded secret of the British Government until 1970. The United States Navy, aided to some extent by the British, builds a machine capable of breaking not only the German code but the Japanese code as well.

In 1943 development begins on the Electronic Numerical Integrator And Computer (ENIAC) in earnest at Penn State. Designed by **John Mauchly** and **J. Presper Eckert** of the Moore School, they get help from **John von Neumann** and others. In 1944, the Havard Mark I is introduced. Based on a series of proposals from **Howard Aiken** in the late 1930's, the Mark I computes complex tables for the U.S. Navy. It uses a paper tape to store instructions and Aiken hires **Grace Hopper** ("Amazing Grace") as one of three programmers working on the machine. **Thomas J. Watson Sr.** plays a pivotal role involving his company, IBM, in the machine's development.

Early in 1945, with the Mark I stopped for repairs, Hopper notices a moth in one of the relays, possibly causing the problem. From this day on, Hopper refers to fixing the system as "debugging". The same year Von Neumann proposes the concept of a "stored program" in a paper that is never officially published.

Work completes on ENIAC in 1946. Although only three years old the machine is woefully behind on technology, but the inventors opt to continue while working on a more modern machine, the EDVAC. Programming ENIAC requires it to be rewired. A later version eliminates this problem. To make the machine appear more impressive to reporters during its unveiling, a team member (possibly Eckert) puts translucent spheres (halved ping pong balls) over the lights. The US patent office will later recognize this as the first computer.

The next year scientists employed by Bell Labs complete work on the transistor (**John Bardeen**, **Walter Brattain** and **William Shockley** receive the Nobel Prize in Physics in 1956), and by 1948 teams around the world work on a "stored program" machine. The first, nicknamed "Baby", is a prototype of a much larger machine under construction in Britain and is shown in June 1948.

The impetus over the next 5 years for advances in computers is mostly the government and military. UNIVAC, delivered in 1951 to the Census Bureau, results in a tremendous financial loss to its manufacturer, Remington-Rand. The next year Grace Hopper, now an employee of that company proposes "reusable software," code segments that could be extracted and assembled according to instructions in a "higher level language." The concept of compiling is born. Hopper would revise this concept over the next twenty years and her ideas would become an integral part of all modern computers. CBS uses one of the 46 UNIVAC computers produced to predict the outcome of the 1952 Presidential Election. They do not air the prediction for 3 hours because they do not trust the machine.

IBM introduces the 701 the following year. It is the first commercially successful computer. In 1956 FORTRAN is introduced (proposed 1954, it takes nearly 3 years to develop the compiler). Two additional languages, LISP and COBOL, are added in 1957 and 1958. Other early languages include ALGOL and BASIC. Although never widely used, ALGOL is the basis for many of today's languages.

With the introduction of Control Data's CDC1604 in 1958, the first transistor powered computer, a new age dawns. Brilliant scientist **Seymour Cray** heads the development team. This year integrated circuits are introduced by two men, **Jack Kilby** and **John Noyce**, working independently. The second network is developed at MIT. Over the next three years computers begin affecting the day-to-day lives of most Americans. The addition of MICR characters at the bottom of checks is common.

In 1961 Fairchild Semiconductor introduces the integrated circuit. Within ten years all computers use these instead of the transistor. Formally building sized computers are now room-sized, and are considerably more powerful. The following year the Atlas becomes operational, displaying many of the features that make today's systems so powerful including virtual memory, pipeline instruction execution and paging. Designed at the University of Manchester, some of the people who developed Colossus thirty years earlier make contributions.

On April 7, 1964, IBM introduces the System/360. While a technical marvel, the main feature of this machine is business oriented...IBM guarantees the "upward compatibility" of the system, reducing the risk that a business would invest in outdated technology. Dartmouth College, where the first network was demonstrated 25 years earlier, moves to the forefront of the "computer age" with the introduction of TSS(Time Share System) a crude(by today's standards) networking system. It is the first Wide Area Network. In three years Randy Golden, President and Founder of Golden Ink, would begin working on this network.

Within a year MIT returns to the top of the intellectual computer community with the introduction of a greatly refined network that features shared resources and uses the first minicomputer (DEC's PDP-8) to manage telephone lines. Bell Labs and GE play major roles in its design.

In 1969 Bell Labs, unhappy with the direction of the MIT project, leaves and develops its' own operating system, UNIX. One of the many precursors to today's Internet, ARPANet, is quietly launched. **Alan Keys**, who will later become a designer for Apple, proposes the "personal computer." Also in 1969, unhappy with Fairchild Semiconductor, a group of technicians begin discussing forming their own company. This company, formed the next year, would be known as Intel. The movie Colossus: The Forbin Project has a supercomputer as the villain. Next year, The Computer Wore Tennis Shoes was the first feature length movie with the word computer in the title. In 1971, Texas Instruments introduces the first "pocket calculator." It weighs 2.5 pounds.

With the country embroiled in a crisis of confidence known as Watergate, in 1973 a little publicized judicial decision takes the patent for the computer away from Mauchly and Eckert and awards it to Atanasoff. Xerox introduces the mouse. Proposals are made for the first local area networks.

In 1975 the first personal computer is marketed in kit form. The Altair features 256 bytes of memory. **Bill Gates**, with others, writes a BASIC compiler for the machine. The next year Apple begins to market PC's, also in kit form. It includes a monitor and keyboard. The earliest RISC platforms become stable. In 1976, Queen Elizabeth goes on-line with the first royal email message.

During the next few years the personal computer explodes on the American scene. Microsoft, Apple and many smaller PC related companies form (and some die). By 1977 stores begin to sell PC's. Continuing today, companies strive to reduce the size and price of PC's while increasing capacity. Entering the fray, IBM introduces it's PC in 1981(it's actually IBM's second attempt, but the first failed miserably). Time selects the computer as its Man of the Year in 1982. Tron, a computer-generated special effects extra-vaganza is released the same year.

GENERATIONS OF COMPUTERS

Each generation of computer is characterized by a major technological development that fundamentally changed the way computers operate, resulting in increasingly smaller, cheaper, more powerful and more efficient and reliable devices.

The history of computer development is often referred to in reference to the different generations of computing devices. Each generation of computer is characterized by a major technological development that fundamentally changed the way computers operate, resulting in increasingly smaller, cheaper, more powerful and more efficient and reliable devices.

First Generation Computers (1949-1959) Vacuum Tubes

The first computers used vacuum tubes for circuitry and magnetic drums for memory, and were often enormous, taking up entire rooms. They were very expensive to operate and in addition to using a great deal of electricity, generated a lot of heat, which was often the cause of malfunctions.

First generation computers relied on machine language, the lowest-level programming language understood by computers, to perform operations, and they could only solve one problem at a time. Input was based on punched cards and paper tape, and output was displayed on printouts.

IBM 701, IBM 650, UNIVAC and ENIAC computers are examples of first-generation computing devices. The UNIVAC was the first commercial computer delivered to a business client, the U.S. Census Bureau in 1951.

Second Generation Computers (1959-1965) Transistors

Transistors replaced vacuum tubes and ushered in the second generation of computers. The transistor was invented in 1947 but did not see widespread use in computers until the late 1950s. The transistor was far superior to the vacuum tube, allowing computers to become smaller, faster, cheaper, more energy-efficient and more reliable than their first-generation predecessors. Though the transistor still generated a great deal of heat that subjected the computer to damage, it was a vast improvement over the vacuum tube. Second-generation computers still relied on punched cards for input and printouts for output.

Second-generation computers moved from cryptic binary machine language to symbolic, or assembly, languages, which allowed programmers to specify instructions in words. High-level programming languages were also being developed at this time, such as early versions of COBOL and FORTRAN. These were also the first computers that stored their instructions in their memory, which moved from a magnetic drum to magnetic core technology.

PDP-8, IBM 7090 and IBM 70941 are the come under second generation computers. The first computers of this generation were developed for the atomic energy industry.

Third Generation Computers (1965-1970) Integrated Circuits

The development of the integrated circuit was the hallmark of the third generation of computers. Transistors were miniaturized and placed on silicon chips, called semiconductors, which drastically increased the speed and efficiency of computers.

Instead of punched cards and printouts, users interacted with third generation computers through keyboards and monitors and interfaced with an operating system, which allowed the device to run many different applications at one time with a central program that monitored the memory. Computers for the first time became accessible to a mass audience because they were smaller and cheaper than their predecessors.

Examples: IBM 360, CDC 7600

Fourth Generation Computers (1970-1985) Integrated Chips

The microprocessor brought the fourth generation of computers, as thousands of integrated circuits were built onto a single silicon chip. What in the first generation filled an entire room could now fit in the palm of the hand. The Intel 4004 chip, developed in 1971, located all the components of the computer—from the central processing unit and memory to input/output controls—on a single chip.

In 1981 IBM introduced its first computer for the home user, and in 1984 Apple introduced the Macintosh. Microprocessors also moved out of the realm of desktop computers and into many areas of life as more and more everyday products began to use microprocessors.

As these small computers became more powerful, they could be linked together to form networks, which eventually led to the development of the Internet. Fourth generation computers also saw the development of GUIs, the mouse and handheld devices.

Example: Apple 11

Fifth Generation Computers (1985-onwards) Artificial Intelligence

Fifth generation computing devices, based on artificial intelligence, are still in development, though there are some applications, such as voice recognition, that are being used today. The use of parallel processing and superconductors is helping to make artificial intelligence a reality. Quantum computation and molecular and nanotechnology will radically change the face of computers in years to come. The goal of fifth-generation computing is to develop devices that respond to natural language input and are capable of learning and self-organization.

Example: VLSIC

BLOCK DIAGRAM OF COMPUTER

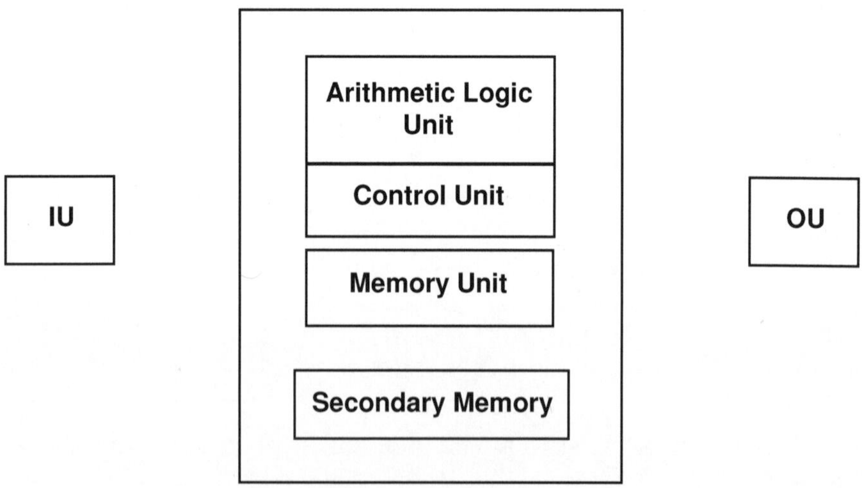

Fig-12: Computer Block Diagram

Input Unit (IU): Computer will collect data from the user through this input unit. The keyboard is a standard input unit. Pictures can be entered to the computer through scanner. Example: Keyboard, mouse, scanner, touch screen, light pen.

Central Processing Unit (CPU): The CPU of the computer has Arithmetic Unit, Logic Unit, Central Unit and a set of registers. The logic unit performs logical operations. The arithmetic unit performs arithmetic operations. The control unit controls all the other unit of computers. The logic unit can understand the instructions of a procedure. It will read instructions from the memory one after the other.

Output Unit (OU): Output devices are for giving results. The standard output unit of the computer is monitor. Monitor looks like a TV. Other output units are printers, plotters, monitor, Liquid Crystal Display (LCD)

Memory:

i) Primary Memory: The RAM (Random Access Memory) and ROM (Read Only Memory) are treated as primary memory units.

ii) Secondary Memory: Hard disk is the secondary memory of the computer. All the software loaded into the computer is stored into the memory.

PARTS OF A COMPUTER

If you use a desktop computer, you might already know that there isn't any single part called the "computer." A computer is really a system of many parts working together. The physical parts, which you can see and touch, are collectively called hardware. (Software, on the other hand, refers to the instructions, or programs, that tell the hardware what to do.)

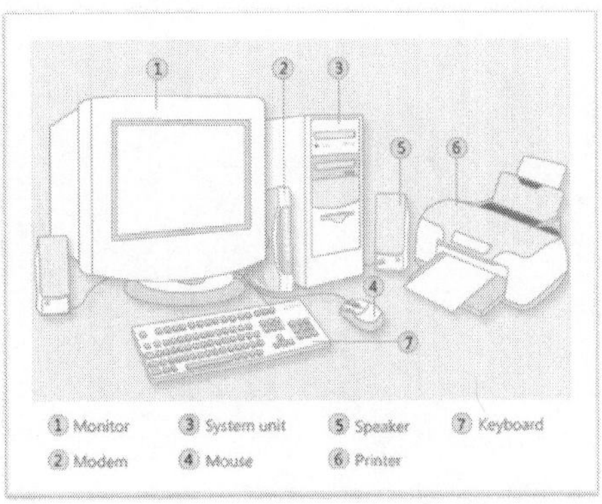

Fig-1: Desktop computer system

The illustration below shows the most common hardware in a desktop computer system. Your system may look a little different, but it probably has most of these parts. A laptop computer has similar parts but combines them into a single notebook-sized package.

System unit

The system unit is the core of a computer system. Usually it's a rectangular box placed on or underneath desk. Inside this box are many electronic components that process information. The most important of these components is the central processing unit (CPU), or microprocessor, which acts as the "brain" of computer. Another component is random access memory (RAM), which temporarily stores information that the CPU uses while the computer is on. The information stored in RAM is erased when the computer is turned off. Read Only Memory (ROM), as the name itself implies, holds permanent data or instruction that can only be read from, but not written onto, i.e. information is permanently recorded so that it cannot be changed by the programmers. The contents of ROM are not lost when the computer is switched off.

Almost every other part of computer connects to the system unit using cables. The cables plug into specific ports (openings), typically on the back of the system unit. Hardware that is not part of the system unit is sometimes called a peripheral device or device.

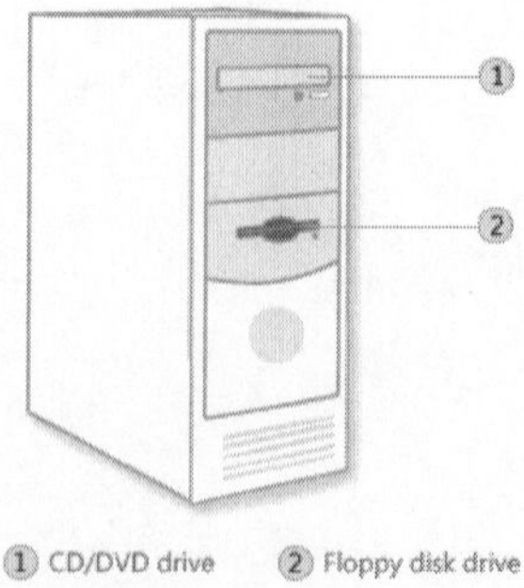

Fig-2: System unit

Storage

Your computer has one or more disk drives—devices that store information on a metal or plastic disk. The disk preserves the information even when your computer is turned off.

Hard disk drive

Your computer's hard disk drive stores information on a hard disk, a rigid platter or stack of platters with a magnetic surface. Because hard disks can hold massive amounts of information, they usually serve as your computer's primary means of storage, holding almost all of your programs and files. The hard disk drive is normally located inside the system unit.

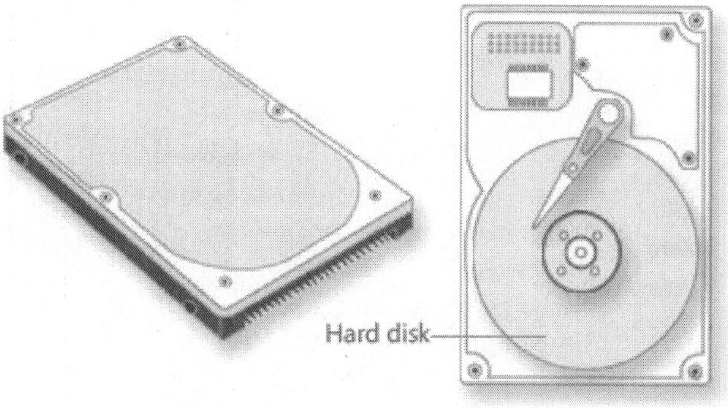

Fig-3: Hard disk drive

CD and DVD drives

Nearly all computers today come equipped with a CD or DVD drive, usually located on the front of the system unit. CD drives use lasers to read (retrieve) data from a CD, and many CD drives can also write (record) data onto CDs. If you have a recordable disk drive, you can store copies of your files on blank CDs. You can also use a CD drive to play music CDs on your computer.

DVD drives can do everything that CD drives can, plus read DVDs. If you have a DVD drive, you can watch movies on your computer. Many DVD drives can record data onto blank DVDs.

Fig-4: CD

Tip

If you have a recordable CD or DVD drive, periodically back up (copy) your important files to CDs or DVDs. That way, if your hard disk ever fails, you won't lose your data.

Floppy disk drive

Floppy disk drives store information on floppy disks, also called floppies or diskettes. Compared to CDs and DVDs, floppy disks can store only a small amount of data. They also retrieve information more slowly and are more prone to damage. For these reasons, floppy disk drives are less popular than they used to be, although some computers still include them.

Fig-5: Floppy disk

Why are floppy disks "floppy"? Even though the outside is made of hard plastic, that's just the sleeve. The disk inside is made of a thin, flexible vinyl material.

Mouse

A mouse is a small device used to point to and select items on your computer screen. Although mice come in many shapes, the typical mouse does look a bit like an actual mouse. It's small, oblong, and connected to the system unit by a long wire that resembles a tail. Some newer mice are wireless.

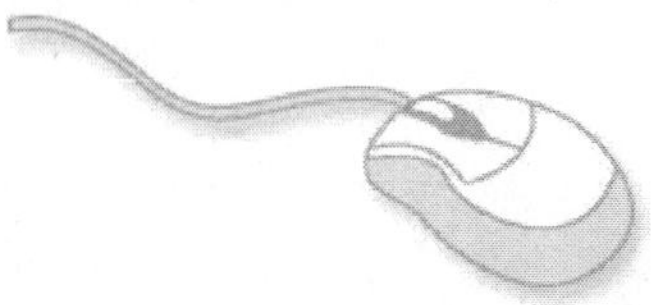

Fig-6: Mouse

A mouse usually has two buttons: a primary button (usually the left button) and a secondary button. Many mice also have a wheel between the two buttons, which allows you to scroll smoothly through screens of information.

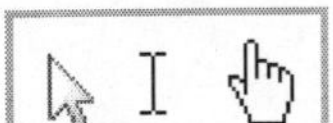

When you move the mouse with your hand, a pointer on your screen moves in the same direction. (The pointer's appearance might change depending on where it's positioned on your screen.) When you want to select an item, you point to the item and then click (press and release) the primary button. Pointing and clicking with your mouse is the main way to interact with your computer.

Keyboard

A keyboard is used mainly for typing text into your computer. Like the keyboard on a typewriter, it has keys for letters and numbers, but it also has special keys:

- The function keys, found on the top row, perform different functions depending on where they are used.
- The numeric keypad, located on the right side of most keyboards, allows you to enter numbers quickly.

- The navigation keys, such as the arrow keys, allow you to move your position within a document or webpage.

Fig-7: Keyboard

You can also use your keyboard to perform many of the same tasks you can perform with a mouse.

Monitor

A monitor displays information in visual form, using text and graphics. The portion of the monitor that displays the information is called the screen. Like a television screen, a computer screen can show still or moving pictures.

There are two basic types of monitors: CRT (cathode ray tube) monitors and LCD (liquid crystal display) monitors. Both types produce sharp images, but LCD monitors have the advantage of being much thinner and lighter. CRT monitors, however, are generally more affordable.

Fig-8: LCD monitor CRT monitor

Printer

A printer transfers data from a computer onto paper. You don't need a printer to use your computer, but having one allows you to print e mail, cards, invitations, announcements, and other materials. Many people also like being able to print their own photos at home.

The two main types of printers are inkjet printers and laser printers. Inkjet printers are the most popular printers for the home. They can print in black and white or in full color and can produce high-quality photographs when used with special paper. Laser printers are faster and generally better able to handle heavy use.

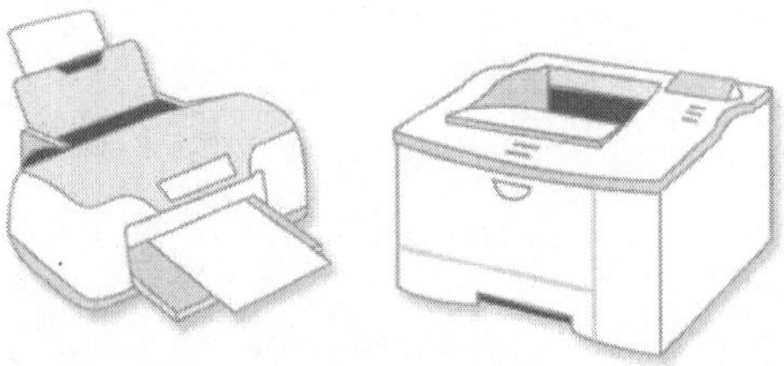

Fig-9: Inkjet printer laser printer

Speakers

Speakers are used to play sound. They may be built into the system unit or connected with cables. Speakers allow you to listen to music and hear sound effects from your computer.

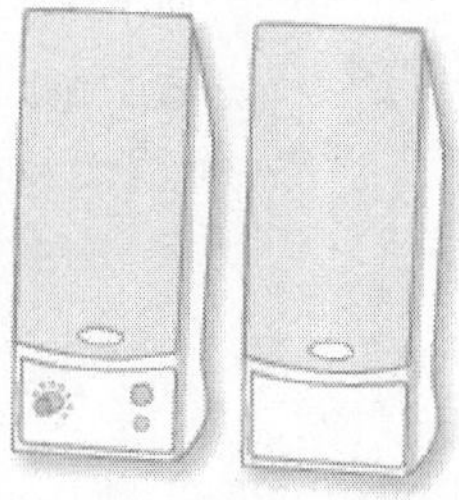

Fig-10: Computer speakers

Modem

To connect your computer to the Internet, you need a modem. A modem is a device that sends and receives computer information over a telephone line or high-speed cable. Modems are sometimes built into the system unit, but higher-speed modems are usually separate components.

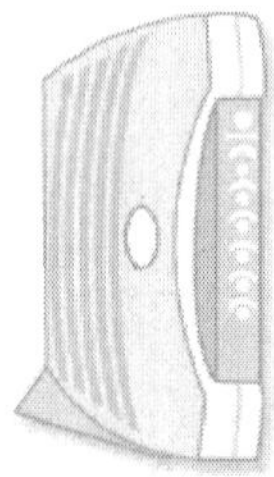

Fig-11: Cable modem

In addition to these components, many others make it possible for the basic components to work together efficiently. For example, every computer requires a bus that transmits data from one part of the computer to another.

INPUT AND OUTPUT DEVICES

Input Devices: Keyboard, Mouse, Scanner, Joystick

Output Devices: Speakers, Headphones, Screen (Monitor), Printer

CHARACTERISTICS OF A COMPUTER

The characteristics of computer are Speed, Accuracy, Automatic, Endurance, Versatility, Storage, Reduction of cost and Intelligent quotient.

Celerity (High Speed)

It denotes the speed of a computer. The computer present in the modern world has the speed of nano and pico second. The various speeds that are used by the computers from the former generations are as follows:

1 milli second=1*10^-3 second
1 micro second=1*10^-6 second
1 nano second=1*10^-9 second
1 pico second=1*10^-12 second
Thus the speeds are measured.

Authenticity (Accuracy)

It denoted the **accuracy** of the computer. They are reliable and robust. It ever makes a mistake. Most probably the error occurs due to the user rather than the computer. There may be certain hardware mistake but with the advanced technique in hand they are overcome.

Example: Only accurate robots are used to perform the operations for the patients since human hands are not flexible for making operations.

Spontaneous (Automatic)

The computers are automatic. It may execute the process without any intervention of user once they are assigned to a work. Once the data or instruction are fetched from the secondary devices such as optical disks, hard disks etc. Immediately they get stored into RAM (primary memory) and then sequentially they get executed.

Pertinacity (Endurance)

This denotes that the computers never get tried as the humans do. If there are surplus amount of executions to be made then each and every execution will be executed at the same time period. They can perform their assigned task without taking any refreshment.

Example: Computers which are used for controlling the satellites.

Adaptability (Versatile)

In our day to day life computers has been a part, with their extended flexibility they are used, all over the world. They can be used as personal computers, for home uses, for business oriented tasks, weather forecasting, space explorations, teaching, railways, banking, medicine etc. All Modern computers can perform different kind of tasks simultaneously.

Storehouse (Memory)

Secondary storage devices are the key for the data storage. They store the data for which the user wants to retrieve these data for future use. The examples for various secondary devices are Floppy disk, Optical disks (CS and DVD), Zip drives, Thumb drives etc. The data of smaller size can be easily fetched and they can be copied to the primary memory (RAM).

Example: Data Warehousing made by IBM.

Cheaper (Reduction of cost)

Computers are short term investment in order to achieve a long term gain. Though the investment is high they reduce the cost of each and every transaction. They reduce man power and leads to an elegant and efficient way for computing various tasks.

Needs a User interface

The only drawback of computer is it cannot make the decision of its own. It needs a guidance to enhance the process. After all computers is a machine

The two principal characteristics of a computer are:

⇒ It responds to a specific set of instructions in a well-defined manner.

⇒ It can execute a prerecorded list of instructions (a program).

CLASSIFICATION OF COMPUTERS

a) Based on type of input or based on logic computers are divided into three types

i) Analog Computers

ii) Digital Computers

iii) Hybrid Computers

i) **Analog Computers**: This system uses physical relationships for measurements and automobile speedometer is an analog computer system. This will convert the physical measurement i.e. distance travelled in a value.

ii) **Digital Computers**: The logic in this system is binary. This is also called as digital logic. Today personal computers are the best examples for digital computers.

iii) **Hybrid Computers**: This system is a combination of analog and digital computers.

Note: Modem converts analog to digital and digital to analog.

b) Based on size, cost and performance computers are divided into 5 types

i) Super Computers
ii) Mainframe Computers
iii) Mini Computers
iv) Personal Computers
v) Laptop and Palmtop Computers

i) **Super Computers**: The super computer requires special type of atmosphere. It requires continuous maintenance. These are heavy systems. The cost will be very high. They are share by a large number of users. Government organizations provide such systems for very large number of users. The speed and memory capacity and other attributes of this system are very high (that can perform hundreds of millions of instructions per second). These systems are used in space research and weather prediction.

ii) **Mainframe Computers**: A powerful multi-user computer capable of supporting many hundreds or thousands of users simultaneously.

iii) **Minicomputer:** A multi-user computer capable of supporting from 10 to hundreds of users simultaneously.

iv) **Personal Computer**: A small, single-user computer based on a microprocessor. In addition to the microprocessor, a personal computer has a keyboard for entering data, a monitor for displaying information, and a storage device for saving data.

v) **Laptop and Palmtop Computers**: A laptop computer is a PC in the form of a book. It is portable. One can carried this for information feeding and retrieval even on sites. These can be used in flights, buses and trains. Top officials and businessmen use this for save their time.

A palmtop computer is a computer system in the size of a calculator. Nowadays they are coming with internet connection. Like cellular phone one can carried palmtop computer and browse the websites freely from any place.

NUMERICAL SYSTEM

The reason that "hex" and octal are popular in computing is that it's easy to translate to and from the binary system that computers *really* use. People use decimal primarily because they have ten fingers, but it's just not that convenient to switch back and forth from 10011010010 to 1234. These are all called radix numbers because the method for figuring out how to represent the value (remember the rocks in a bag) is the same. The only real difference between them is the base that they use.

Binary - base 2
Octal - base 8
Decimal - base 10
Hexadecimal - base 16

One thing that should be kept in mind is that the number system used to represent the value of the base above is actually expressed as a decimal, or base 10 number. That is, we don't normally say hexadecimal is base 10 in hex. We say it's base 16 in decimal.

8

Introduction to Operating System

Definition of Operating System

An operating system (OS) is a set of programs that manage computer hardware resources and provide common services for application software. The operating system is the most important type of system software in a computer system. A user cannot run an application program on the computer without an operating system, unless the application program is self booting.

Operating system acts as an interface between the computer user and physical computer hardware.

Functions of Operating System

1) Command Interpretation
2) Memory Management
3) Device Management
4) Process Management

The computer system can be divided into the following modules:

i. The hardware, CPU, Input & Output devices, memory, all connections of computer etc.

ii. Operating system is a tool to manage hardware resources
iii. Application programmes, compilers, database, software applications etc.
iv. The computer used such as programmers, clients, administrators.

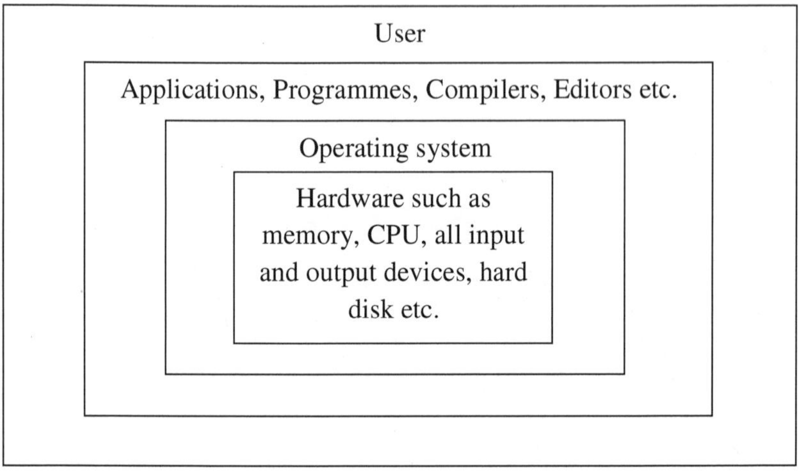

1) Command Interpretation:

If we want to do any piece of work with the help of computers then we have to give instructions to the computer. In computer language these instructions are called commands. But we are giving commands in high level languages. But the computer can understand only machine language. So we need interface between these two languages. This command interpretation interprets the command given by the user.

2) Memory Management:

If many users use the computer as the same user run more than one application at a time. The main memory allocated and de-allocated to all these jobs by the operating system in an efficient ways.

3) Device Management:

All the hardware input, output devices such as printer, modem, CD drivers, floppy drives are managed by the operating system.

4) Process Management:

If more than one job is submitted to the CPU of the computer then the operating system allows a time schedule for each job. Then all jobs are completed in an efficient way by the operating system.

Types of Operating System

a) Character user interface operating system (CUI): DOS

Every computer that is to be operated by an individual requires a user interface. The user interface is not actually a part of the operating system—it generally runs in a separate program usually referred to as a shell, but is essential if human interaction is to be supported. The user interface requests services from the operating system that will acquire data from input hardware devices, such as a keyboard, mouse or credit card reader, and requests operating system services to display prompts, status messages and such on output hardware devices, such as a video monitor or printer. The two most common forms of a user interface have historically been the command-line interface, where computer commands are typed out line-by-line, and the graphical user interface, where a visual environment is present.

b) Graphical user interface operating system (GUI): Windows

Most of the modern computer systems support graphical user interfaces (GUI), and often include them. In some computer systems, such as the original implementation of Mac OS, the GUI is integrated into the kernel (the kernel is the main component of most computer operating systems; it is a bridge between applications and the actual data processing done at the hardware level). Modern releases of Microsoft Windows such as Windows Vista implement a graphics subsystem that is mostly in user-space; however the graphics drawing routines of versions between Windows NT 4.0 and Windows Server 2003 exist mostly in kernel space. Windows 9x had very little distinction between the interface and the kernel. Many computer operating systems allow the user to install or create any user interface they desire.

Introduction & History of Windows

Windows is the operating system sold by the Seattle-based company Microsoft. Microsoft, originally christened "Traf-O-Data" in 1972, was renamed "Micro-soft" in November 1975, then "Microsoft" on November 26, 1976.

Microsoft entered the marketplace in August 1981 by releasing version 1.0 of the operating system Microsoft DOS (MS-DOS), a 16-bit command-line operating system

The first version of Microsoft Windows (Microsoft Windows 1.0) came out in November 1985. It had a graphical user interface, inspired by the user interface of the Apple computers of the time. Windows 1.0 was not successful with the public, and Microsoft Windows 2.0, launched December 9, 1987, did not do much better.

It was on May 22, 1990 that Microsoft Windows became a success, with Windows 3.0, then Windows 3.1 in 1992, and finally Microsoft Windows for Workgroups, later renamed Windows 3.11, which included network capabilities. Windows 3.1 cannot be considered an entirely separate operating system because it was only a graphical user interface running on top of MS-DOS.

On August 24, 1995, Microsoft launched the operating system Microsoft Windows 95. Windows 95 signified Microsoft's willingness to transfer some of MS-DOS's capabilities into Windows, but this new version was based more heavily on 16-bit DOS and retained the limitations of the FAT16 file system, so that it was not possible to use long file names.

After minor revisions of Microsoft Windows 95, named Windows 95A OSR1, Windows 95B OSR2, Windows 95B OSR2.1 and Windows 95C OSR2.5, Microsoft released the next version of Windows on June 25, 1998: Windows 98. Windows 98 natively supported features other than those of MS-DOS but was still based upon it. What's more, Windows 98 suffered from poor memory handling when multiple applications were running, which could cause system malfunctions. A second edition of Windows 98 came out on February 17, 2000; it was named Windows 98 SE (for "Second Edition").

On September 14, 2000, Microsoft released Windows Me (for Millennium Edition), also called Windows Millennium. Windows Millennium was based largely on Windows 98 (and therefore on MS-DOS), but added additional multimedia and software capabilities. Furthermore, Windows Millennium included a system-restore mechanism for returning to a previous state in the event of a crash.

Concurrent with these releases, Microsoft had been selling (since 1992) an entirely 32-bit operating system (which therefore was not based on MS-DOS) for professional use, at a time when business primarily used mainframes. It was Windows NT (for Windows "New Technology"). Windows NT was not a new version of Windows 95 or an improvement on it, but an entirely different operating system

On May 24, 1993, the first version of Windows NT was released. It was called Windows NT 3.1, and was followed by Windows NT 3.5 in September 1994 and Windows 3.51 in June 1995. With Windows NT 4.0, launched for sale on August 24, 1996, Windows NT finally became a true success.

In July 1998, Microsoft released Windows NT 4.0 TSE (Terminal Server Emulation), the first Windows system that allowed terminals to be plugged into a server, i.e. use thin clients to open a session on the server.

On February 17, 2000, the next version of NT 4.0 was renamed Windows 2000 (instead of Windows NT 5.0) in order to highlight the unification of "NT" with the "Windows 9x" systems. Windows 2000 is an entirely 32-bit system with characteristics of Windows NT, as well as an improved task manager and full compatibility with USB and FireWire peripherals.

Utilities of Windows (95-2000)

What is MS-DOS?

Microsoft Disc Operating System: MS-DOS acts like a traffic cop. It enforces basic rules that all programs must follow. MS-DOS controls how a program interacts with you. They help you:

- Manage your files.
- Deal with peripheral devices such as your printer, plotters, scanners etc.
- Control and optimize your computer.

Internal and External Commands

Internal Commands

- BREAK
- CALL
- CHCP
- CHDIR(CD)
- CLS
- COPY
- CTTY
- DATE
- DEL(ERASE)
- DIR
- ECHO
- EXIT
- FOR
- GOTO
- IF
- MKDIR(MD)
- PATH
- PAUSE
- PROMPT
- REM
- RENAME(REN)
- RMDIR(RD)
- SET
- SHIFT
- TIME
- TYPE
- VER
- VERIFY
- VOL

External Commands

- APPEND.EXE
- ASSIGN.COM
- ATTRIB.EXE
- BACKUP.EXE
- CHKDSK.EXE
- COMMAND.COM
- COMP.EXE
- DEBUG.EXE
- DISKCOMP.COM
- DISKCOPY.COM
- DOSKEY.COM
- DOSSHELL.COM
- EDIT.COM
- EDLIN.EXE
- EMM386.EXE
- EXE2BIN.EXE
- EXPAND.EXE
- FASTOPEN.EXE
- FC.EXE
- FDISK.EXE
- FORMAT.COM
- GRAFTABLE.COM
- GRAPHICS.COM
- HELP.EXE
- JOIN.EXE
- KEYB.COM
- LABEL.EXE
- MEM.EXE
- MIRROR.COM
- MODE.COM
- MORE.COM
- NLSFUNC.EXE
- PRINT.EXE
- QBASIC.EXE

- o RECOVER.EXE
- o REPLACE.EXE
- o RESTORE.EXE
- o SETVER.EXE
- o SHARE.EXE
- o SORT.EXE
- o SUBST.EXE
- o SYS.COM
- o TREE.COM
- o UNDELETE.EXE
- o UNFORMAT.COM
- o XCOPY.EXE

Command	Explanation	Syntax	Example	Notes
DIR	The DIR commands displays all the sub directories and files of the current drive and directory. It also shows the size of the files and the date and time they were last modified.	C:\DIR DRIVE	C:\DIR	Displays the contents of the C: If you give just DIR then the result will be same as DIR C:, since your current drive is C:
CLS	CLS command is used to clear the screen	C:CLS	C:CLS	If the screen is full with the information and you want to clear the screen the CLS command can be used and the C: will appear on the top of the screen.
DATE	Date command is used to display the system's current date	C:\DATE	C:\DATE	DOS displays the current date and asks you to enter the new date Current date is Mon 11-14-2011 Enter New Date (mm-dd-yy)
TIME	TIME command is used to display the system's current time	C:\TIME	C:\TIME	DOS displays the current time and asks you to enter new time Current time is 12:55:25:34p Enter new time:
MD	The Make Directory command is used to create a new directory. Directories are created to organize the	MD DRIVE PATH\ DIRECTOR Y	C:\MD\ DATA	A directory will be created under C: by name DATA. If the path is not given

	programmes and data systematically	NAME		the directory will be created in the current drive.
CD	The Change Directory command will allow you to move to the directory	CD PATH	C:\DATA>	The C prompt appears with a new directory DATA
RD	The Remove Directory command will allow you to remove the directory.	RD DRIVE PATH	C:\RD DATA	To remove a directory, first you should come to one level above the current directory and then remove. If the directory you are removing contains any other directories of files, first those should be removed and then the directory should be removed.
MOVE	Move command allows to move the file from one source to another.	MOVE SOURCE DESTINATION	C:\DATA\LETTER> MOVE TEST.EXT \DATA	In this example, file TEXT.EXT is moved from LETTER directory to DATA directory. Here the source is LETTER directory and destination is DATA directory.
DELETE	Delete command erase the files which are not required any more.	DEL DRIVE PATH FILE NAME	C:\ DATA\LETTER> DEL TEXT.EXT	This TEXT.EXT file from the LETTER directory will be deleted
COPY	Copy command is used to make an exact copy of the files and place them in a new location	COPY SOURCE DESTINATION	C:\COPY TEXT EXT A:	TEXT.EXT from C drive will be copied to A:

a) Arranging Windows

Arrange windows side by side on the desktop using Snap

You can use Snap to arrange windows side by side, which can be especially helpful when comparing two documents or when moving files from one place to another.

To arrange windows side by side

1. Drag the title bar of a window to the left or right side of the screen until an outline of the expanded window appears.

2. Release the mouse to expand the window.
3. Repeat steps 1 and 2 with another window to arrange the windows side by side.

To return the window to its original size, drag the title bar away from the top of the desktop and then release.

b) Creating & Renaming Folders (Files)

Creating a file or folder

1. **Open My Documents**
2. Under **File and Folder Tasks**, click **Make a new folder**. A new folder is displayed with the default name, **New Folder**, selected.
3. Type a name for the new folder, and then press ENTER.

Rename a file or folder

1. Click on Start, and then click on My Documents
2. Click on the file or folder you want to rename.
3. Under File, click Rename.
4. Type the new name, and then press ENTER key.
5. File or folder can also be renamed by right clicking it and then clicking Rename.

c) Creating Desktop shortcuts

To create a shortcut on the desktop to a program or file, there are two possible methods to choose from.

Method 1

1. Right-click an open area on the desktop, point to **New**, and then click **Shortcut**.
2. Click **Browse**.
3. Locate the program or file to which you want to create a shortcut, click the program or file, click **Open**, and then click **Next**.
4. Type a name for the shortcut. If a **Finish** button appears at the bottom of the dialog box, click it. If a **Next** button appears at the bottom of the dialog box, click it, click the icon you want to use for the shortcut, and then click **Finish**.

Method 2

1. Click **Start**, point to **Programs**, and then right-click the program you want to create the shortcut to.
2. Click **Create Shortcut**.
3. The shortcut is now at the end of the Programs list. For example, if you created a shortcut to Microsoft Word, to find that program, click **Start**, and then point to **Programs**. You will find the shortcut, named "Microsoft Word (2)" (without the quotation marks), at the bottom of the Program list.
4. Drag the shortcut to the Desktop.

d) Creating & saving files

Creating a File

1. In the menu bar click file menu.
2. Select New from the list that appears.
3. New file appears in the form of window.

Save a File in Windows

1. In the top toolbar (menu bar) click File.
2. Select Save As from the list that appears.
   The Save As dialog box appears.
3. In the top of the Save As dialog box there is a dropdown list. Click the arrow on the right of the dropdown list and navigate to the folder you wish to save the file too.
4. At the bottom of the Save As dialog box there is a section with the label File name. In the box beside that label type in the name of the file. Include the extension to be sure it is saved in the correct format.

e) Copying file to a different location

In the realm of computer file management, file copying is the creation of a new file which has the same content as an existing file. All computer operating systems include file copying provisions in the user interface, like the command, "cp" in Unix and "copy" in MS-DOS; operating systems with a graphical user interface, or GUI, usually provide copy-and-paste or drag-and-drop methods of file copying. File manager applications, too, provide an easy way of copying files.

f) Search & Delete file

To search for a file or folder

1. Click Start, and click on Search.
2. Select All files and folders from the left-hand side of the windows.
3. Type the name of the file or folder in part or full or type a word or phrase that exists in the file to be searched.
4. If you do not know either piece of information selects one or more of the remaining options:
   - In Look in, click the drive, folder, or network you want to search.
   - Click on when was it modified? To look for files that were created or modified on or between specific dates.
   - To look for files of a specific size, click on what size is it? Select a size.
   - Click on More advanced options to specify additional search criteria.
5. Once you finish specifying the search criteria, click on Search to locate the file. Similarly you can search for specific information on Internet, or people in your address book, search for a printer or a computer on your network.

Delete a file or folder

1. Click on Start, and then click on My Documents
2. Click on the file or folder you want to delete.
3. Under File, click Delete.
4. Files or folders can also be deleted by right clicking the file or folder and then clicking Delete.
5. Deleted files or folders are stored in the Recycle Bin, till they are permanently removed from the Recycle Bin.
6. To retrieve a deleted file, double-click the Recycle Bin icon on the desktop. Right-click on the file to retrieve, and then click Restore.

7. To permanently delete a file, press and hold down SHIFT and drag it to the Recycle Bin.

2.6 Exploring Windows

Securing Files/Folders

Until recently, the only way to password-protect individual files or folders in Windows 98 and Me was to buy additional software. Password protection of files has always been available in Windows 2000 or Windows XP, if the hard drive is formatted as NTFS rather than as FAT. But now there's a new way to password-protect your files in Windows Me and XP, regardless of your hard drive's format: Simply store sensitive files and folders in a compressed folder and use that folder's built-in password protection option.

If you're using Windows Me, start by making sure that the folder compression feature is installed on your PC: Choose Start, Settings and click or double-click Control Panel. In the Control Panel window, double-click Add/Remove Programs and click the Windows Setup tab. Select System Tools and click Details. If there is no check mark next to 'Compressed Folders', click the box to check it; then click OK and follow the prompts to add this compression feature to your system.

To compress a folder, right-click the desktop or inside any folder, and choose New, Compressed Folder (in Windows Me) or New, Compressed (zipped) Folder (in Windows XP; see FIGURE 1). This adds a new folder in that location with the default name 'New Compressed Folder'. Type a name for the folder and press Enter. Double-click the folder to open it.

Now open Windows Explorer or any folder window (if you have a Windows keyboard, press Windows-E to launch Explorer), and select the folders and/or files you want to password-protect. Use the right mouse button to drag the items into the new compressed folder. When you release the mouse button, choose Move Here. (If you left-drag, only copies will be added to the compressed folders, leaving the originals unprotected.)

If necessary, click the title bar of the compressed-folder window to activate it. Choose File, Encrypt in Windows Me or File, Add a password in Windows XP. Type your desired password in the 'Password' and 'Confirm Password' boxes, and then click OK. From now on, only users who know the password will be able to open, extract, copy, or move the files and subfolders to another folder; Windows will prompt you for your password before permitting any of these operations. If you send the folder to people who don't have Windows XP or Me, they can uncompress the folder using a program such as WinZip, but they'll still need to know the password before they can access the contents.

Keep these things in mind when you add passwords to files and folders:

"Private" isn't "impervious": Compressed-folder passwords keep files private, but they don't protect them (or even the entire compressed folder) from being deleted. If your sensitive files are important, keep backups of them in a safe place.

Add files before protecting: All of the files in your compressed folder are password-protected at the time you create the password. Any files you add to the folder subsequently will not be password-protected, so make sure the compressed folder contains every file you need to protect before you create the password. To protect files that you add later, open the compressed folder and use the File, Decrypt or File, Remove Password command, and then the File, Encrypt or File, Add a Password command again to password-protect all the files in the folder. You could also compress individual files and give each its own password.

Undo the lock: If you decide to remove the password protection from a file or folder, you have two options. The first is to extract all the contents, either by dragging the file (or files) out of their window or by right-clicking the folder and choosing Extract All (if you prefer the "wizard" approach). Your second option is to open the compressed folder and choose File, Decrypt (in Windows Me) or File, Remove Password (in Windows XP). Either way, Windows will prompt you for your original password (see FIGURE 2).

Keep folder contents a secret: A password-protected folder's file names are visible even though the files themselves are inaccessible without the password. To hide them, compress a folder inside another compressed folder and password-protect the topmost folder (see FIGURE 3). Other users can open the top compressed folder, but not the subfolder holding the files.

Protect files on Windows 98 and on OSs using the FAT file system: If you use Windows 98 or Windows 2000 with FAT rather than NTFS, you can use the free AxCrypt encryption program to protect your files. Browse to AxCrypt - AES-128 File Encryption, Compression to download a copy

What is "file security"?

File Security is a feature of your file system which controls which users can access which files, and places limitations on what users can do to files. For example, a file may be secured so that everyone can view it but only certain specific people may change it, while another is secured so that only the owner may view it. Folders may also be secured in this way.

Users of Windows 95 or Windows 98 may not have encountered file security before, because the FAT file system does not support file security. Users of Windows NT who have NTFS volumes may be familiar with file security, because NTFS supports this feature. File security consists of two key elements: authentication and permissions. Authentication is how the computer finds out who you are — you tell it this by providing a username and password when you begin using it, also known as "logging on". Permissions are the properties of a file or folder that specify who can access it (a list of users) and how (the type of access they are allowed). Normally, you modify the permissions of a file or folder from its properties dialog in the Windows Explorer.

Whenever a user accesses a file or folder, the file security feature kicks in. This is called an access check. The file system considers the user's identity, and what kind of action the user is performing, and consults the file's permissions. If the permissions do not allow the action, the user gets an "Access Denied" error.

Protecting files on the Network

A set of guidelines to protecting home computers and networks:

1. On Windows systems, unbind file and print sharing from TCP/IP
2. Use anti-virus software
3. Employ some type of firewall software or hardware
4. On Windows systems, be sure to display file extensions
5. Never open an attachment unless it comes from someone you know and you are expecting it
6. Turn off Java, JavaScript, ActiveX, etc. on your browser unless you are at a known, "safe" site

1. Unbind file and print sharing from TCP/IP

The most dangerous issue for any computer running any version of the Windows operating system is that file and print sharing is, by default, enabled and bound to TCP/IP. That means, simply, that the same capability that allows peer-to-peer networking and file sharing on your home/office LAN is available to anyone on the Internet!! In particular, the following ports are open and listening:

- UDP port 137, nbname (NetBIOS name service)
- UDP port 138, nbdatagram (NetBIOS datagram service)
- TCP port 139, nbsession (NetBIOS session service)

There is no reason for file and print sharing to use TCP/IP. Before connecting in any way to the Internet, Windows users should block file and print sharing over TCP/IP. This is simply done; go into the Network configuration under Control Panel, and unbind "Client for Microsoft Networks" and "File and print sharing for Microsoft Networks" in the TCP/IP properties for all adapters using TCP/IP (Screen #1). You can still do all of the file and print sharing that you want over the LAN because Microsoft networks use the NetBIOS protocol and don't need to have these functions bound to TCP/IP.

The situation is somewhat clouded in Windows 2000, however. With that operating system, Microsoft decided that TCP/IP was the only communications protocol to employ so that file sharing has to use it. In this case, you will find TCP port 445 open on your computer.

Although counter to Microsoft's wishes, my advice (consistent with many others) is to install the NetBEUI protocol onto your Windows 2000 system and then unbind file and print sharing from TCP/IP.

2. Employ Anti-Virus Software

It is imperative that all users on the Internet run and maintain anti-virus (AV) software. Installing AV software alone is not sufficient; users also have to use the option to run the software at all times (sometimes called *auto-protect*) and to routinely update the AV signature files. There are well over 50,000 known virus signatures today and that number continues to grow; AV software vendors generally update their signature database file at least weekly. If your software has the option, consider having the software automatically check the vendor's Web site for update and automatically download and install new signature files when they are available (sometimes called *live update*). Note that although the vast majority of viruses target Windows operating systems, Mac, Unix/Linux, and other operating systems are **not** immune.

There are many vendors of AV software, some of which are listed below; costs vary but US$35-50 is a rough estimate. Obtain a reputable product; AV software on your PC is often your first and only defense against viruses:

- AntiViral Toolkit Pro (AVP) — www.avp.ch/avpve
- F-Secure — www.f-secure.com/virus-info
- McAfee Anti-Virus — www.mcafee.com/anti-virus/
- Norton AntiVirus — www.symantec.com/avcenter/
- Sophos Anti-Virus — www.sophos.com/products/software/antivirus/
- Trend Micro PC-cillin — www.antivirus.com/vinfo/

3. Employ a Personal Firewall

If you are on the Internet, you should use some form of personal firewall. Personal firewall software runs on your computer and protects against attempts by outsiders to break into your computer. If you have a LAN at home, a hardware firewall might make more sense both economically and practically; most home hardware firewalls also double as a LAN hub/switch and personal firewall software might block local peer-to-peer networking which you want. You will need one copy of personal firewall software for each machine that you want to protect, while a single hardware firewall can protect all systems on the local network.

Some of the available personal firewall software products for Windows are listed below; prices vary from free to US$90. Good, independent reference information for choosing personal firewall software can be found at the *Home PC Firewall Guide* (www.firewallguide.com).

- BlackICE PC Protection — http://blackice.iss.net/product_pc_protection.php
- ConSeal PC Firewall — www.consealfirewall.com
- CyberArmor Personal Firewall — www.cyberarmor.com/products/pf/index.html
- Internet Firewall 2000 (IFW2000) for Personal Computers — www.digitalrobotics.com/IFW2000.htm
- Norton Personal Firewall & Norton Internet Security — www.symantec.com/consumer_products/home-is.html
- Tiny Personal Firewall and WinRoute — www.tinysoftware.com
- ZoneAlarm — www.zonelabs.com/

There are also a number of cable modem/DSL hardware products that provide firewall capabilities; prices here range from about US$75-200:

- D-Link home broadband products — www.dlink.com/products/DigitalHome/Broadband/
- Linksys EtherFast Cable/DSL Router family — www.linksys.com
- Macsense *X*Router family — www.xsense.com/Product/xrouter/index.html
- SonicWALL SOHO2 — www.sonicwall.com/products/soho/index.html

4. Show File Extensions

By default in Windows, Windows Explorer and other Microsoft applications do not show the extension of files if the extension is "known" to the operating system. This is potentially dangerous with the many viruses that are distributed today with a so-called "double extension"; e.g., a file named *foo.jpg.exe*. This is an executable file because of the *.exe* extension. If extensions are hidden, however, the user will only see the name *foo.jpg* and might open this, mistaking it for a JPEG file.

5. Take Care Opening Attachments

E-mail attachments are the most common way in which viruses are propagated on the Internet. You should **never** open an e-mail attachment unless it comes from someone you know **and** you are expecting it. An attachment coming from someone you know is not sufficient proof that it is ok to open; most of today's viruses and worms use a compromised address book to find new targets.

As a side note, some e-mail software will automatically execute some attachment types when you preview a message; this feature should be turned off, if possible. Outlook and Outlook Express are among the worst offenders in this regard; consider using another e-mail client if you can.

6. Secure Your Browser

Malicious code can be sent to your computer through your browser; Internet Explorer is particularly prone to this so-called *malware*. Turn off all active-content mechanisms on your browser — Java, JavaScript, and ActiveX — unless you are at a known, "safe" Web site.

9

Introduction to Word

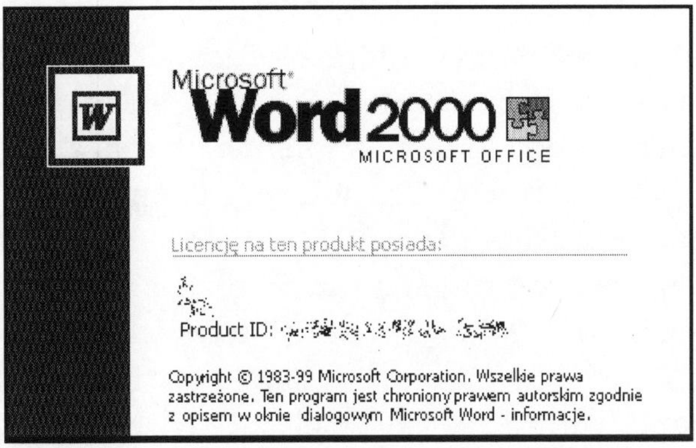

SCREEN LAYOUT

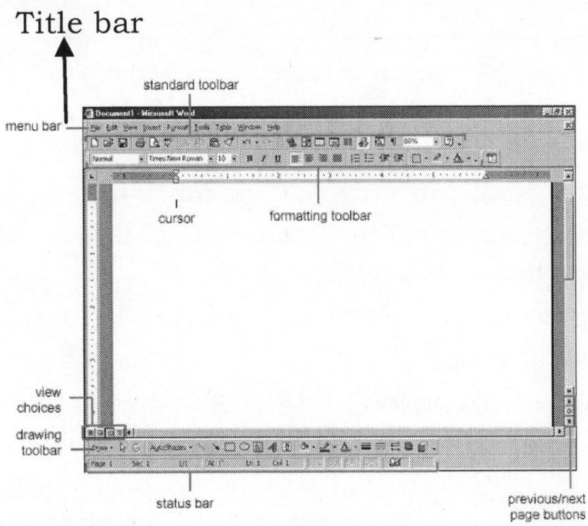

Clear and organized writing is one of the most important skills for success in today's world. Word 2000 can help students develop those skills as well as help you with your own writing needs. Word 2000 provides an easy way to create handouts, worksheets, student papers, and other printed documents, and also makes it easy to save your documents to the Web or send them through e-mail. Some of Word 2000's new features also make it an excellent tool for collaboration and for teaching and learning foreign languages.

Word 2000 can encourage the use of a writing process from developing ideas and content, through revising multiple drafts and publishing student work. **For example:**

- Developing ideas and content. Students can use Word 2000's Outline view to brainstorm an outline for their writing project. Outline view shows the document's organization and makes it easy for students to restructure a document by moving text and headings up or down.
- Producing drafts. Students can produce a rough draft knowing that Word 2000 offers them the freedom to easily edit and revise. Students can even save multiple drafts of their documents within the same file using the Versions feature, so they can easily refer to previous drafts. Educators may find this useful when reviewing earlier versions of a student's work.
- Organizing documents. Students can use Word 2000's Outline view to determine how well their writing is organized. In Outline view, you can collapse a document to show only the headings and body text you want. This makes it easy to view the document's organization, move through the document, and rearrange large chunks of text.
- Revising writing. Students can refine their writing through individual or peer editing. With the Reviewing toolbar, students or educators can easily Insert Comments, Track Changes, Highlight areas of text with color, Save Versions, and even Send Mail. They can also proof using the spelling and grammar checkers. Rewriting becomes a challenging, exciting

opportunity to improve quality, rather than a time-consuming chore.

- Formatting papers. Students can select styles, font sizes, and colors, and align and space words, bullets, numbered lists, tables, and drop caps. They can set margins, borders, page borders, shading, and document layout.
- Publishing. You and your students can print documents, submit documents electronically, or save files to HTML for publishing on the Internet or an intranet. With built-in HTML support, you simply select Save As HTML and all text, graphics, and tables are converted to HTML format. Once in this format, new Word 2000 features let you add scrolling text, background sound, background effects, and more. You can also create PowerPoint presentations from Word 2000 outlines and documents.

The following features in Word 2000 make it even easier to create Web, e-mail, and print documents.

- **Click-n-type**: In Page Layout view, you can move the cursor anywhere on a page, double-click, and then start typing. This simplifies complex document layout.
- **Collect and paste**: Gather information from multiple sources and place up to 12 items on the Microsoft Office Clipboard at a time.
- **Personalized menus**: Commands that you use most often are prominently featured on the menus. Menus are easily expanded to reveal all commands.
- **Tables**: Create nested tables (tables within table cells), floating tables (text wraps around a table), arbitrarily positioned tables including side-by-side tables, and integrated header rows (header rows integrated with the outside border).
- **Thesaurus**: Word 2000 has a new thesaurus developed for Microsoft by Bloomsbury Publishing Plc. Right-click a word, point to synonyms, and then you can select a word from the synonyms list.

FILE MENU

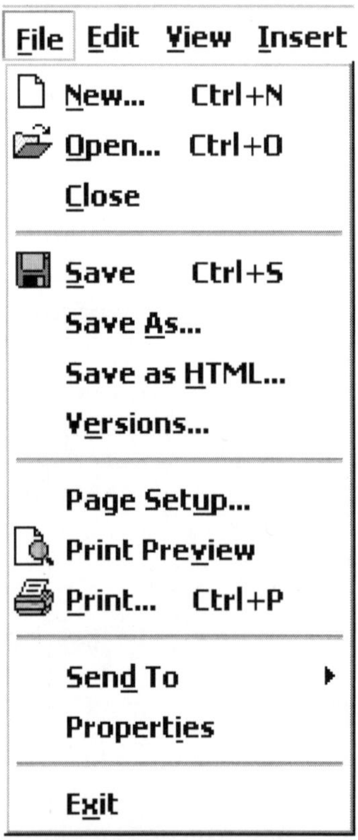

New - Opens a new document. If you use the keyboard combination indicated on the right a blank document opens immediately. Selecting the New menu item with your cursor gives the opportunity to open a large number of types of documents.

Open - Opens a previously saved document.

Close - Closes the active document but does not quit the application.

Save - Saves the active document with its current file name, location and format.

Save As - Saves by opening a window which gives the opportunity to change the file name, location or format.

Page Setup - Sets margins, paper size, orientation and other layout options.

Print Preview - Shows how the file will look when you print it.

Print - Prints the active file, also gives the opportunity to change print options

Exit - Closes Microsoft Word.

EDIT MENU

Undo ... - The actual entry of this item will depend on what you did last. In my example I had cut text, so that was displayed. This selection can be repeated several times.

Repeat ...- After an action has been undone, it can be reinstated in the document.

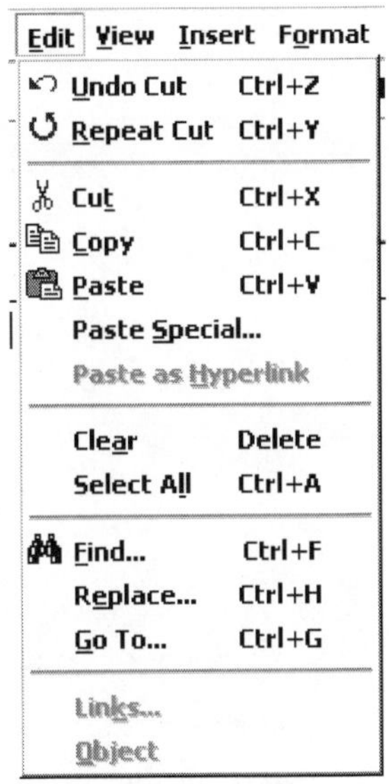

Cut - Removes the selection from the active document and places it on the clipboard.

Copy - Copies the selection to the clipboard

Paste - Inserts the contents of the clipboard at the insertion point (cursor) or whatever is selected.

Clear - Deletes the selected object or text, but does not place it on the clipboard.

Select All - Selects all text and graphics in the active window.

Find - Searches for specified text in the active document

Replace - Searches for and replaces specified text and formatting.

VIEW MENU

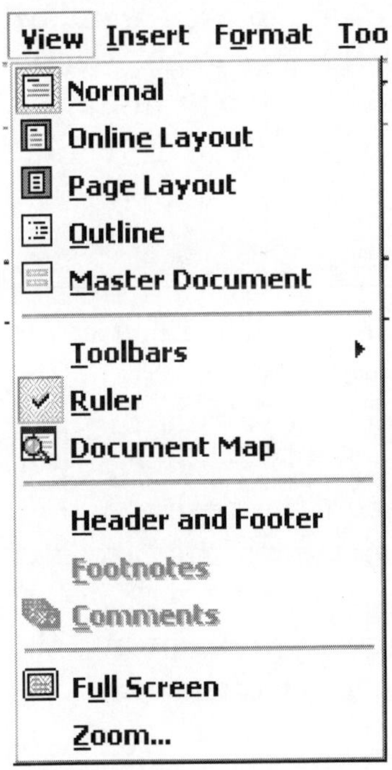

Normal - The default document view for most word processing tasks.

Page Layout - An editing view that displays your document as it will look when printed. This view takes more system memory and scrolling may be slow.

Toolbars - Displays or hides toolbars. The right pointing arrow indicates a list of toolbars. To add one slide down to the name of the toolbar and click to select.

Ruler - Displays or hides horizontal and vertical rulers at the top and left side of the document.

Header and Footer - Adds or changes the text that is displayed at the top or bottom of every page of the document

Full Screen - Hides most screen elements so you can see more of your document

Zoom - Controls how large, or small, the current document appears on the screen.

INSERT MENU

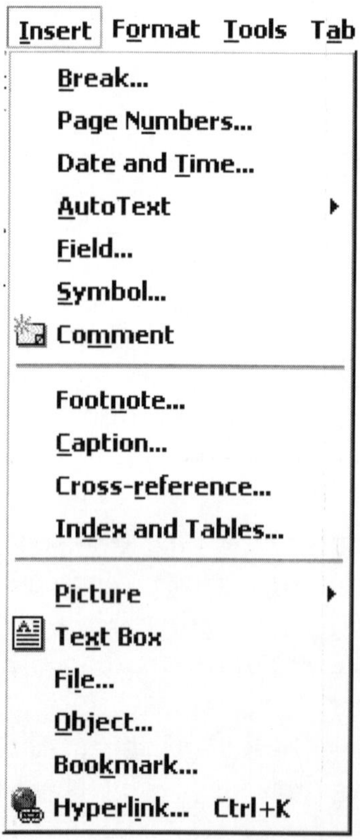

Page Break - Use this command to send your cursor to the top of the next page even though the text does not extend to the bottom of the previous page

Date and Time - Choose from seventeen formats for displaying date, time, or date and time.

Auto Text - Insert any of several pre-set text lines, or create your own.

Symbol - Insert a symbol from each of your symbol fonts, or any standard font which includes symbols. There are more than you might think!

Footnote - Place a footnote at the bottom of the page or the end of the document.

Picture - Insert pictures from clip art or a file. You can also insert auto shapes, word art, or a chart.

Text Box (Frame) - Use this to place captions near tables or drawings, or to set off text at the beginning of a page. Click and draw the box after making this selection.

File - Insert a saved document into the active document at the cursor.

Object - Insert an object such as clip art, word art, an equation or much more.

Hyperlink - An interesting use of hyperlinks is to place a link to any document stored on your computer. You can later open that document by clicking on the link. Neat?

FORMAT MENU

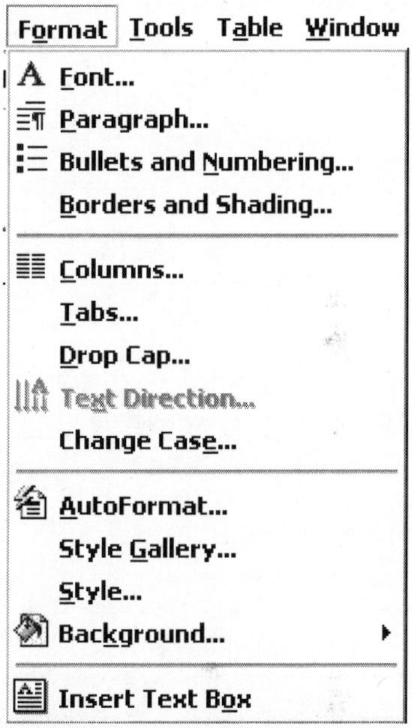

Font - Change font style, size, color and a large number of other features. You can also change the spacing between letters here.

Paragraph - Indent a paragraph using either margin or place some chosen amount of space before or after the paragraph.

Bullets and Numbering - As promised in the Insert menu, if you wish to change the bullet, it can be done here. Your bullets can be literally any symbol you wish them to be

Border - Create borders around blocks of text, or around the entire document. On the Page Border tab, under the Art pull down menu you can find a huge selection of graphic borders; hearts, stars, planets and much more.

Drop Cap - Make the first letter of a paragraph or chapter large enough to span several lines.

Style - If you prefer not to use the Formatting toolbar, document style can be changed here.

Background - Another task which can be handled in the Formatting toolbar, you can choose the color to highlight selected text in your document.

Change Case - DO YOU EVER FORGET THE CAPS LOCK? If so, some to this sub-menu and change the case of the highlighted text. This is a cool feature!

Bold, Italic, Underline - Format selected text; Bold , *Italic*, or Underlined.

Object - Make changes to any selected object; image, word art, auto shape or any other object inserted into the document.

TOOLS MENU

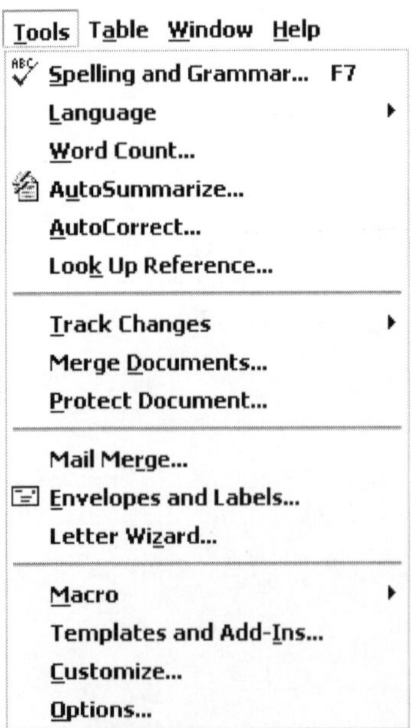

Spelling and Grammar - Choose either sub-menu and the same window opens. Questioned spelling is in red , grammar in green .

Language/Thesaurus - Have you used the word "like" too many times? Highlight the word, select Thesaurus and get suggestions like similar and analogous.

Word Count - Need to know how many words are in your document? Select Word Count and find out how many pages, words, characters, paragraphs, and lines.

Auto Summarize - Exactly what it sounds like, Word summarizes the document, reducing the length of the document, keeping the meaning.

Auto Correct - Word will automatically correct some things. If this feature is irritating to you, come here to change what is corrected.

Customize- Opens the same window that you get by going to the View menu and selecting Toolbar/ Customize.

Options - Modify Word settings here. Modify print, editing, spelling and other options from this sub-menu.

WINDOW MENU

New Window - This opens another window with a copy of the active document.

Arrange All - Displays all open files in the window. This makes dragging and dropping from one document to another much easier.

Split - Splits the active window into panes.

Open Document List - There is no need to drag windows to the side so you can see other documents open in Word. Come to the bottom of this window for a listing of all open documents. The active document has a check mark beside it.

HELP MENU

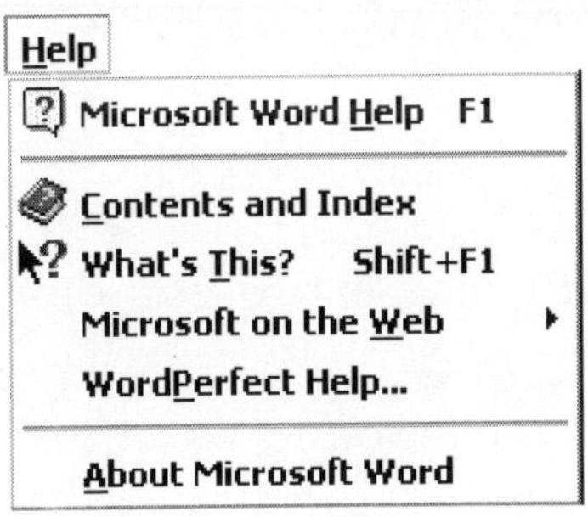

Microsoft Word Help - Open Word's Assistant and get a search box to type in. Word displays possible matches for you to read about.

Contents and Index - See an index of all topics available in Word's Help documentation.

Microsoft on the Web - That's right! It is exactly what it sounds like. Select a link and a Microsoft help page is opened in your browser. If you are not online, Word will make the connection and then display the page.

About Microsoft Word - Not sure which version of Word you working with.

Check here for version information and for the produce ID number.

COMMONLY USED KEYBOARD COMBINATIONS

To use one of these combinations Hold the Ctrl or Alt key down and strike the letter key

Ctrl+N	Open a new word document quickly.
Ctrl+X	Cut- Removes the selection from the active document and places it on the clipboard.
Ctrl+O	Opens a previously saved document.
Ctrl+C	Copies the selection to the clipboard
Ctrl+W	Closes the active window, but does not Exit Word.
Ctrl+V	Paste - Inserts the contents of the clipboard at the insertion point (cursor) or whatever is selected.
Ctrl+S	Saves the active document with its current file name, location and format.
Ctrl+A	Selects all text and graphics in the active window.
Ctrl+P	Prints the active file, also gives the opportunity to change print options
Ctrl+F	Find - Searches for specified text in the active document
Alt+F4	Exit - Closes Microsoft Word.
Ctrl+B	Bold - Formats selected text; make text bold, or remove bold formatting
Ctrl+Z	Undo the last action. This selection can be repeated several times.
Ctrl+I	Italic - Formats selected text; make text italic or remove italic
Ctrl+Y	Redo - After an action has been undone, it can be reinstated in the document.
Ctrl+U	Underline - Formats selected text; make text underlined or remove underline

LESS COMMONLY USED KEYBOARD COMBINATIONS

Ctrl+Shift+>	Increase selected text two points	Ctrl+Shift++	Apply superscript formatting
Ctrl+Shift+<	Decrease selected text two points	Ctrl+=	Apply subscript formatting

Ctrl+]	Increase selected text one point	Ctrl+Shift+C	Copy formats
Ctrl+[	Decrease selected text one point	Ctrl+Shift+V	Paste formats
Shift+F3	Change case of the letters	Ctrl+1	Single space lines
Ctrl+Shift+W	Underline words but not spaces	Ctrl+5	Set 1.5 line spacing
Ctrl+Shift+D	Double underline text	Ctrl+2	Double space lines
Ctrl+E	Center a paragraph	Ctrl+Backspace	Delete one word to the left
Ctrl+J	Justify a paragraph	Ctrl+Del	Delete one word to the right
Ctrl+L	Left align a paragraph	Ctrl+R	Right align a paragraph
Ctrl+M	Indent a paragraph from the left	Shift+Enter	Insert a line break
Ctrl+T	Create a hanging indent	Ctrl+Shift+T	Reduce a hanging indent

If text is already selected and you want to extend the selection area

Shift+←	Extend selection one character to the left	Shift+→	Extend selection one character to the right
Ctrl+Shift+→	Extend selection to the end of a word	Ctrl+←	Extend selection to the beginning of a word

If you want to move the cursor

→	One character to the right	←	One character to the left
Ctrl+→	One word to the right	Ctrl+←	One word to the left
Ctrl+End	To the end of a document	Ctrl+Home	To the beginning of a document

CREATING A NEW FILE

1. From Microsoft Word, Choose **File/New/Blank Document** -or-

   Click **New** Icon 

   The cursor should be blinking in the work area. If it is not blinking, click once in the work area.

SAVING FILE

1. Choose **File/Save As**

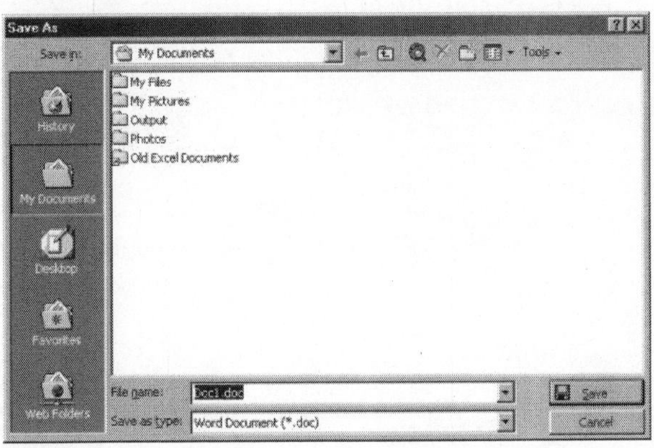

a. Make sure **correct drive letter** has been selected in the Save in area.
b. Type your **filename** in the Filename box.
c. Click **Save**.

PRINT PREVIEW

Print Preview allows you to see how your file looks before you print, preventing a waste of paper and ink!

To Access Print Preview:

- Choose **File→ Print Preview** from the menu bar.

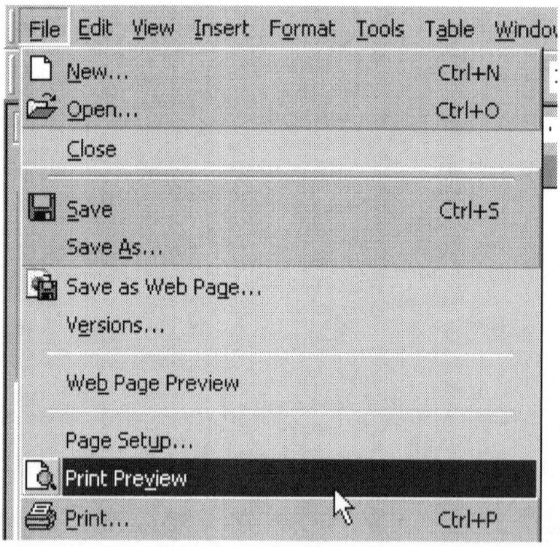

Or, Use the Toolbar:

- Click the **Print Preview** button  on the **Standard** toolbar.

Once you have accessed Print Preview, your document will now be in **Print Preview mode**. It will look something like this:

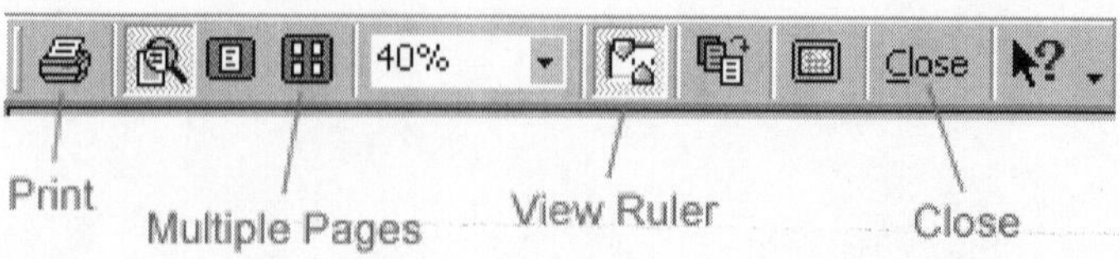

Print Preview mode displays how your file is formatted. If you would like to take a closer look, use the **Zoom** feature. The Zoom feature "zooms" closer, giving you a better view of your file.

Let's "zoom" in and take a look at the **Print Preview** toolbar:

- The **Print** button prints a file.
- The **View Ruler** button displays the Vertical or Horizontal rulers. Rulers help edit margin settings.
- If your file consists of multiple pages, the **Multiple Pages** button allows you to either view **one page** or several pages at a time.
- Use **Zoom**, and then use the **Scroll bars** to view your file.
- Use the **Shrink to Fit** button to "fit" your information to one page.
- If you want to **exit/close** Print Preview, simply click **Close** on the **Print Preview** toolbar.

PRINTING OUTPUT

1. Choose **File/Print Preview**.

   Look at your preview. Click **Close**.

2. Choose **File/Print/OK**.

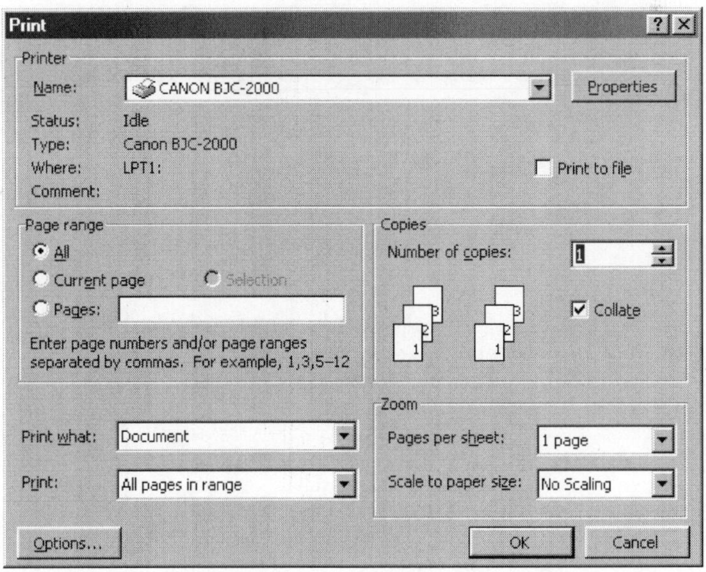

CHECKING THE SPELLING IN YOUR DOCUMENT

1. Choose **Tools/Spelling and Grammar**.

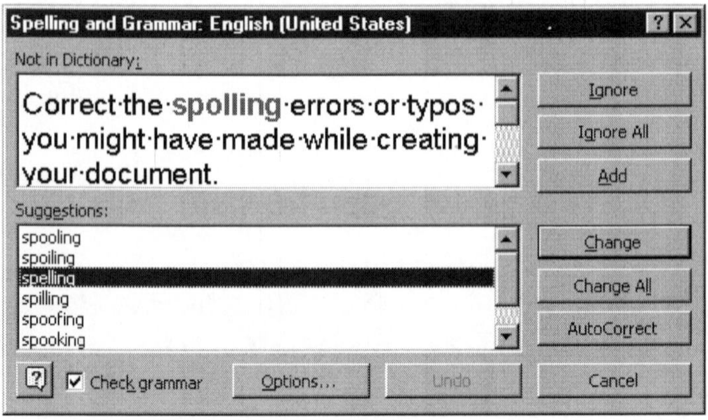

USING THE THESAURUS

1. Select word to lookup using the Thesaurus. In this example, the word "lesson" was selected, but you may choose any word you like.
2. Choose **Tools/Thesaurus**.

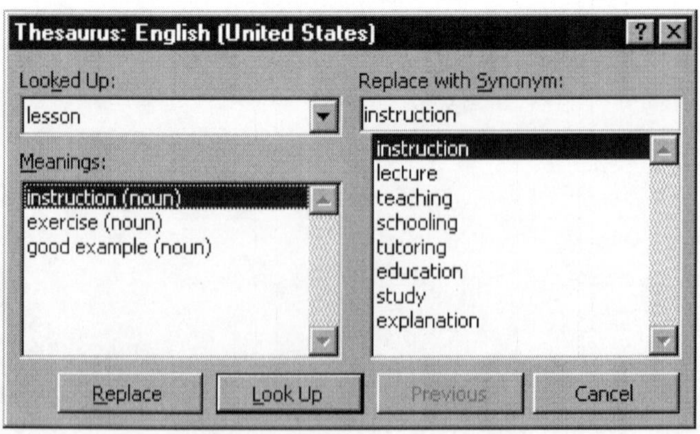

a. Select replacement word from list.

b. Click on the **Replace** button.

That's all there is to using the Thesaurus

CHANGING FONTS IN DOCUMENT

1. Select the text to change by highlighting (dragging the mouse over the text).
2. Choose **Format/Font**.

   The following dialog box will appear.

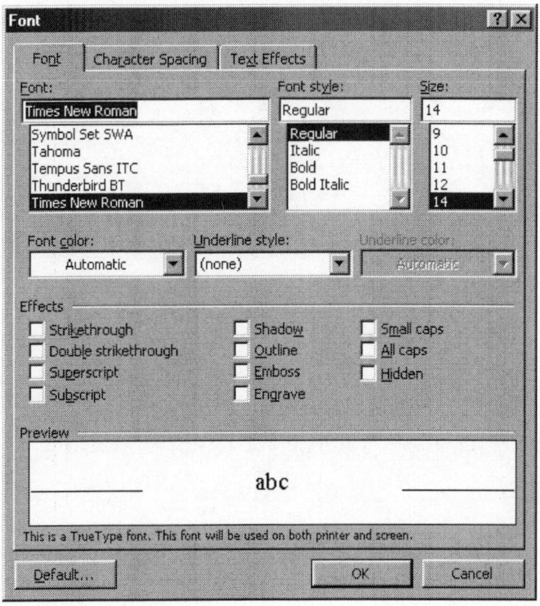

a. Select the Font **Typeface** (example, Times New Roman)
b. Select the Font **Style** (example, Bold)
c. Select the Font **Size** (small numbers represent small letters)
d. Select underlining mode, text color, and special effects, (Superscript or Subscript, for example), if desired.
e. Click **OK**

INSERTING SPECIAL CHARACTERS (SYMBOLS)

Occasionally you will need to insert special characters called **symbols** into your document. Place the cursor at the location you wish to insert a symbol.

1. Choose **Insert/Symbol**.

   The following dialog box will appear.

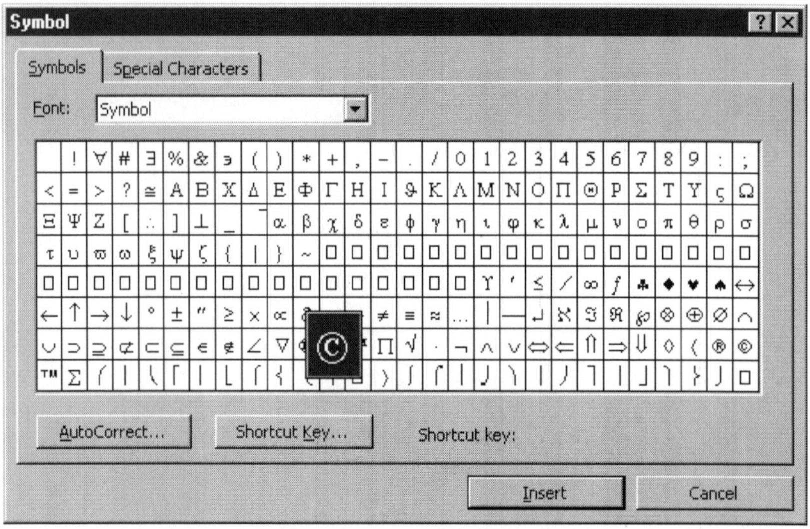

a. Select Font **Typeface**. (Here we have selected Symbol, but there are typefaces for musical notation, mathematical notation.)
b. Select the symbol you wish to insert into your document. Clicking on the symbol shows you an enlarged view as the arrow shown below.
c. Click **Insert.**

2. To enlarge or reduce the size of the symbol, highlight it in your document after the symbol has been inserted and change the Font Size.

The symbol shown below has been increased from 14 pt to 48 pt.

USING BULLETS AND NUMBERING IN DOCUMENT

Occasionally you will want to list items in your document You may type the numbers yourself or WORD will number the list items for you.

1. On the formatting Tool Bar, click on either the **Number button** or the **Bullet button**. Press Enter/Return after each list item.

- As You
- Type

- The Items
- Will Be
- Bulleted

1. Or
2. Preceded
3. With A
4. Number

To change the appearance of bullets or numbers,

1. Select **your list** by highlighting the text.
2. Choose **Format/Bullets and Numbering**.

   The following dialog box will appear.

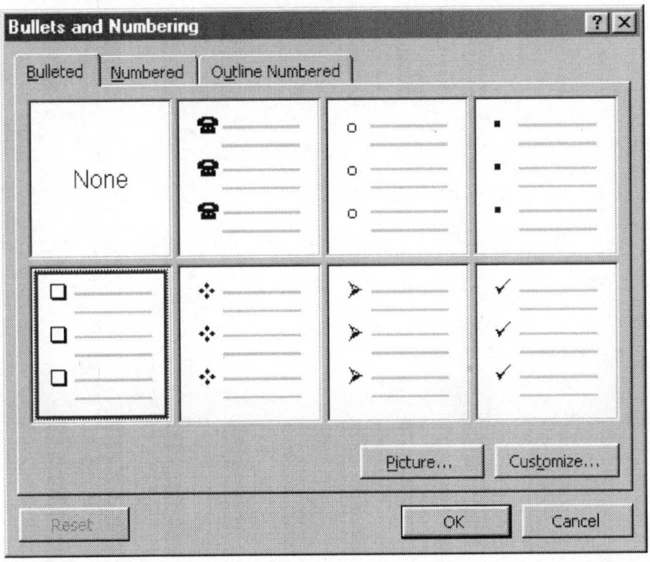

a. Select from the **Bulleted**, **Numbered**, or **Multilevel** tabs.

b. Select the bullet or number **style** you wish to use.

c. Click **OK**.

SEND A DOC AS AN EMAIL ATTACHMENT

If you'd like to share a doc in a format, such as Microsoft Word, you can email it as an attachment. Here's how:

1. Open the doc or file you'd like to share.
2. Go to the **File** menu, and select **Email as attachment....**
3. Select a file type from the drop-down menu.
4. Enter the email address of the people to whom you'd like to send the doc or file. If you'd like, you can also add a subject and a message.
5. Click **Send**. People to whom you're emailing this doc will receive it as a downloadable attachment in the file format you selected in Step 2.

CREATING A DOCUMENT FROM A DOCUMENT TEMPLATE

When you select **New** on the **File** menu, you open the **New Document** task pane.

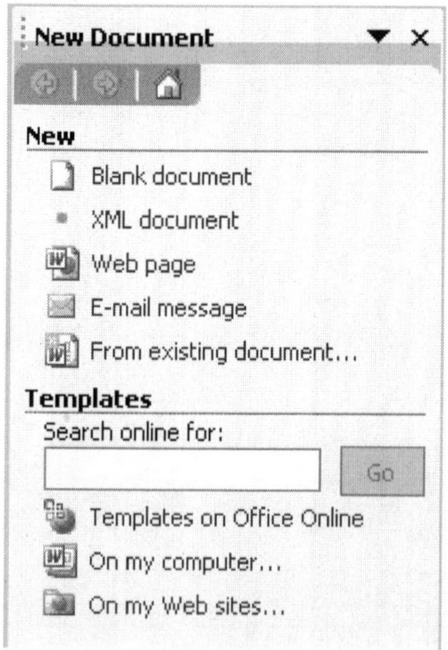

Fig-1: The New Document task pane

There are four sections: the one we want is labeled **New from template**. Click the **General Templates** link to see the selection available on your computer.

When you pick a template and then create a new document based on that template, the template remains "attached" to the document. Any text that is in the template will be available in your new document.

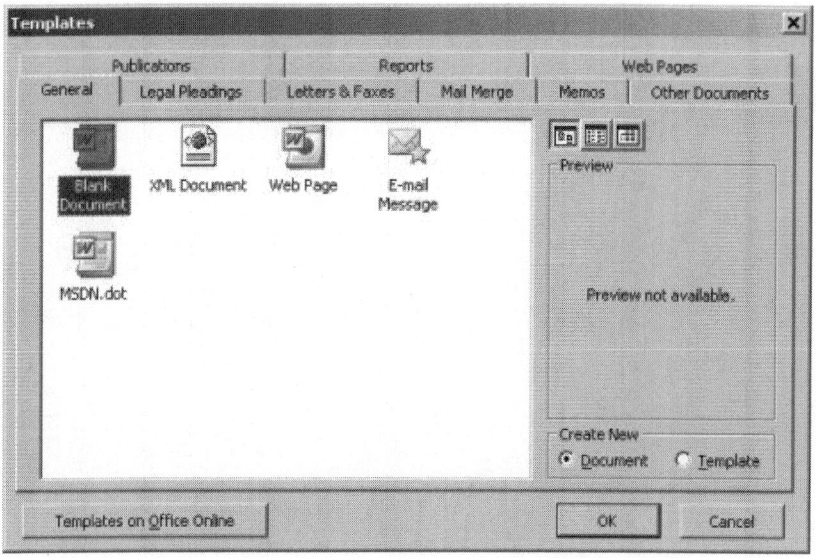

Fig-2: The Templates dialog box

Any template styles used in the document (whether in the template's text or in text that you type or insert) become defined in the document and will stay with the document even if the attachment is later broken. If the template's style definition is changed after it is used in the document, the document style will not change unless the template is reattached or the style is otherwise copied into the document again. (More on attaching a template to an existing document shortly)

AutoText entries, macros, keyboard customizations, and toolbars in the template are available to the document so long as the document remains attached to the template, but are not normally transferred into the document. (Documents cannot hold AutoText entries but can have keyboard customizations, macros, and toolbars.)

SAVING DOCUMENT AS A WORD TEMPLATE

Once you have outlined your document and are ready to create your Word template, follow these simple steps:

1. Click the **File** menu and select **Save**

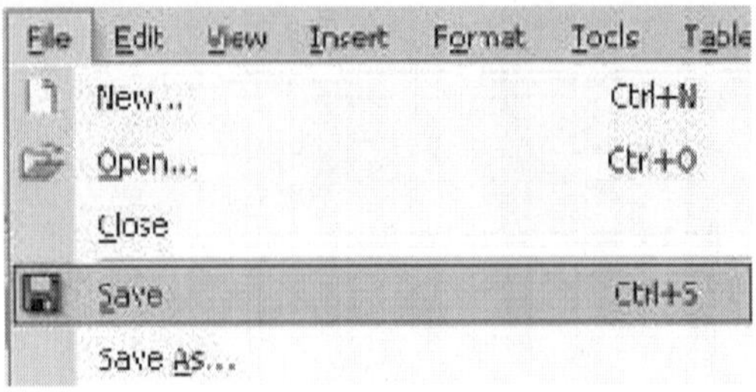

2. In the **File Name** box, give your template a name that will be easily recognizable.

3. In the **Save as type** box, select **Document Templates (*.dot)**

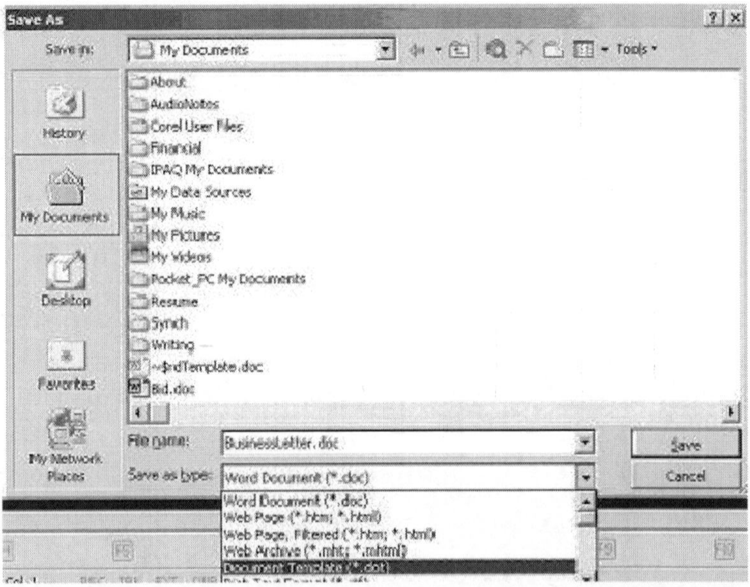

4. Word will automatically open the default save location for Templates (generally **...\Application Data\Microsoft\Templates**). If you would prefer to save the template in another location, you can do so by navigating through the folders on your hard drive, but keep in mind that templates saved in locations other than the default location will not appear in the **Templates** dialog box.

5. Click **Save**

10

Introduction to Excel

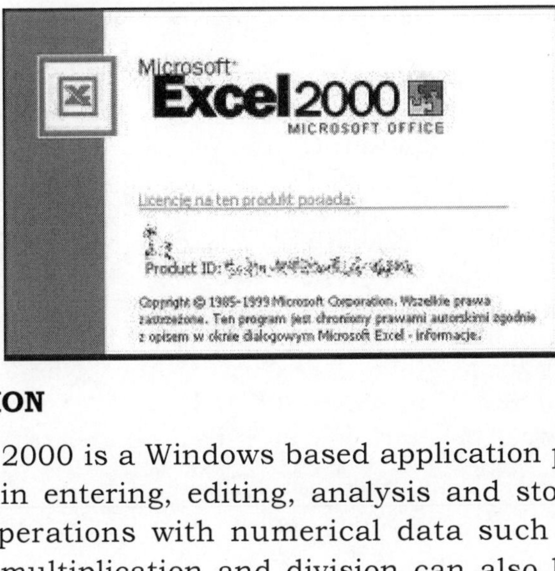

INTRODUCTION

MS-Excel 2000 is a Windows based application package. It is quite useful in entering, editing, analysis and storing of data. Arithmetic operations with numerical data such as addition, subtraction, multiplication and division can also be done with Excel. You can sort the numbers/characters according to some given criteria (like ascending, descending etc.) and solve simple financial, mathematical and statistical formulas.

Excel allows you to create spreadsheets much like paper ledgers that can perform automatic calculations. Each Excel file is a workbook that can hold many worksheets. The worksheet is a grid of columns (designated by letters) and rows (designated by numbers). The letters and numbers of the columns and rows (called labels) are displayed in gray buttons across the top and left side of the worksheet. The intersection of a column and a row is called a cell. Each cell on the spreadsheet has a cell address that is the column letter and the row number. Cells can contain either text, numbers, or mathematical formulas.

EXCEL FEATURES

There are a number of features that are available in Excel to make your task easier. Some of the main features are:

1. AutoFormat - lets you to choose many preset table formatting options.
2. AutoSum - helps you to add the contents of a cluster of adjacent cells.
3. List AutoFill - automatically extends cell formatting when a new item is added to the end of a list.
4. AutoFill - feature allows you to quickly fill cells with repetitive or sequential data such as chronological dates or numbers, and repeated text. AutoFill can also be used to copy functions. You can also alter text and numbers with this feature.
5. AutoShapes toolbar will allow you to draw a number of geometrical shapes, arrows, flowchart elements, stars and more. With these shapes you can draw your own graphs.
6. Wizard - guides you to work effectively while you work by displaying various helpful tips and techniques based on what you are doing. Drag and Drop - feature will help you to reposition the data and text by simply dragging the data with the help of mouse.
7. Charts - features will help you in presenting a graphical representation of your data in the form of Pie, Bar, Line charts and more.
8. PivotTable - flips and sums data in seconds and allows you to perform data analysis and generating reports like periodic financial statements, statistical reports, etc. You can also analyse complex data relationships graphically.

9. Shortcut Menus - commands that are appropriate to the task that you are doing appear by clicking the right mouse button.

MICROSOFT EXCEL 2000 SCREEN ELEMENTS

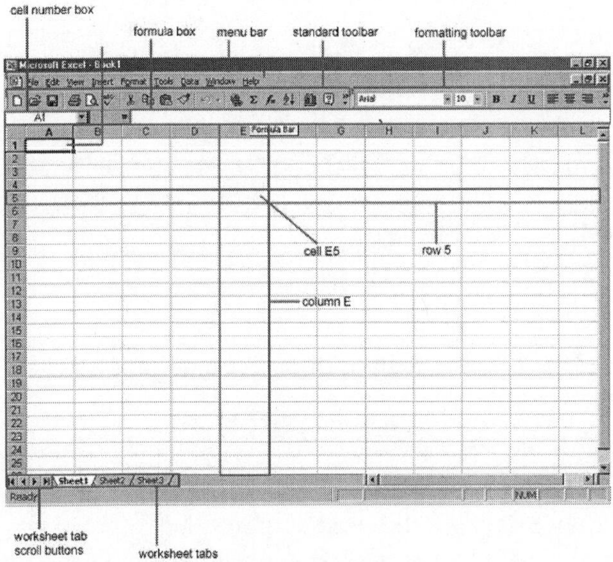

MENUS

FILE MENU

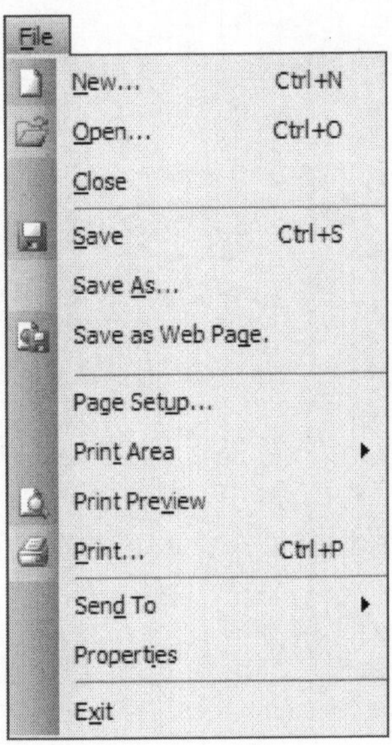

New - Opens a new document. If you use the keyboard combination indicated on the right a blank document opens immediately. Selecting the New menu item with your cursor gives the opportunity to open a large number of types of documents.

Open - Opens a previously saved document.

Close - Closes the active document but does not quit the application.

Save - Saves the active document with its current file name, location and format.

Save As - Saves by opening a window which gives the opportunity to change the file name, location or format.

Page Setup - Sets margins, paper size, orientation and other layout options. Grid lines don't show up when you print? Go to the sheet tab in this window

Print Preview - Shows how the file will look when you print it.

Print - Prints the active file, also gives the opportunity to change print options

Exit - Closes Microsoft Excel

EDIT MENU

Undo - The actual entry of this item will depend on what you did last. In my example I had typed, so that was displayed. This selection can be repeated several times.

Redo - After an action has been undone, it can be reinstated in the document.

Cut - Removes the selection from the active document and places it on the clipboard.

Copy - Copies the selection to the clipboard, the cell from which information is copied remains highlighted

Paste - Inserts the contents of the clipboard at the insertion point (cursor) or whatever is selected.

Paste Special - Ten choices are available when making this selection; examples include pasting formulas, values, and comments.

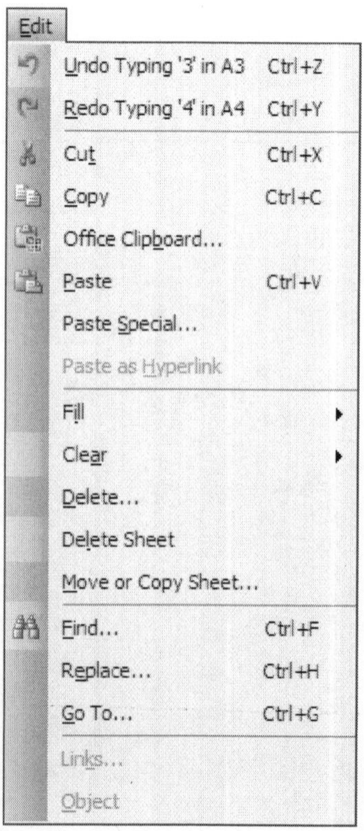

Fill - Fill contents of a selected cell Up, Down, Left or Right

Clear - Deletes the selected object or text, but does **not** place it on the clipboard. Four choices are available; All, Format, Contents or Comments

Delete - This menu entry can be used to delete entire rows or columns.

Find - Searches for specified text in the active document

Replace - Searches for and replaces specified text and formatting.

VIEW MENU

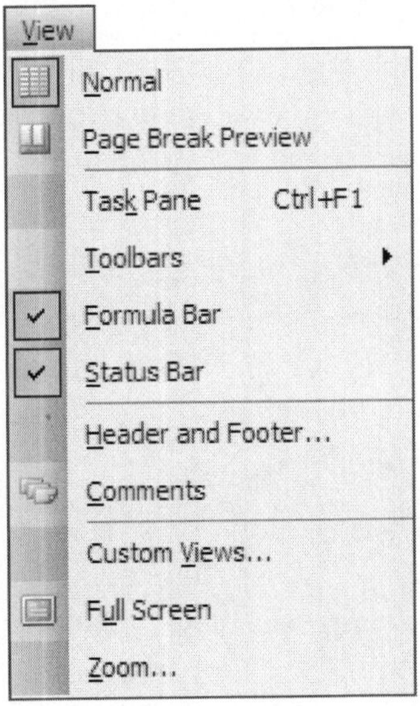

Normal - The default document view for most word processing tasks.

Page Break Preview - Before printing, make sure the page breaks appear where you want them

Toolbars - Displays or hides toolbars. The right pointing arrow indicates a list of toolbars. To add one slide down to the name of the toolbar and click to select.

Formula Bar - Remove or display the bar which displays cell address and data entered into the active cell

Header and Footer - Adds or changes the text that is displayed at the top or bottom of every page of the document

Comments - Hidden comment give further information about cell contents. Comments are displayed when you move the cursor into the cell; however this command causes all comments on a page to be displayed.

Full Screen - Hides most screen elements so you can see more of your document

Zoom - Controls how large, or small, the current document appears on the screen.

INSERT MENU

Cells - Use this command to insert a cell. A pop-up window allows you to move existing data down or to the right. You can also insert rows or columns with this window.

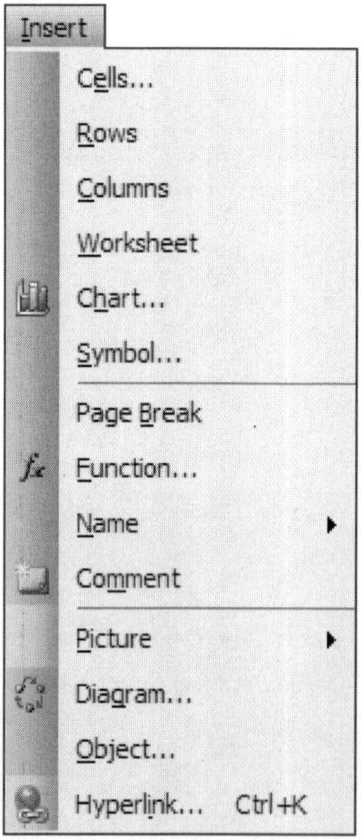

Rows - Inserts a new row in the spreadsheet, above the row that contains the active cell.

Columns - Inserts a new column in the spreadsheet, to the left of the column that contains the active cell.

Worksheet - By default, an Excel workbook is made up of three worksheets. You may insert as many additional sheets as you require. Sheets are inserted in front of the current worksheet.

Chart - This adds a chart of the selected data or of the entire worksheet if you have no data selected.

Page Break - Inserts page breaks above and to the left of the active cell. To avoid adding a page break to the left, make sure a cell in Column A is selected before inserting the break.

Function - Opens the Paste Function window allowing the selection of a specific equation to go in the active cell.

Comment- Have something to say about the contents of a cell? Add a small note with the appearance of a Post-It note.

Picture - Insert pictures from clip art or a file. You can also insert auto shapes, word art, or a chart.

Object - Insert an object such as clip art, word art, an equation or much more.

Hyperlink - An interesting use of hyperlinks is to place a link to any document stored on your computer. You can later open that document by clicking on the link. If you want to see an example of an Excel worksheet using hyperlinks to Internet sites, download a copy and open it with Excel.

FORMAT MENU

Cells - Format the way a number is displayed; alignment of data in the cell(s), font (size, color, style, etc.), borders and colors for the selected cells, and you may also lock the contents of a cell here.

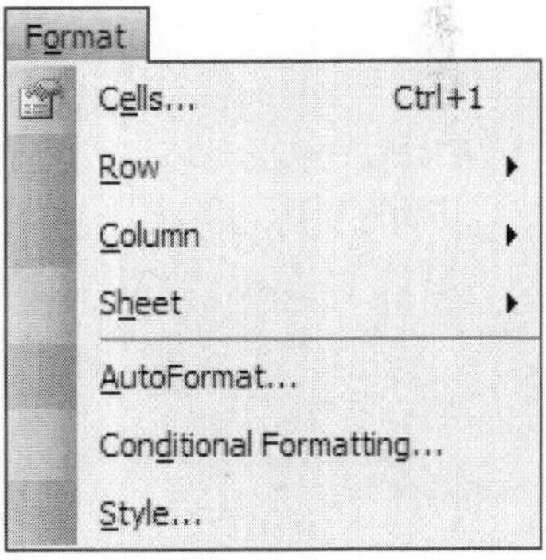

Row - Specify a row height, choose auto-fit, and hide or un-hide the selected row.

Column - Specify a column width, choose auto-fit, hide or un-hide the selected column, or choose the standard width for a column.

Sheet - Here you can rename the sheet if sheet 1 is not descriptive enough (and it's not), you can hide or un-hide a sheet, or you can tile an image in the background of the entire sheet.

Auto Format- There are sixteen pre-designed formats to change the look of your spreadsheet. You may apply the format to the entire sheet or only to selected cells.

Style - Opens a **Style** window which will lead to the **Format Cells** window if you wish to **Modify** the format.

TOOLS MENU

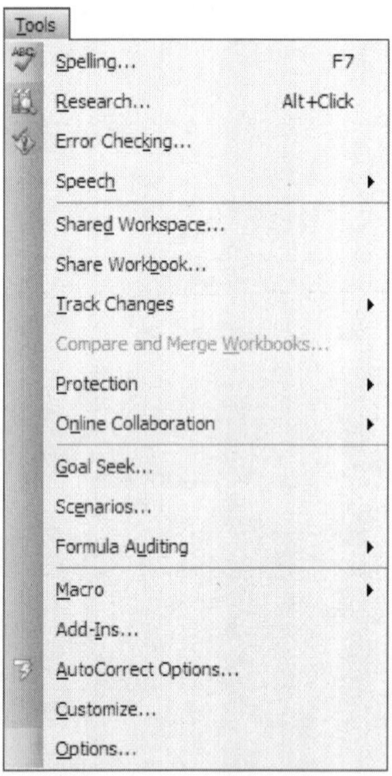

Spelling... - Check spelling in your document

AutoCorrect... - Define, or turn off automatic corrections. If you tend to make a particular keystroke error often, and it is not in the dictionary, you can add it here.

Share Workbook... - Choose this option if you want several users to work on the data in the same workbook simultaneously. Make it available on your network and anyone with access can make changes.

Protection - You can password protect a single sheet of a workbook, or the entire workbook. One obvious application would be to protect a worksheet which you are using as your grade book.

Customize... - Select/Deselect toolbars to be displayed with your workbook, or add buttons to existing toolbars.

Options... - If you do not like something Excel does automatically, or if you know it should be doing something automatically and it is not, this is where you turn those features on or off. One thing I use a lot here is removing gridlines from a worksheet so I can draw a graphic organizer.

DATA MENU

Sort Sort Makes it easy to sort columns of data alphanumerically

Filter Allows you to filter a list of data based on whether or not it meets specified criteria.

Form... Lets you display your data as a form with field names based on your column headings. Very useful for lists of names and addresses.

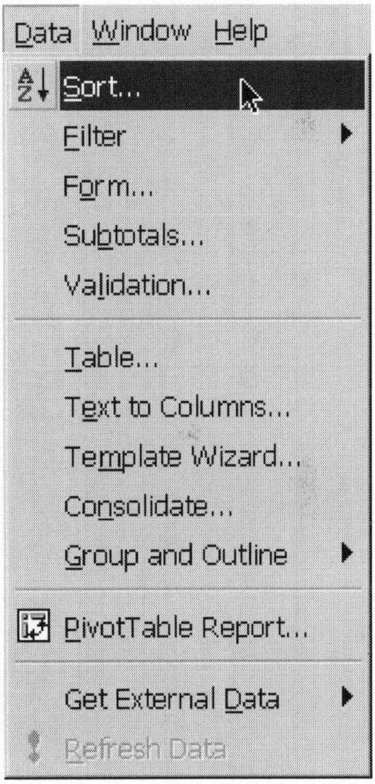

Subtotals... Use functions such as =SUM(A1:A25) to calculate subtotals for a given range of data.

Validation... Checks to see if data fits a specified format such as text, number, date, whole number, zip code or a custom format that you create.

Table... Calculate data tables by selecting row and column inputs.

Text to Columns... Converts a column of delimited text into separate columns of a specified format. For example, use to separate last name, first name data into two columns.

Template Wizard... Creates a template and a database from your Workbook. Each time you enter data into the template, it will be copied into the database.

Consolidate... Lets you combine multiple data sources into one.

Group and Outline Lets you group and outline data with up to eight levels of detail. For example, you can list by (1)Name Only, (2)Name & Phone Number, (3) Name, Phone & Address, etc., etc.

PivotTable Report... A convenient way to sort and analyze data interactively.

Get External Data Makes it easy to query the web, an external database or a custom data source to input data into Excel.

Refresh Data Repeats the query (see Get External Data) to update the data in Excel.

WINDOW MENU

New Window Opens a new window to view the current document. It is not the same as selecting New... from the file menu - no new file is created by this command. Like two windows looking into the same room, two windows looking into the same Workbook show the same contents, just from a different perspective. Windows are denoted by Workbookname: Window Number. For example, changes made in one window of a Workbook (Filemaker Data.xls:1) will affect the Workbook in another window (FilemakerData.xls:2). This is most useful for viewing two sheets of the same workbook at the same time.

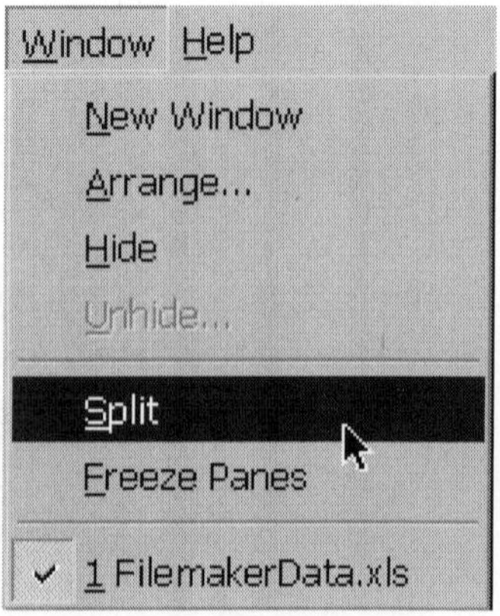

Arrange Lets you arrange all of your open windows on the screen in the following layouts: **Tiled**, **Horizontal**, **Vertical**

and **Cascade** (one on top of the other). Checking the box labeled **Windows of active workbook** will make it so windows of other workbooks are unarranged.

Hide Makes your window disappear from sight completely.

Unhide... Lists the hidden window and allows you to select which ones to show.

Split Breaks the active window into four panes which can be scrolled up and down or left and right independently, allowing you to see the beginning of a large Worksheet in the left pane and the end in the right pane, for example. You can get rid of the pane dividers by double-clicking on them or by selecting **Remove Split** from the Window menu.

Freeze Panes This is very useful for locking the heading row of a long list of data onto the top of the screen so that when you scroll down it will remain visible. First move a horizontal split below the column heading row or to the right of a row heading column, then Freeze Panes.

Open Windows List Allows you to bring any open, non-hidden window to the foreground so that you can work on it.

HELP MENU

Microsoft Excel Help Launches the sometimes-annoying Office Assistant where you can type questions to find what you're looking for.

Contents and Index An index of help topics, along with a nice search function.

What's This? Lets you click on an area of the screen to find out what it does.

Microsoft on the Web Online resources such as product updates and news, along with a web tutorial.

Lotus 1-2-3 Help... Help for people accustomed to using Lotus 1-2-3.

About Microsoft Excel Displays product version and licensing information. Also contains a link for information about your computer system and a link for **tech support**.

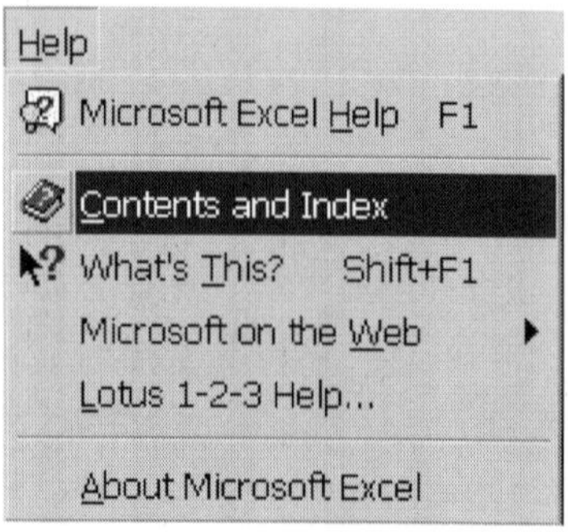

Adding and Renaming Worksheets

The worksheets in a workbook are accessible by clicking the worksheet tabs just above the status bar. By default, three worksheets are included in each workbook. To add a sheet, select **Insert | Worksheet** from the menu bar. To rename the worksheet tab, right-click on the tab with the mouse and select **Rename** from the shortcut menu. Type the new name and press the **ENTER** key.

The Standard Toolbar

This toolbar is located just below the menu bar at the top of the screen and allows you to quickly access basic Excel commands.

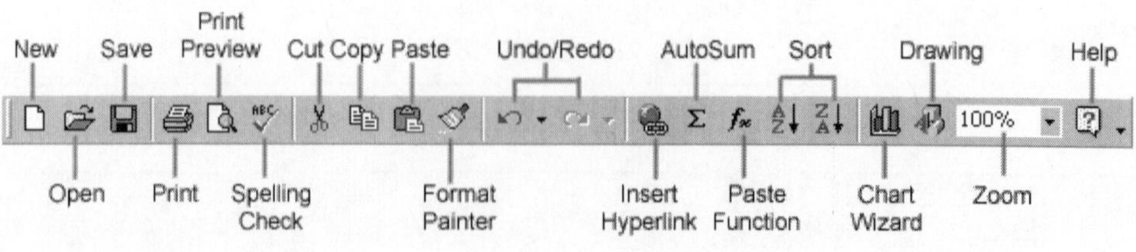

Moving Through Cells

Use the mouse to select a cell you want to begin adding data to and use the keyboard strokes listed in the table below to move through the cells of a worksheet.

Movement	Key stroke
One cell up	up arrow key
One cell down	down arrow key or **ENTER**
One cell left	left arrow key
One cell right	right arrow key or **TAB**
Top of the worksheet (cell A1)	**CTRL+HOME**
End of the worksheet (last cell containing data)	**CTRL+END**
End of the row	**CTRL**+right arrow key
End of the column	**CTRL**+down arrow key
Any cell	**File | Go To** menu bar command

Adding Worksheets, Rows, and Columns

- **Worksheets** - Add a worksheet to a workbook by selecting **Insert | Worksheet** from the menu bar.
- **Row** - To add a row to a worksheet, select **Insert | Rows** from the menu bar, or highlight the row by clicking on the row label, right-click with the mouse, and choose **Insert**.
- **Column** - Add a column by selecting **Insert | Columns** from the menu bar, or highlight the column by click on the column label, right-click with the mouse, and choose **Insert**.

Resizing Rows and Columns

There are two ways to resize rows and columns.

- **Resize a row** by dragging the line below the label of the row you would like to resize. **Resize a column** in a similar manner by dragging the line to the right of the label corresponding to the column you want to resize.

  - OR -
- Click the row or column label and select **Format | Row | Height** or **Format | Column | Width** from the menu bar to enter a numerical value for the height of the row or width of the column.

Selecting Cells

Before a cell can be modified or formatted, it must first be selected (highlighted). Refer to the table below for selecting groups of cells.

Cells to select	Mouse action
One cell	click once in the cell
Entire row	click the row label
Entire column	click the column label
Entire worksheet	click the whole sheet button
Cluster of cells	drag mouse over the cells or hold down the **SHIFT** key while using the arrow keys

To activate the contents of a cell, double-click on the cell or click once and press **F2**.

Moving and Copying Cells

Moving Cells

To cut cell contents that will be moved to another cell select **Edit | Cut** from the menu bar or click the **Cut** button on the standard toolbar.

Copying Cells

To copy the cell contents, select **Edit | Copy** from the menu bar or click the **Copy** button on the standard toolbar.

Pasting Cut and Copied Cells

Highlight the cell you want to paste the cut or copied content into and select **Edit | Paste** from the menu bar or click the **Paste** button on the standard toolbar.

Drag and Drop

If you are moving the cell contents only a short distance, the drag-and-drop method may be easier. Simply drag the highlighted border of the selected cell to the destination cell with the mouse.

FORMULAS & FUNCTIONS

The distinguishing feature of a spreadsheet program such as Excel is that it allows you to create mathematical formulas and execute functions. Otherwise, it is not much more than a large table for displaying text. This page will show you how to create these calculations.

Formulas

Formulas are entered in the worksheet cell and must begin with an equal sign "=". The formula then includes the addresses of the cells whose values will be manipulated with appropriate operands placed in between. After the formula is typed into the cell, the calculation executes immediately and the formula itself is visible in the formula bar. See the example below to view the formula for calculating the sub total for a number of textbooks. The formula multiplies the quantity and price of each textbook and adds the subtotal for each book.

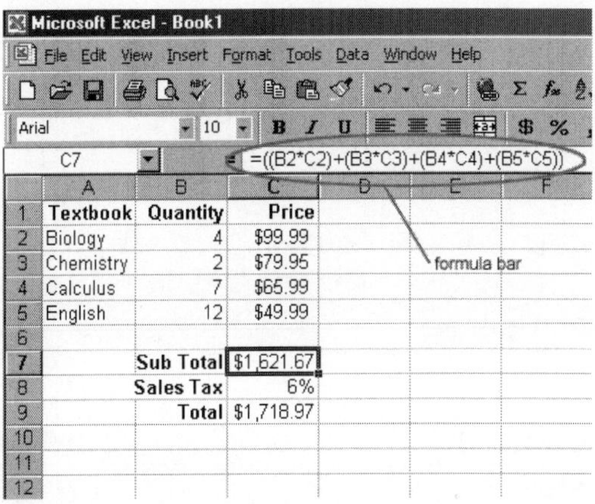

Linking Worksheets

You may want to use the value from a cell in another worksheet within the same workbook in a formula. For example, the value of cell A1 in the current worksheet and cell A2 in the second worksheet can be added using the format "sheetname!celladdress". The formula for this example would be "=A1+Sheet2!A2" where the value of cell A1 in the current worksheet is added to the value of cell A2 in the worksheet named "Sheet2".

Relative, Absolute, and Mixed Referencing

Calling cells by just their column and row labels (such as "A1") is called **relative referencing**. When a formula contains relative referencing and it is copied from one cell to another, Excel does not create an exact copy of the formula. It will change cell addresses relative to the row and column they are moved to. For example, if a simple addition formula in cell C1 "=(A1+B1)" is copied to cell C2, the formula would change to "=(A2+B2)" to reflect the new row. To prevent this change, cells must be called by **absolute referencing** and this is accomplished by placing dollar signs "$" within the cell addresses in the formula. Continuing the previous example, the formula in cell C1 would read "=(A1+B1)" if the value of cell C2 should be the sum of cells A1 and B1. Both the column and row of both cells are absolute and will not change when copied. **Mixed referencing** can also be used where only the row OR column fixed. For example, in the formula "=(A$1+$B2)", the row of cell A1 is fixed and the column of cell B2 is fixed.

Basic Functions

Functions can be a more efficient way of performing mathematical operations than formulas. For example, if you wanted to add the values of cells D1 through D10, you would type the formula "=D1+D2+D3+D4+D5+D6+D7+D8+D9+D10". A shorter way would be to use the SUM function and simply type "=SUM(D1:D10)". Several other functions and examples are given in the table below:

Function	Example	Description
SUM	=SUM(A1:100)	finds the sum of cells A1 through A100
AVERAGE	=AVERAGE(B1:B10)	finds the average of cells B1 through B10
MAX	=MAX(C1:C100)	returns the highest number from cells C1 through C100
MIN	=MIN(D1:D100)	returns the lowest number from cells D1 through D100
SQRT	=SQRT(D10)	finds the square root of the value in cell D10
TODAY	=TODAY()	returns the current date (leave the parentheses empty)

Function Wizard

View all functions available in Excel by using the Function Wizard.

- Activate the cell where the function will be placed and click the **Function Wizard** button on the standard toolbar.
- From the **Paste Function** dialog box, browse through the functions by clicking in the **Function category** menu on the left and select the function from the **Function name** choices on the right. As each function name is highlighted a description and example of use is provided below the two boxes.

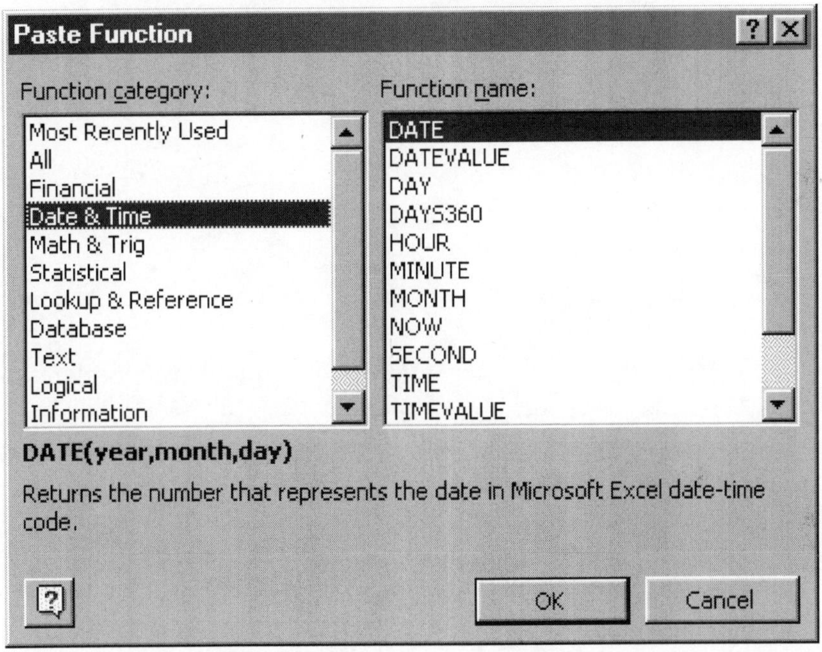

- Click **OK** to select a function.
- The next window allows you to choose the cells that will be included in the function. In the example below, cells B4 and C4 were automatically selected for the sum function by Excel. The cell values {2, 3} are located to the right of the **Number 1** field where the cell addresses are listed. If another set of cells, such as B5 and C5, needed to be added to the function, those cells would be added in the format "B5:C5" to the **Number 2** field.

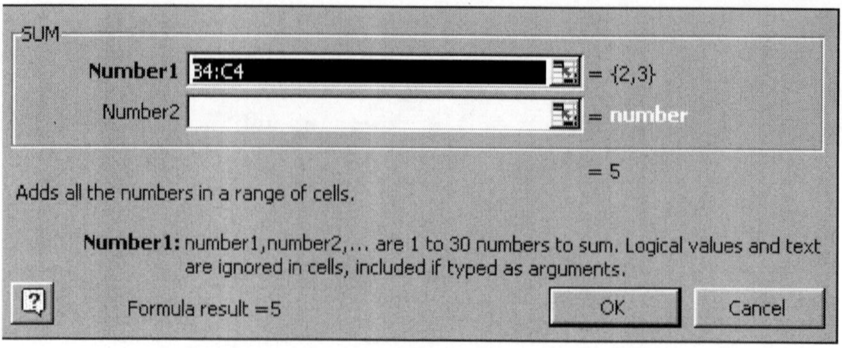

- Click **OK** when all the cells for the function have been selected.

Autosum

Use the Autosum function to add the contents of a cluster of adjacent cells.

- Select the cell that the sum will appear in that is outside the cluster of cells whose values will be added. Cell C2 was used in this example.
- Click the **Autosum** button (Greek letter sigma) on the standard toolbar.
- Highlight the group of cells that will be summed (cells A2 through B2 in this example).
- Press the **ENTER** key on the keyboard or click the green check mark button on the formula bar .

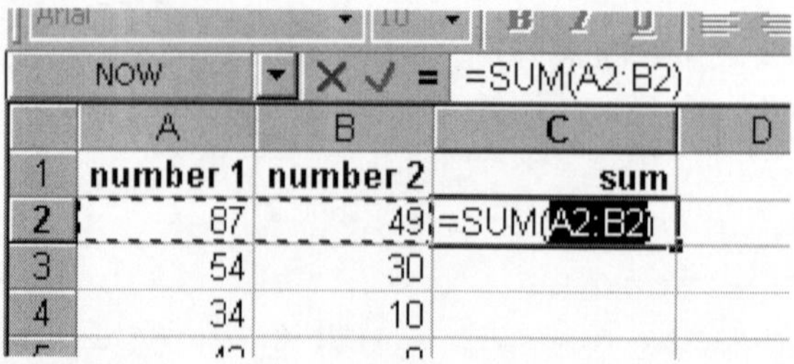

Basic Sorts

To execute a basic descending or ascending sort based on one column, highlight the cells that will be sorted and click the **Sort Ascending** (A-Z) button or **Sort Descending** (Z-A) button on the standard toolbar.

Complex Sorts

To sort by multiple columns, follow these steps:

- Highlight the cells, rows, or columns that will be sorted.
- Select **Data|Sort** from the menu bar.
- From the **Sort** dialog box, select the first column for sorting from the **Sort By** drop-down menu and choose either ascending or descending.
- Select the second column and, if necessary, the third sort column from the **Then By** drop-down menus.

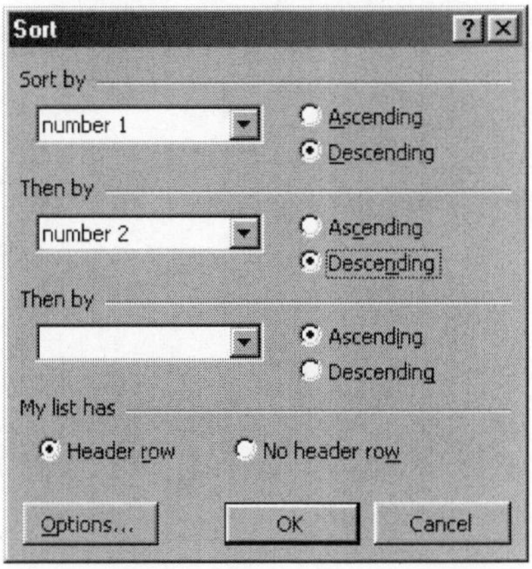

- If the cells you highlighted included the text headings in the first row, mark **My list has**...**Header row** and the first row will remain at the top of the worksheet.
- Click the **Options** button for special non-alphabetic or numeric sorts such as months of the year and days of the week.

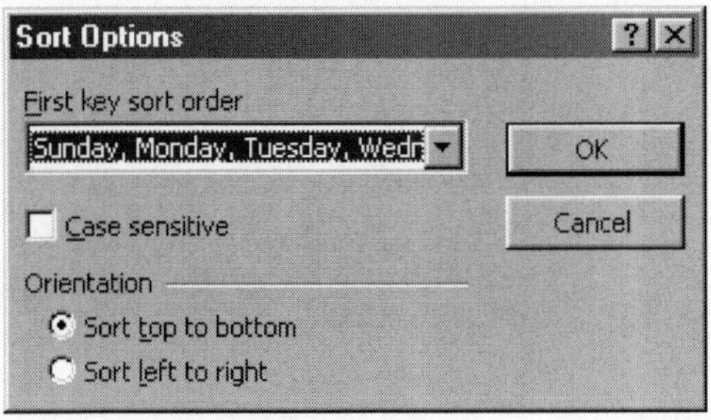

- Click **OK** to execute the sort.

Autofill

The Autofill feature allows you to quickly fill cells with repetitive or sequential data such as chronological dates or numbers, and repeated text.

- Type the beginning number or date of an incrementing series or the text that will be repeated into a cell.
- Select the handle at the bottom, right corner of the cell with the left mouse button and drag it down as many cells as you want to fill.
- Release the mouse button.

If you want to autofill a column with cells displaying the same number or date you must enter identical data to two adjacent cells in a column. Highlight the *two* cells and drag the handle of the selection with the mouse.

Alternating Text and Numbers with Autofill

The Autofill feature can also be used for alternating text or numbers. For example, to make a repeating list of the days of the week, type the seven days into seven adjacent cells in a column. Highlight the seven cells and drag down with the mouse.

Autofilling Functions

Autofill can also be used to copy functions. In the example below, column A and column B each contain lists of numbers and column C contains the sums of columns A and B for each row. The function in cell C2 would be "=SUM(A2:B2)". This function can then be copied to the remaining cells of column C by activating cell C2 and dragging the handle down to fill in the remaining cells. The autofill feature will automatically update the row numbers as shown below if the cells are reference relatively.

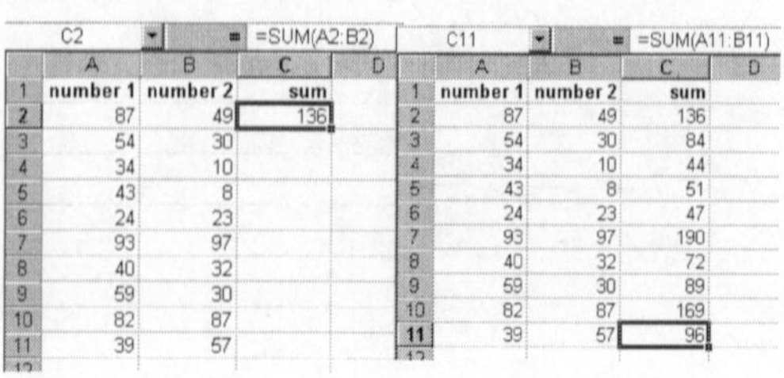

CHART

Chart Wizard

The Chart Wizard brings you through the process of creating a chart by displaying a series of dialog boxes.

1. Enter the data into the worksheet and highlight all the cells that will be included in the chart including headers.

	A	B	C
1		Students	
2	English	34	
3	Biology	32	
4	Calculus	26	
5	Physics	28	
6	History	39	
7			

2. Click the Chart Wizard button on the standard toolbar to view the first **Chart Wizard** dialog box.
3. **Chart Type** - Choose the **Chart type** and the **Chart subtype** if necessary. Click **Next**.

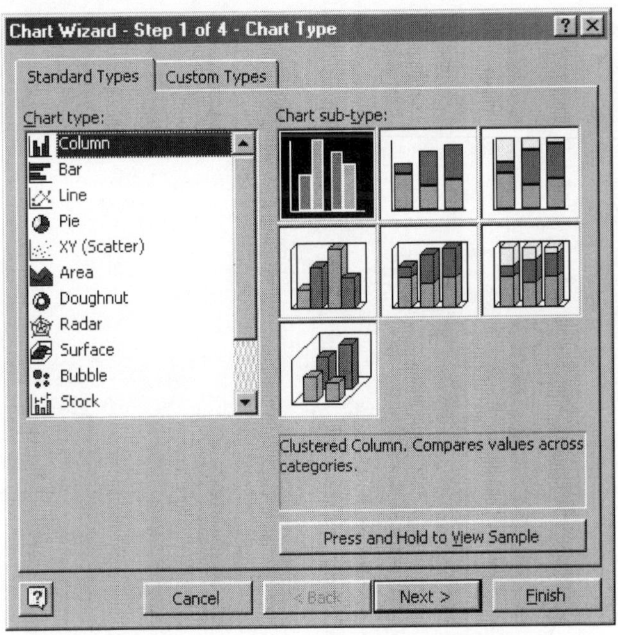

4. **Chart Source Data** - Select the data range (if different from the area highlighted in step 1) and click **Next**.

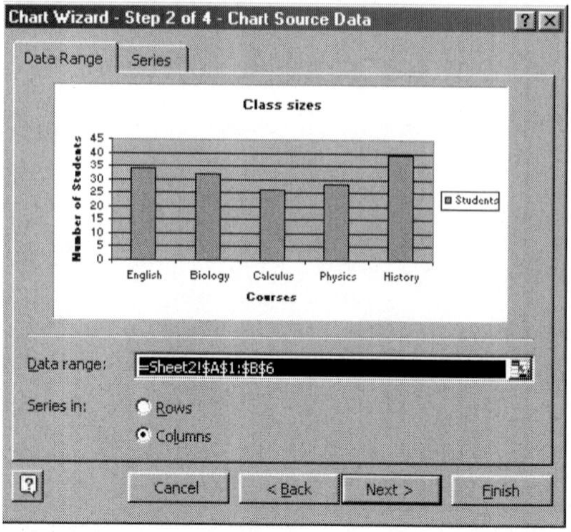

5. **Chart Options - Enter the name of the chart and titles for the X**- and Y-axes. Other options for the axes, grid lines, legend, data labels, and data table can be changed by clicking on the tabs. Press **Next** to move to the next set of options.

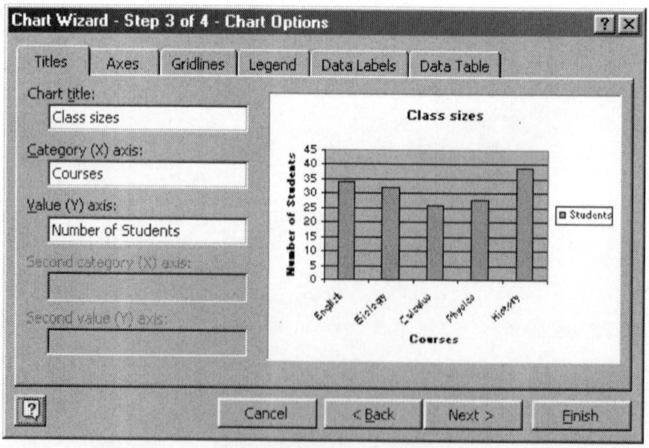

6. **Chart Location** - Click **As new sheet** if the chart should be placed on a new, blank worksheet or select **As object in** if the chart should be embedded in an existing sheet and select the worksheet from the drop-down menu.

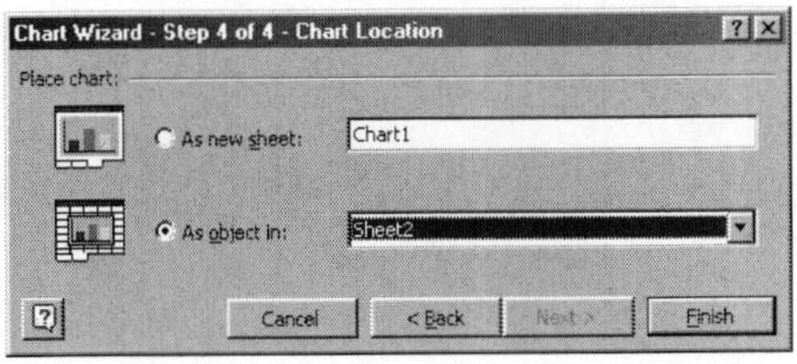

7. Click **Finish** to create the chart.

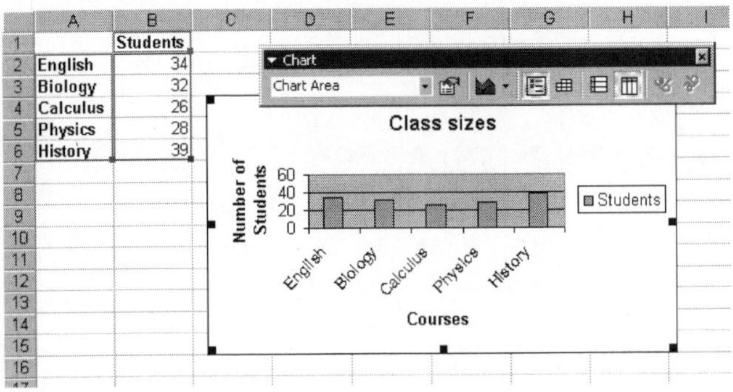

Resizing the Chart

To resize the chart, click on its border and drag any of the nine black handles to change the size. Handles on the corners will resize the chart proportionally while handles along the lines will stretch the chart.

Moving the Chart

Select the border of the chart, hold down the left mouse button, and drag the chart to a new location. Elements within the chart such as the title and labels may also be moved within the chart. Click on the element to activate it, and use the mouse to drag the element to move it.

Chart Formatting Toolbar

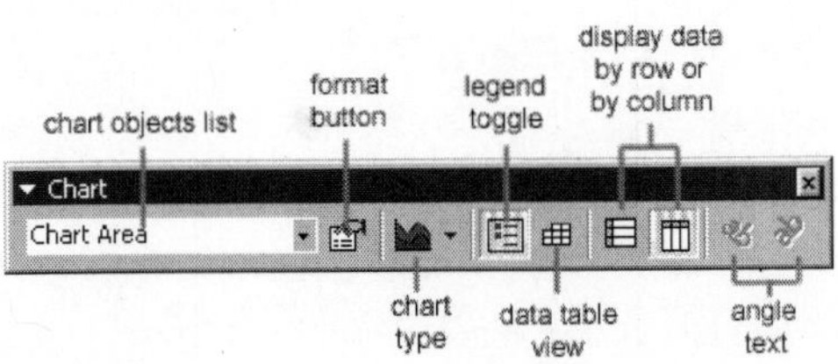

Chart Objects List - To select an object on the chart to format, click the object on the chart or select the object from the **Chart Objects List** and click the **Format button**. A window containing the properties of that object will then appear to make formatting changes.

Chart Type - Click the arrowhead on the chart type button to select a different type of chart.

Legend Toggle - Show or hide the chart legend by clicking this toggle button.

Data Table view - Display the data table instead of the chart by clicking the Data Table toggle button.

Display Data by Column or Row - Charts the data by columns or rows according to the data sheet.

Angle Text - Select the category or value axis and click the **Angle Downward** or **Angle Upward** button to angle the selected by +/- 45 degrees.

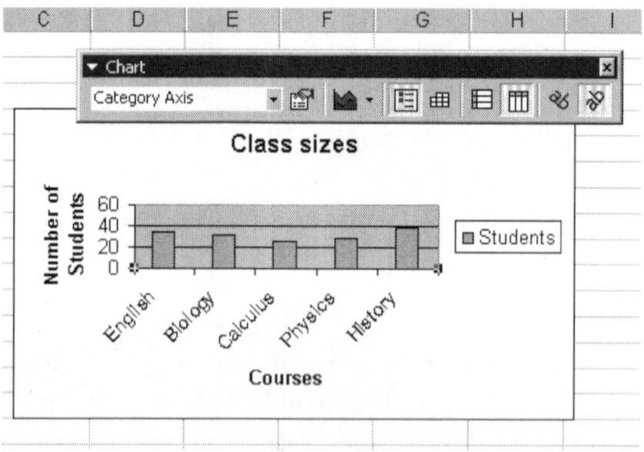

Copying the Chart to Microsoft Word

A finished chart can be copied into a Microsoft Word document. Select the chart and click

Copy. Open the destination document in Word and click **Paste**.

PAGE, PRINT PREVIEW & PRINT

Page Breaks

To set page breaks within the worksheet, select the row you want to appear just below the page break by clicking the row's label. Then choose **Insert|Page Break** from the menu bar. You may need to click the double down arrow at the bottom of the menu list to view this option.

Page Setup

Select **File|Page Setup** from the menu bar to format the page, set margins, and add headers and footers.

- **Page**

Select the **Orientation** under the **Page** tab in the Page Setup window to make the page Landscape or Portrait. The size of the worksheet on the page can also be formatting under **Scaling**. To force a worksheet to print only one page wide so all the columns appear on the same page, select **Fit to 1 page(s) wide**.

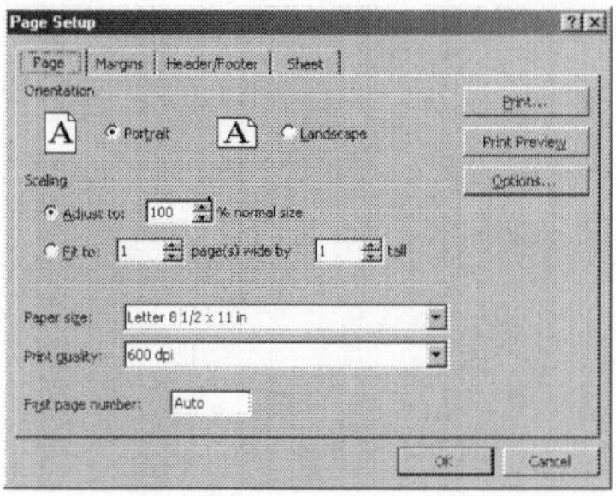

- **Margins**

Change the top, bottom, left, and right margins under the **Margins** tab. Enter values in the header and footer fields to indicate how far from the edge of the page this text should appear. Check the boxes for centering horizontally or vertically on the page.

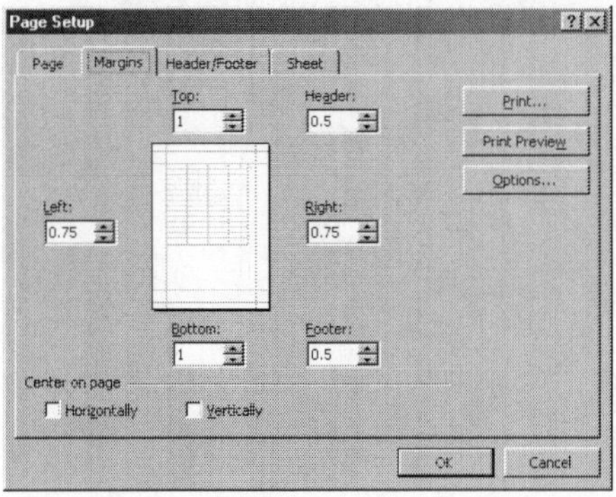

- **Header/Footer**

Add preset headers and footers to the page by clicking the drop-down menus under the Header/Footer tab.

To modify a preset header or footer, or to make your own, click the **Custom Header** and **Custom Footer** buttons. A new window will open allowing you to enter text in the left, center, or right on the page.

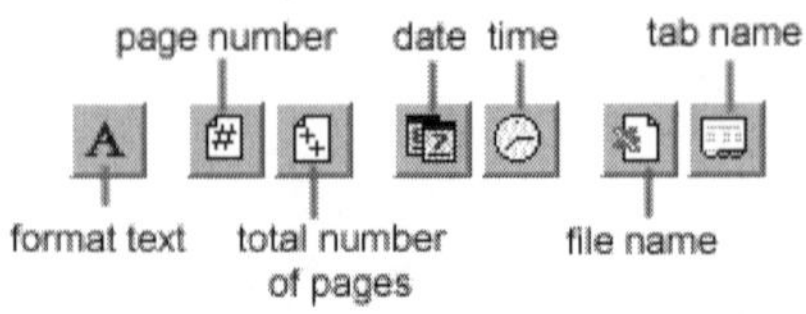

Format Text - Click this button after highlighting the text to change the font, size, and style.

Page Number - Insert the page number of each page.

Total Number of Pages - Use this feature along with the page number to create strings such as "page 1 of 15".

Date - Add the current date.

Time - Add the current time.

File Name - Add the name of the workbook file.

Tab Name - Add the name of the worksheet's tab.

- **Sheet**

Check **Gridlines** if you want the gridlines dividing the cells to be printed on the page. If the worksheet is several pages long and only the first page includes titles for the columns, select **Rows to repeat at top** to choose a title row that will be printed at the top of each page.

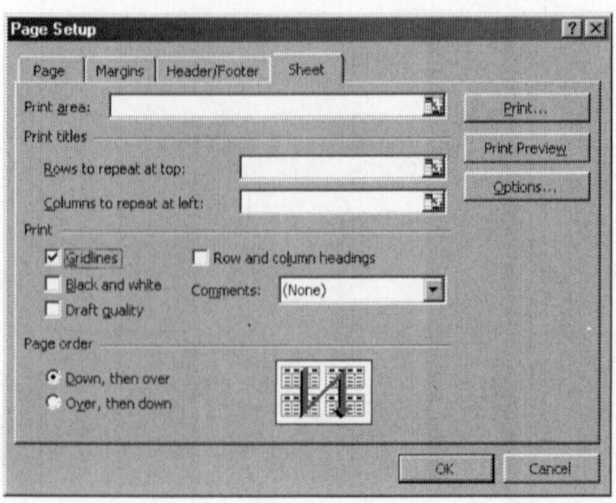

Print Preview

Select **File | Print Preview** from the menu bar to view how the worksheet will print. Click the **Next** and **Previous** buttons at the top of the window to display the pages and click the **Zoom** button to view the pages closer. Make page layout modifications needed by clicking the **Page Setup** button. Click **Close** to return to the worksheet or **Print** to continue printing.

Print

To print the worksheet, select **File | Print** from the menu bar.

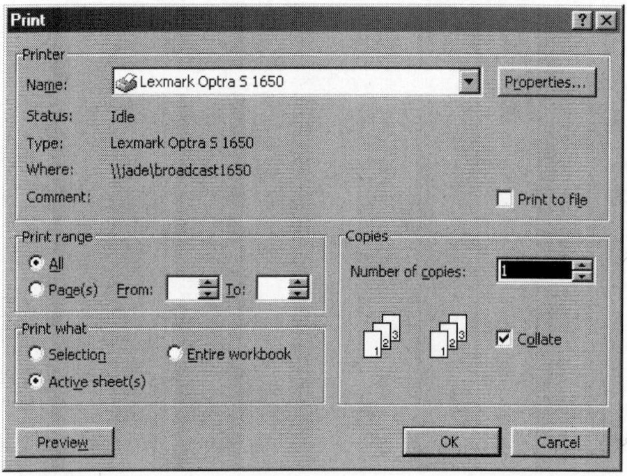

- **Print Range** - Select either all pages or a range of pages to print.
- **Print What** - Select selection of cells highlighted on the worksheet, the active worksheet, or all the worksheets in the entire workbook.
- **Copies** - Choose the number of copies that should be printed. Check the **Collate** box if the pages should remain in order.

Click **OK** to print.

E-MAIL A WORKSHEET

There are many ways to send Excel data through e-mail. One way to send Excel data in e-mail is to use the Microsoft Office Word Mail Merge Wizard. This feature is available in Microsoft

Excel 2000. In Microsoft Excel 2000, this feature is called the Mail Merge Helper. The Word Mail Merge Wizard simplifies many e-mail related tasks, including creating batch mailings, sending e-mail messages, creating postal mailing labels, labeling envelopes for postal mail, and creating directory lists.

If you have Microsoft Outlook® or Outlook Express installed, you can embed a worksheet in an e-mail message and send it directly from Excel. Distributing a worksheet via e-mail allows you to do the following:

- **Quickly share a worksheet with others** Just create the worksheet as usual, specify the recipient information, click a button—and the worksheet is on its way.
- **Embed a worksheet in a message** In effect, the worksheet is the message. There's no need for recipients to locate and open a separate attached file.
- **Use HTML format so almost anyone can view your worksheet** Excel sends the worksheet in HTML format. To view the worksheet, recipients don't need Excel or other special software—just an e-mail program that can read HTML format.

NOTE You can send only an individual worksheet (not an entire workbook) in HTML format. You must send an entire workbook as an attachment. You might also want to send a worksheet as an attachment if you want to collaborate on the worksheet, or if the recipient doesn't have an HTML-compatible e-mail program. An attachment is not converted to HTML format, so anyone using Excel 97 or later can view and modify it. For more information about sending files as an attachment, see Excel Help.

Step 1: Prepare your worksheet

Open or create the worksheet you want to send. Then, because the HTML document that appears in your recipient's e-mail program might not look exactly the same as the original, you might want to make some minor customizations to the worksheet before you send it. For example, to improve readability, you can add cell borders to selected cells by clicking **Cells** on the **Format** menu, and then clicking the **Border** tab.

To improve readability, add borders and shading to your worksheet.

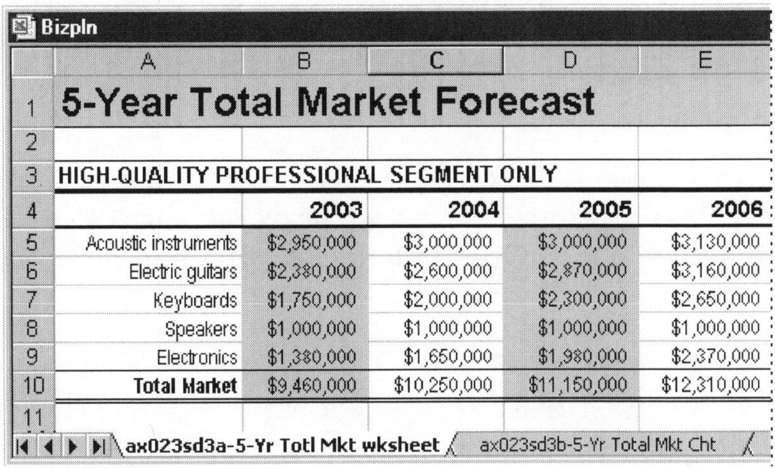

Bizpln

	A	B	C	D	E
1	5-Year Total Market Forecast				
2					
3	HIGH-QUALITY PROFESSIONAL SEGMENT ONLY				
4		2003	2004	2005	2006
5	Acoustic instruments	$2,950,000	$3,000,000	$3,000,000	$3,130,000
6	Electric guitars	$2,380,000	$2,600,000	$2,870,000	$3,160,000
7	Keyboards	$1,750,000	$2,000,000	$2,300,000	$2,650,000
8	Speakers	$1,000,000	$1,000,000	$1,000,000	$1,000,000
9	Electronics	$1,380,000	$1,650,000	$1,980,000	$2,370,000
10	Total Market	$9,460,000	$10,250,000	$11,150,000	$12,310,000
11					

ax023sd3a-5-Yr Totl Mkt wksheet / ax023sd3b-5-Yr Total Mkt Cht

To help your recipients understand the worksheet, you might want to add a comment that describes the worksheet's contents. To do this, click a cell at the top of the worksheet, click **Comment** on the **Insert** menu, and then type your comment.

Step 2: Start an e-mail message in Excel

On the **Standard** toolbar, click the **E-mail** button. Clicking this button displays (and hides, if clicked again) an e-mail header that lets you set e-mail options and send the worksheet, as shown in the following picture.

Now you're ready to address the message. In the **To** and **Cc** boxes, enter the recipient names separated by a semicolon. Or select recipient names from a list by clicking the address book icon next to **To** or **Cc**.

NOTE To send the message to someone privately, you can add the **Bcc** box by clicking **Options** on the e-mail header, and then clicking **Bcc**.

By default, the worksheet's file name appears in the **Subject** box. You can delete this text, if you want, and type your own subject line. For example, "Please review this document by Friday."

Step 3: Set e-mail options

Before you send the worksheet, you might want to include an attached file or set e-mail options, such as a message flag or security level. To attach a file, click the **Insert File** button. To set options, click **Options**, and then choose the options you want.

Step 4: Send the worksheet

When you click **Send this Sheet**, Excel sends a copy of the worksheet, and then closes the e-mail header. The following picture shows how the worksheet looks in your recipient's e-mail program.

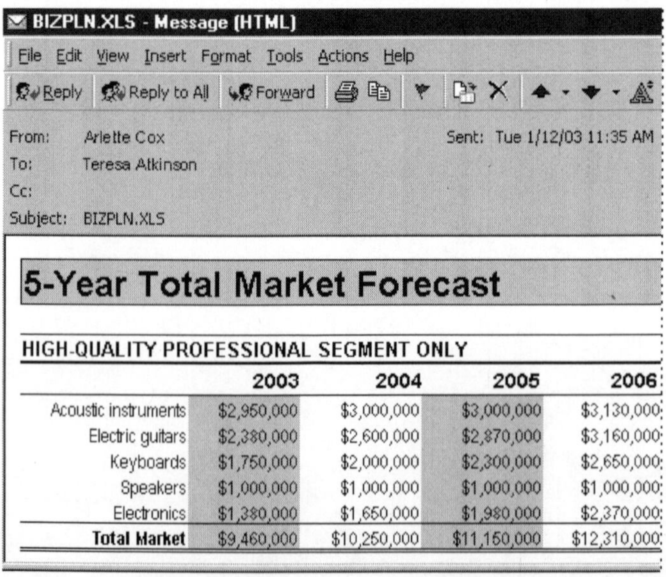

	2003	2004	2005	2006
Acoustic instruments	$2,950,000	$3,000,000	$3,000,000	$3,130,000
Electric guitars	$2,380,000	$2,600,000	$2,870,000	$3,160,000
Keyboards	$1,750,000	$2,000,000	$2,300,000	$2,650,000
Speakers	$1,000,000	$1,000,000	$1,000,000	$1,000,000
Electronics	$1,380,000	$1,650,000	$1,980,000	$2,370,000
Total Market	$9,460,000	$10,250,000	$11,150,000	$12,310,000

In Excel, the original worksheet remains open so that you can continue working on it. When you save the worksheet, the e-mail information (recipient list, e-mail options, and any file attachments) is saved with the worksheet. The next time you send a copy of the worksheet, the e-mail information appears in the e-mail header. This makes it easy to send updates of the worksheet to the same recipients.

Responding to a worksheet message

If you receive a worksheet sent in HTML format, you'll notice that the body of the message contains only a static view of the original worksheet. However, some of the original worksheet information (such as formatting and formulas) is preserved. This means you can make some modifications to the worksheet within your e-mail program. For example, you can add data, use formulas, sort the information, or filter it.

If you have Excel installed, you can click **Edit Message** on the **Edit** menu in Outlook, and the worksheet will open in Excel. Then you can modify the worksheet by using any Excel features you want. When you finish, you can save the worksheet to your local computer or send the revised version back to its originator.

Keyboard shortcuts can save time and the effort of switching from the keyboard to the mouse to execute simple commands. Print this list of Excel keyboard shortcuts and keep it by your computer for a quick reference.

Note: A plus sign indicates that the keys need to be pressed at the same time.

Action	Keystroke
Document actions	
Open a file	CTRL+O
New file	CTRL+N
Save As	F12
Save	CTRL+S
Print	CTRL+P
Find	CTRL+F
Replace	CTRL+H
Go to	F5
Cursor Movement	
One cell up	up arrow
One cell down	down arrow
One cell right	Tab
One cell left	SHIFT+Tab
Top of worksheet (cell A1)	CTRL+Home

Action	Keystroke
End of worksheet (last cell with data)	CTRL+End
End of row	Home
End of column	CTRL+left arrow
Move to next worksheet	CTRL+PageDown
Formulas	
Apply AutoSum	ALT+=
Current date	CTRL+;
Current time	CTRL+:
Spelling	F7
Help	F1
Macros	ALT+F8

Action	**Keystroke**
Selecting Cells	
All cells left of current cell	SHIFT+left arrow
All cells right of current cell	SHIFT+right arrow
Entire column	CTRL+Spacebar
Entire row	SHIFT+Spacebar
Entire worksheet	CTRL+A
Text Style	
Bold	CTRL+B
Italics	CTRL+I
Underline	CTRL+U
Strikethrough	CTRL+5
Formatting	
Edit active cell	F2
Format as currency with 2 decimal places	SHIFT+CTRL+$
Format as percent with no decimal places	SHIFT+CTRL+%
Cut	CTRL+X
Copy	CTRL+C
Paste	CTRL+V
Undo	CTRL+Z
Redo	CTRL+Y
Format cells dialog box	CTRL+1

11

Introduction to Access

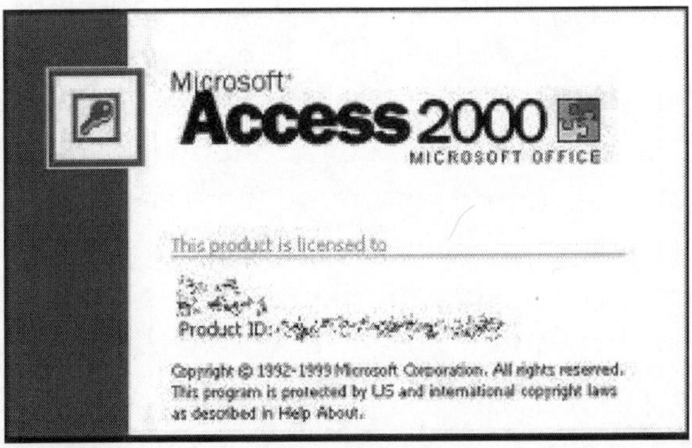

DATABASE: A systematic organization of data is called a database.

- Fields and Records are used to organize database
- A record which gives complete information about one item.
- Field gives unique information of the item.
- A table is a fundamental building block of an access database.

Database Management System (DBMS) contains

1. Tables
2. Queries
3. Forms

4. Reports
5. Data Access Page
6. Macros
7. Modules

A Few Terms

These words are used often in Access so you will want to become familiar with them before using the program.

- **A database** is a collection of related information.
- An **object** is a competition in the database such as a table, query, form, or macro.
- **A table** is a grouping of related data organized in fields (columns) and records (rows) on a datasheet. By using a common field in two tables, the data can be combined. Many tables can be stored in a single database.
- **A field** is a column on a datasheet and defines a data type for a set of values in a table. For a mailing list table might include fields for first name, last name, address, city, state, zip code, and telephone number.
- **A record** in a row on a datasheet and is a set of values defined by fields. In a mailing list table, each record would contain the data for one person as specified by the intersecting fields.
- **Design View** provides the tools for creating fields in a table.
- **Datasheet View** allows you to update, edit, and delete information from a table.

Getting Started

After opening Access, you will be presented with the window shown below. Select one of the first two options if you are creating a new database or the third if you want to edit an existing database. All three choices are explained in detail below.

Blank Access database

- Unlike Word documents, Excel worksheets, and Power Point presentations, you must save an Access database before you start working on it. After selecting “Blank Access database”, you will first be prompted to specify a location and name for the database.

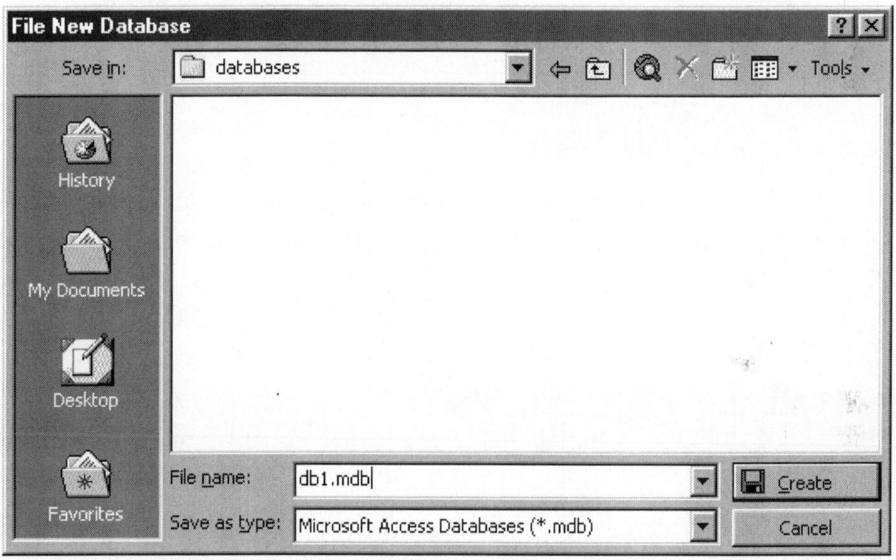

- Find the folder where the database should reside in the **Save in** drop-down menu.
- Type the name of the database in the **File name** line and click the **Create** button.

Access database wizards, pages, and projects

Access’ wizards and layout are existing database structures that only need data input. Select a database type and click **OK**. Name the database on the next screen.

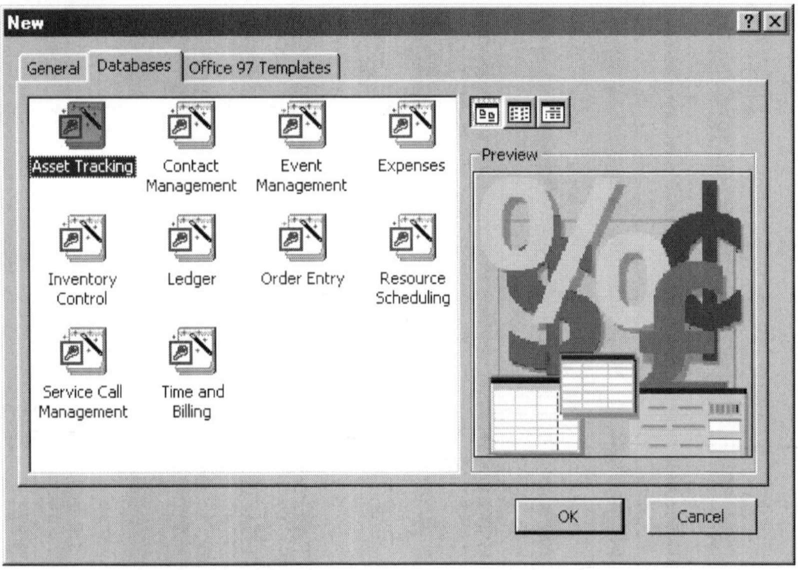

Open an existing database

If the database was opened recently on the computer, it will be listed on the main window. Highlight the database name and click **OK**. Otherwise, highlight "More Files..." in the list and click **OK**. From the subsequent window, click the "Look In:" drop-down menu to find the folder where the database is located, highlight the database name in the listing and click **OK**.

Converting to Access 2000

Before opening an existing file that was created in a previous version of Access, it must first be converted to Access 2000 format. Convert a database by following these steps:

- Open Access and select **Tools | Database Utilities | Convert Database | To Current Access Database Version** from the menu bar.
- Select the database that should be converted and click the **Convert** button.
- The new version will be a completely separate database and the old one will remain intact so you must then name the new version of the database.

Database Window

The Database Window organizes all of the objects in the database. The default tables listing provide links for creating tables and will list all of the tables in the database when they have been added.

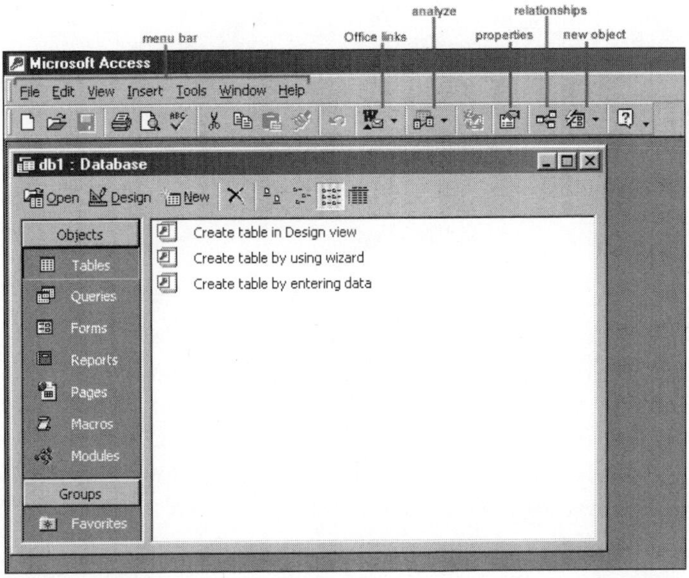

CREATING A NEW DATABASE TABLE AND FORM...

STEP 1 Launch Microsoft Access and select **Blank Access database**

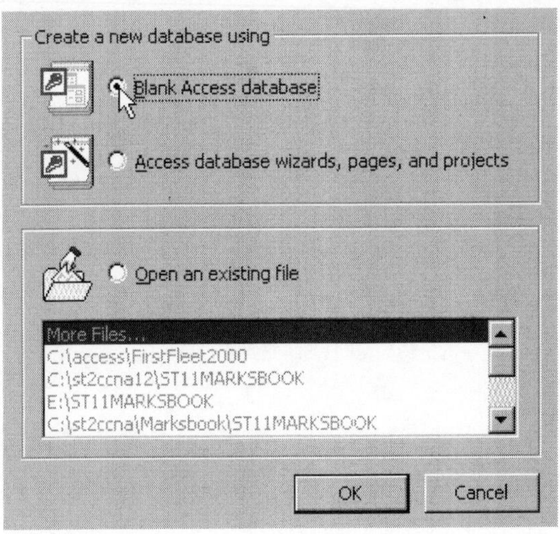

STEP 2 Name your new Database and save it.

STEP 3 Select **Tables** from the **Objects** list and double-click **Create table in Design View**.

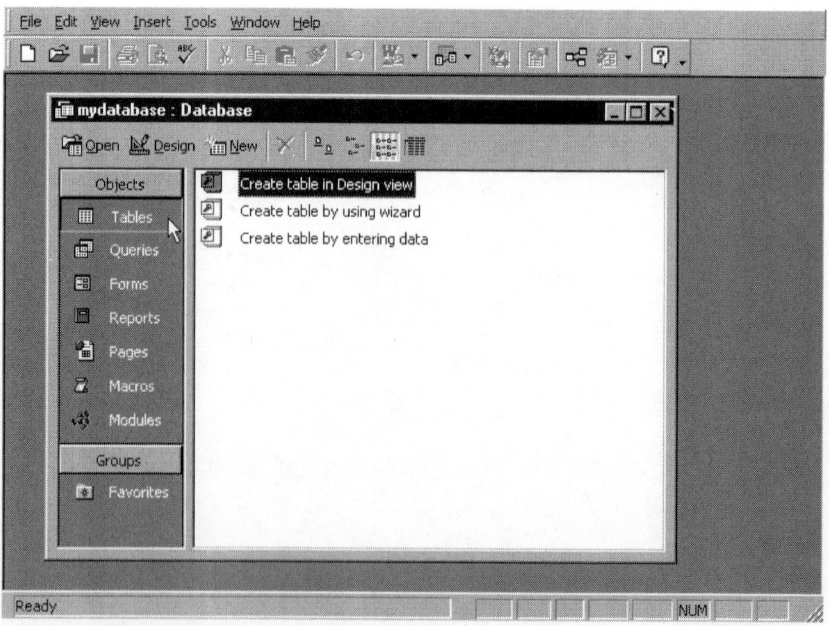

STEP 4 Enter Field names. Select the **Data Types** and add a **Description** where required.

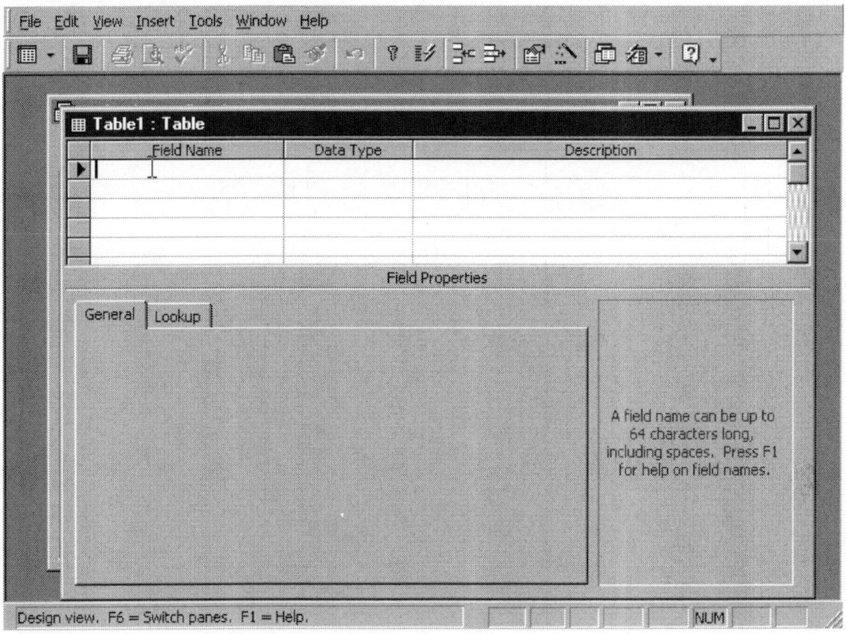

Selecting Data Types ...

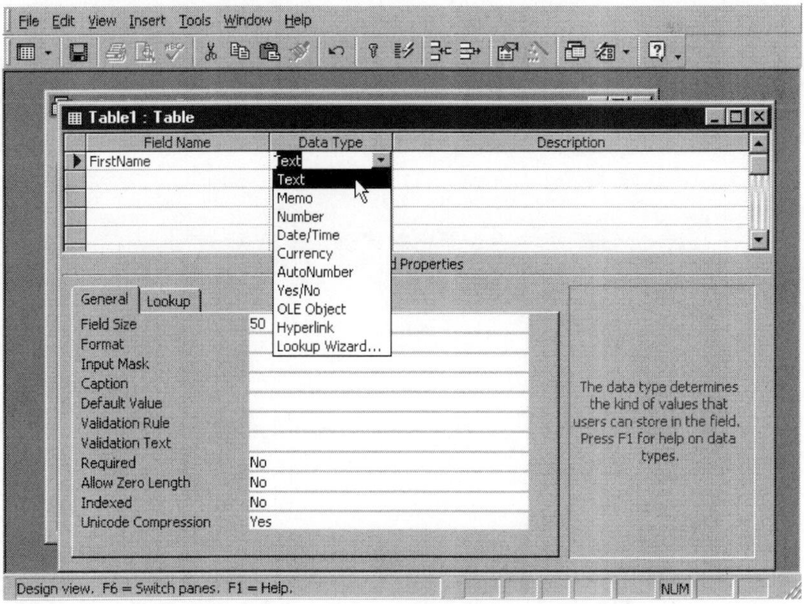

The Data Type selected depends upon how you intend using the data ...

STEP 5 When you have finished creating your Table click the **Close** button

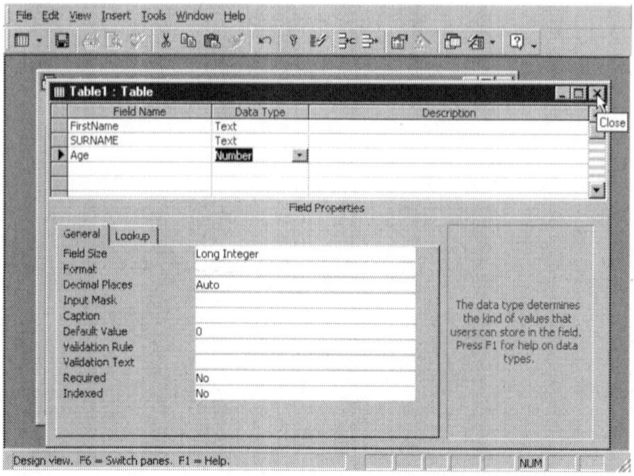

You will be prompted to define a **Primary Key** ...

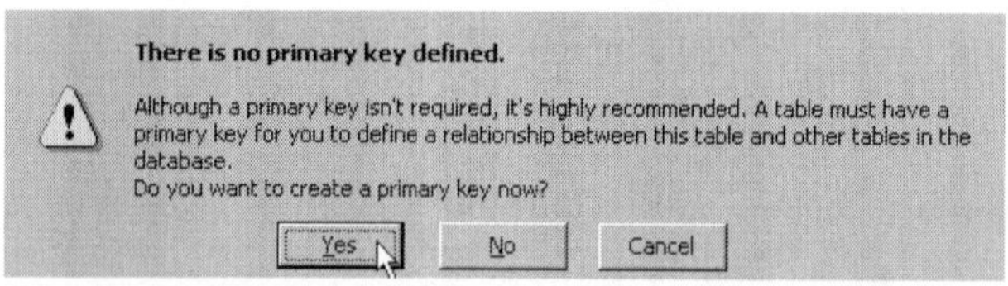

STEP 6 Go to **Forms** on the **Objects** list.

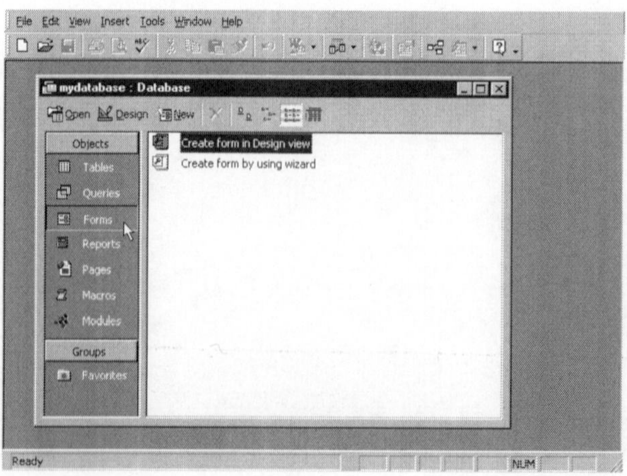

STEP 7 Right-click the top-left Form button with the black centre square.

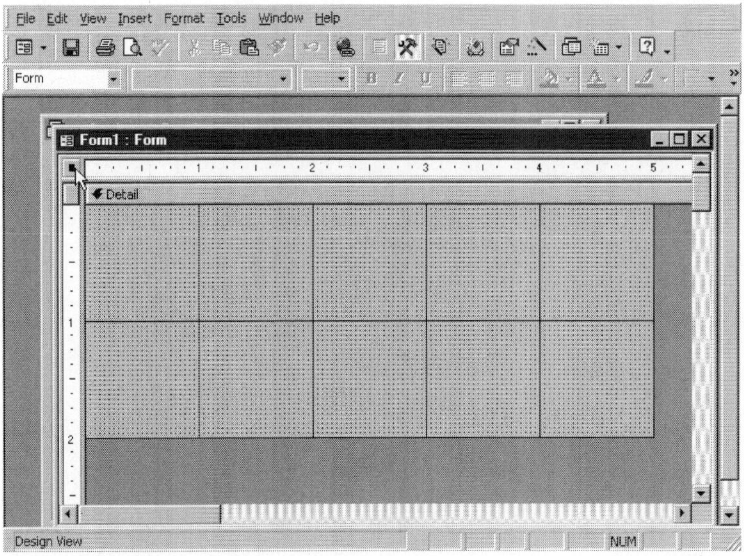

STEP 8 Select **Properties**.

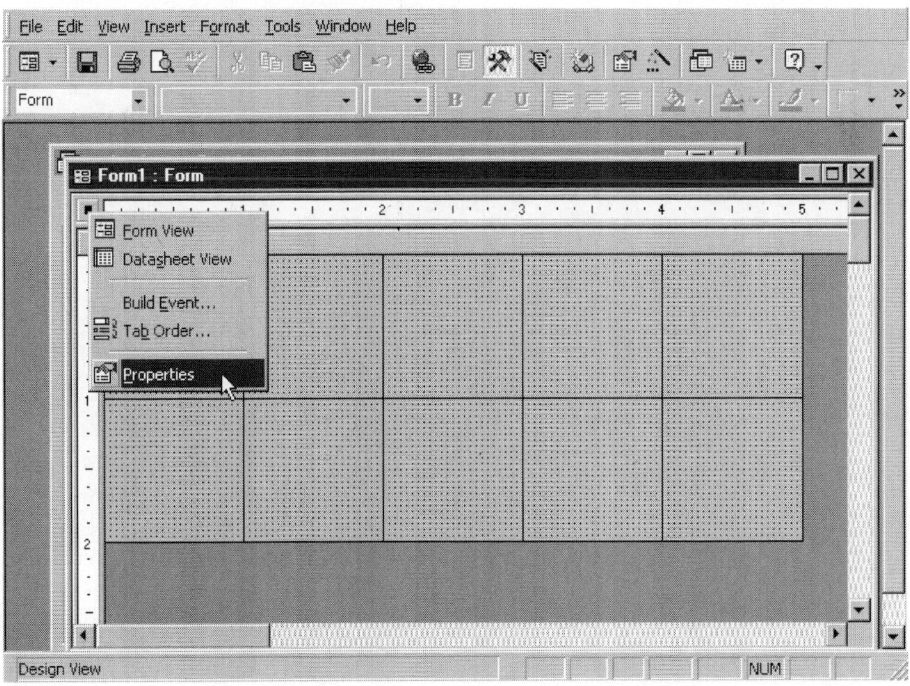

STEP 9 Select the **Data** tab and click on the drop-arrow. Select the Table you intend using.

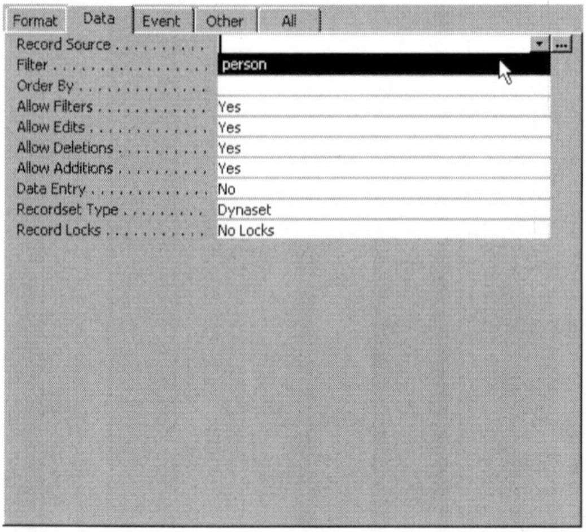

The **Fields List** box appears ...

STEP 10 Drag each of the Fields from the **Fields List** and drop them onto the Form

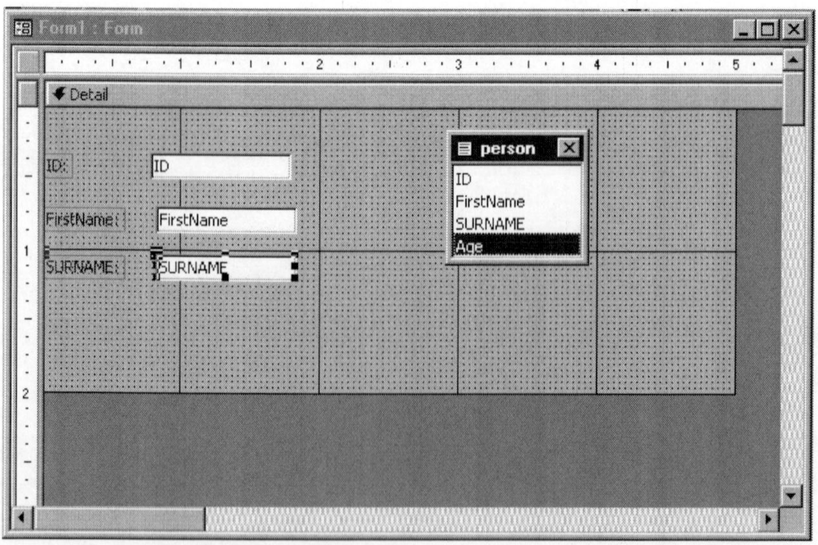

STEP 11 Position the Fields on the Form. Use **Ctrl/arrow Keys** for precise positioning.

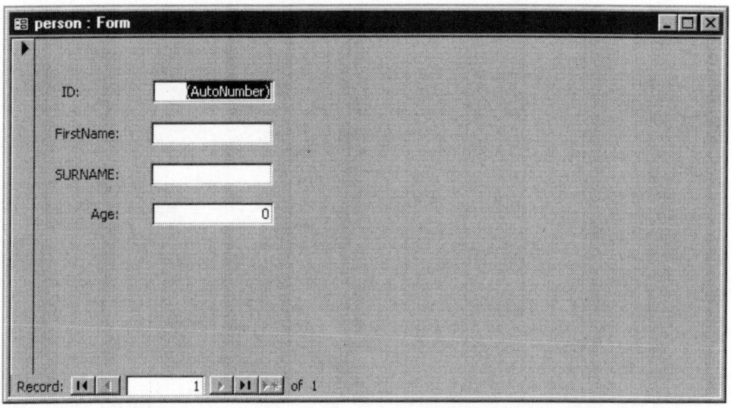

STEP 12 Start adding records to your database.

REPORTS IN ACCESS 2000

If you use **File/Print** to print information from an Access database you have very little control over how the data is printed. A better approach is to design a "Report" that specifies what data is to be printed and where it is to appear on the page.

STEP 1 Setting up a **Report** is similar to setting up a **Form**. There are three sections to the Report - the **Page Header**, the **Detail** section and the **Page Footer**. Each section can contain data, text and images. Anything you can include on a Form can be included in each of the sections. The usual approach would be to have most of the data in the "**Detail**" section.

STEP 2 Go to the report **Properties** menu by right-clicking on the **Form Selection** button.

Select **Properties** from the menu ...

STEP 3 Nominate the source of the data ...

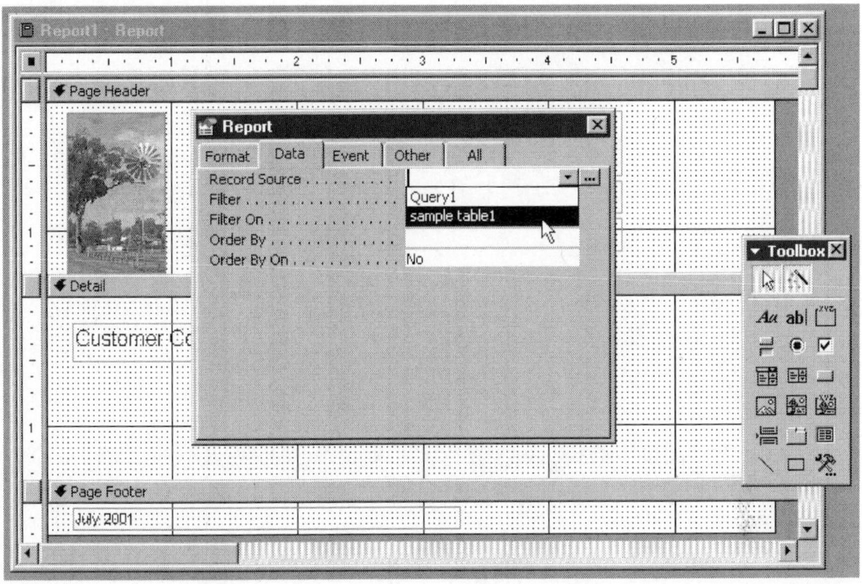

STEP 4 Close the Report properties window and then drag and drop the fields from the **Field List** box onto the Report as you would when creating a Form.

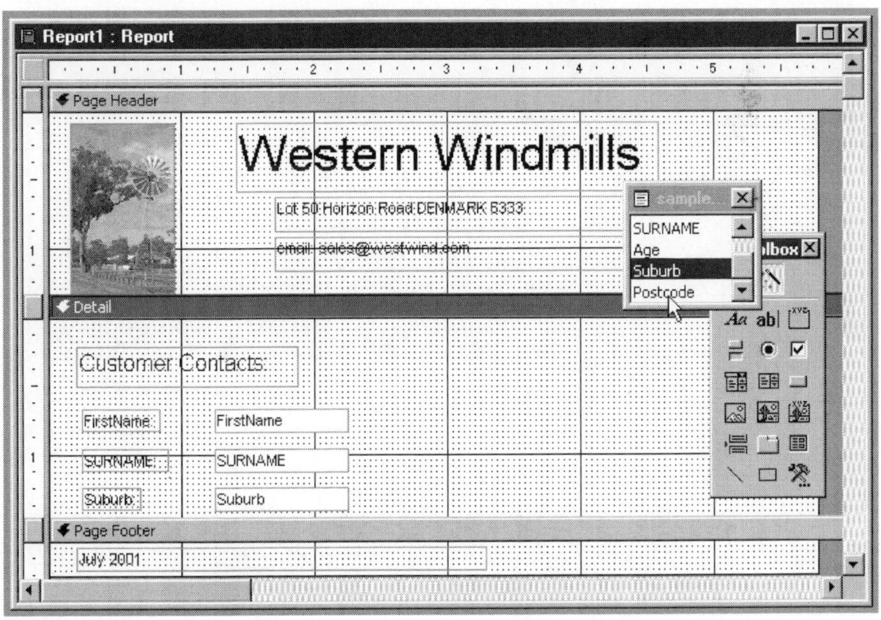

STEP 5 Click on the print **View** button to preview the Report ...

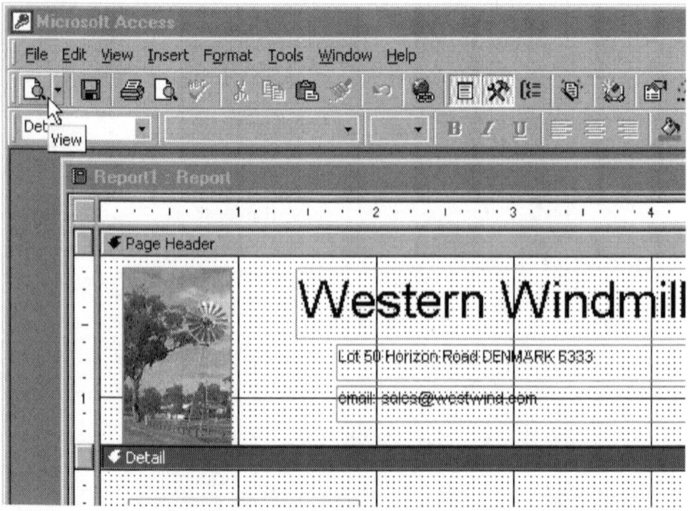

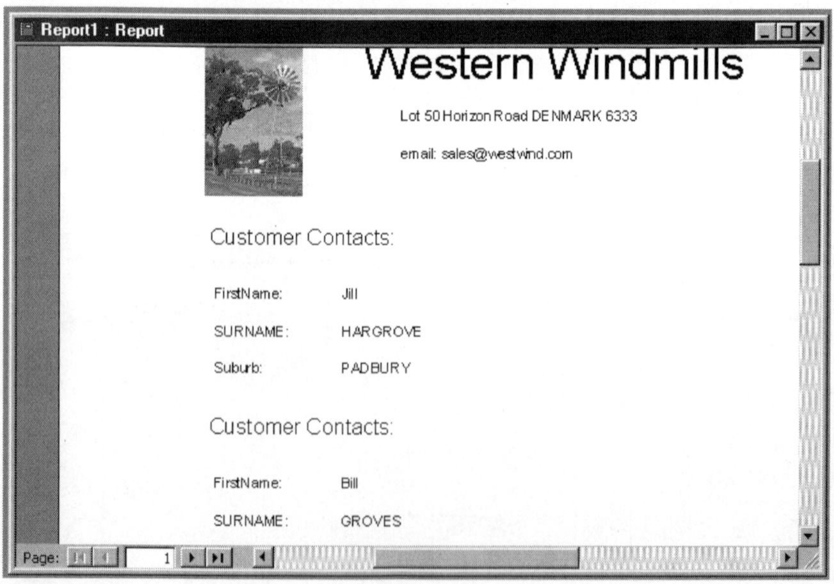

Print out the completed Report.

NOTE:

If you want only one record per page right click the **Section Selector** and then go to **Properties** (or double click the **Section Selector**) as indicated below ...

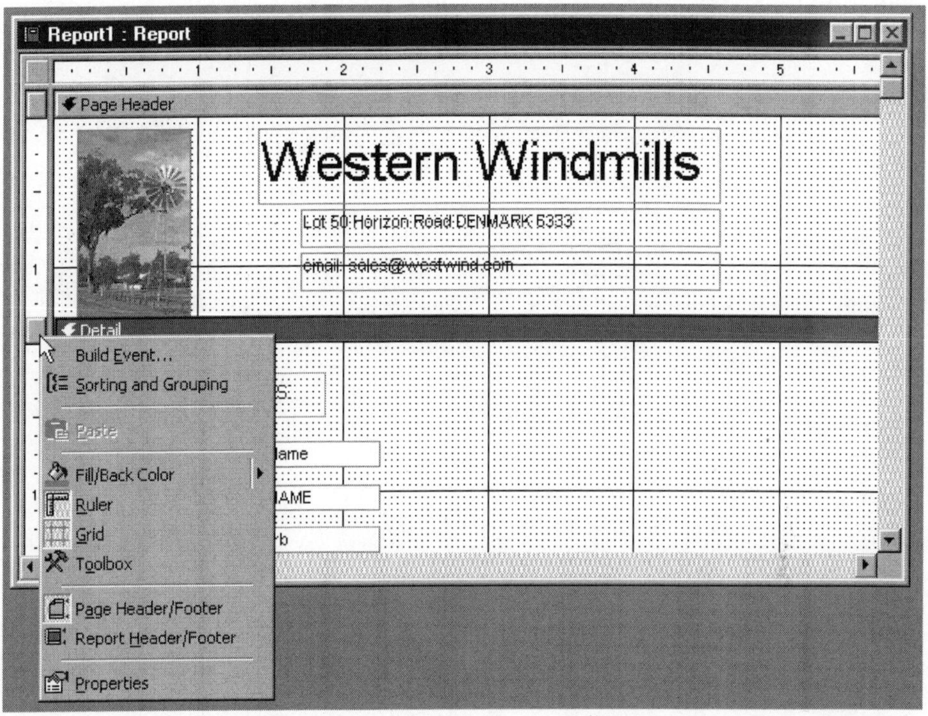

Select **Properties** ...

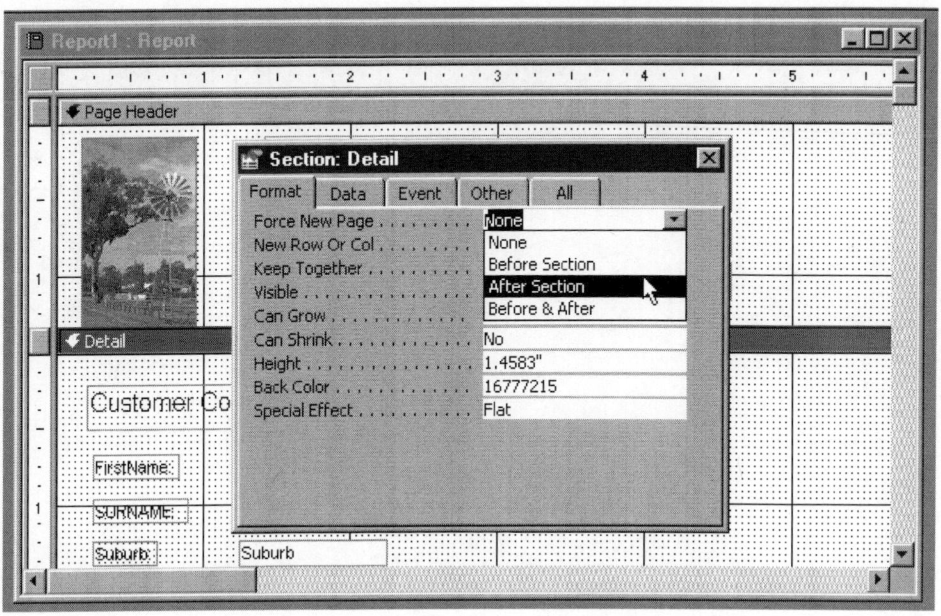

From the **Force New Page** drop-down menu select **After Section**. Each record will be printed on a separate page ...

APPLYING QUERIES IN ACCESS 2000

A "query" is a search condition you apply to your data.

For the following examples, the database below will be used:

sample table1 : Table

ID	FirstName	SURNAME	Age	Suburb	Postcode
1	Jill	HARGROVE	33	PADBURY	6025
2	Bill	GROVES	24	RANGEVIEW	3132
3	Mary	JONES	13	MANDURAH	6210
4	Matthew	CRAIG	45	KALAMUNDA	6076
5	Sydney	TEED	21	PADBURY	6025
6	Julie	WATERS	17	ALBANY	6330
7	Mary	SMITH	45	BENTLY	6102
8	Bill	TEED	24	PADBURY	6025
9	Wendy	JONES	14	COLLIE	6225
10	Brian	JEFFRIES	37	DARWIN	800
mber)			0		0

Record: 10 of 10

You can download this sample database to practice with here (140Kb).

STEP 1 Go to **Create query in Design view** from the **Objects** list.

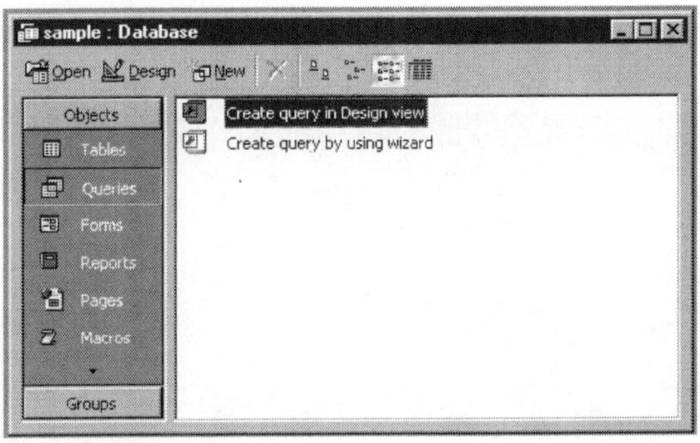

STEP 2 Select the Table to be used from the **Show Table** window

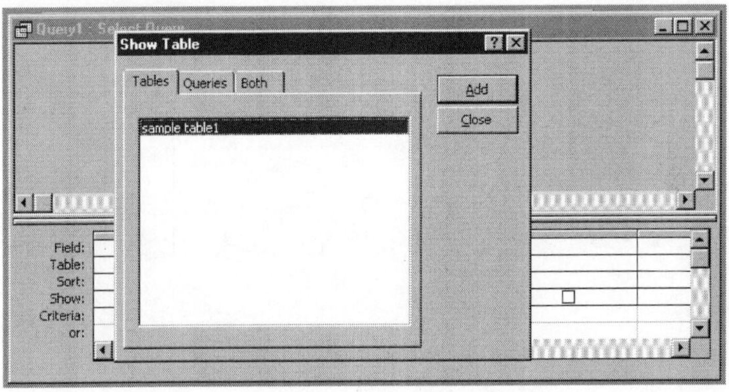

The **Fields List** appears. (Close the **Show Table** window.)

STEP 3 Drag each of the Fields you want to include in your query and drop them into the top cell in each column. At this point you could use the alternate approach of selecting the fields using the Drop-down menu.

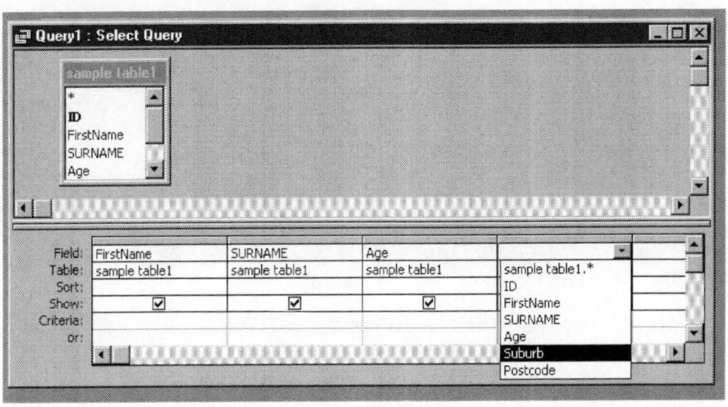

STEP 4 Click the **Run** button to apply your query to the data ...

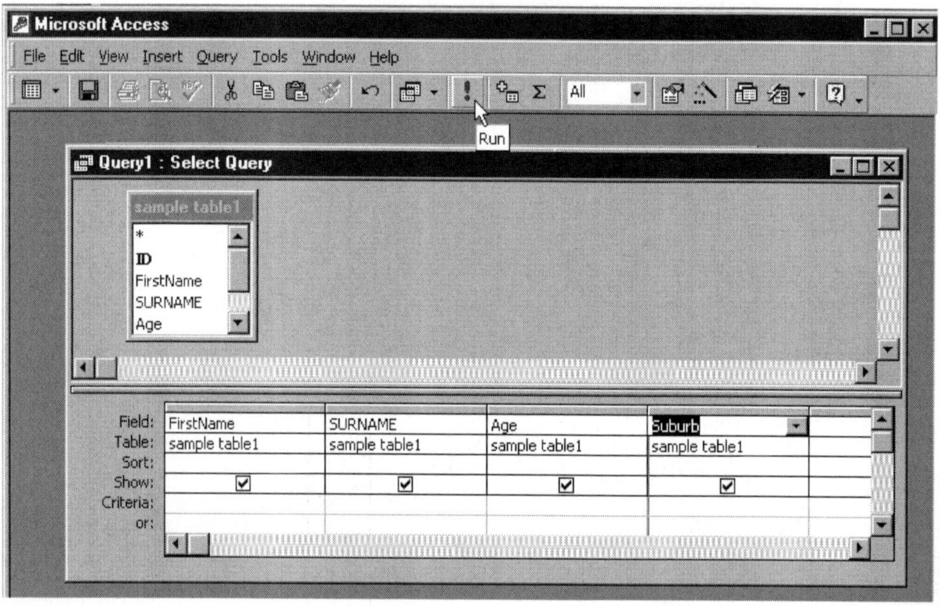

Since no selection "**Criteria**" were defined, this query displays all records under the selected fields...

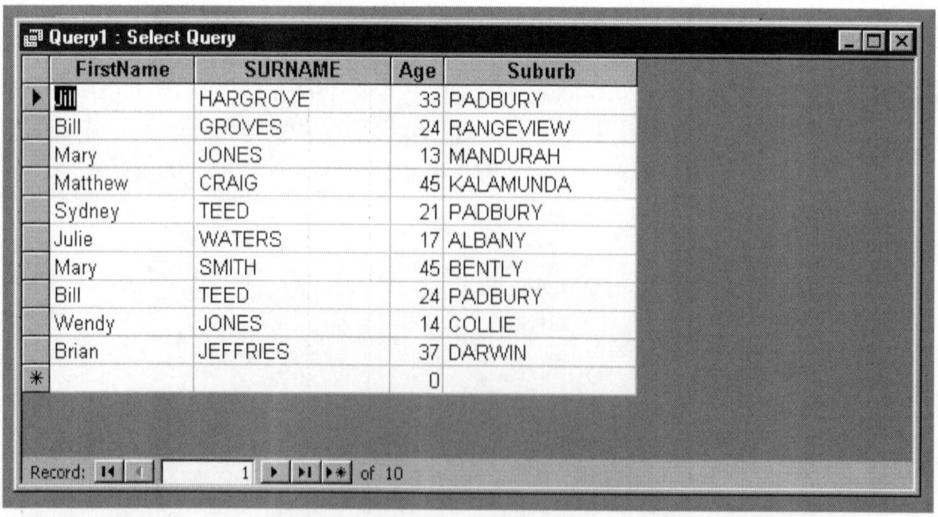

FirstName	SURNAME	Age	Suburb
Jill	HARGROVE	33	PADBURY
Bill	GROVES	24	RANGEVIEW
Mary	JONES	13	MANDURAH
Matthew	CRAIG	45	KALAMUNDA
Sydney	TEED	21	PADBURY
Julie	WATERS	17	ALBANY
Mary	SMITH	45	BENTLY
Bill	TEED	24	PADBURY
Wendy	JONES	14	COLLIE
Brian	JEFFRIES	37	DARWIN
		0	

In the following case the selection criteria was set to: FirstName is "mary"

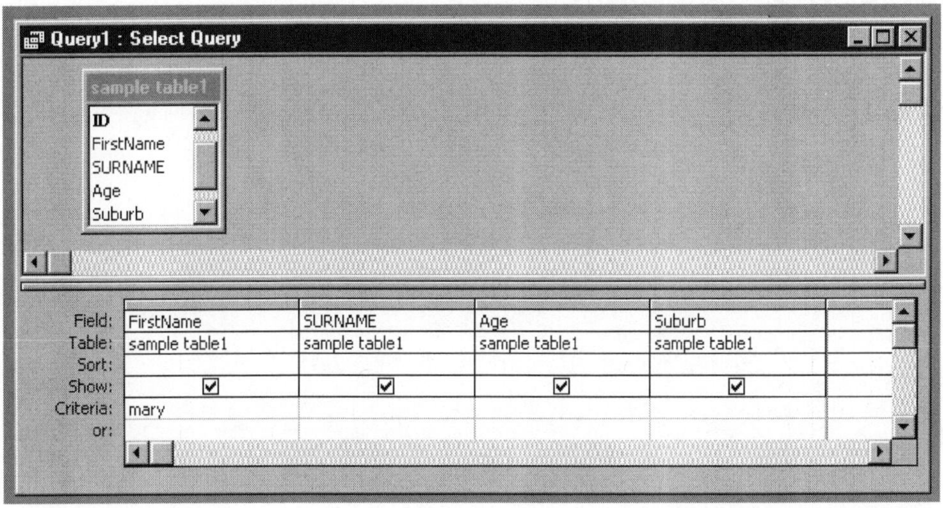

This time, only records containing the FirstName "mary" are selected.

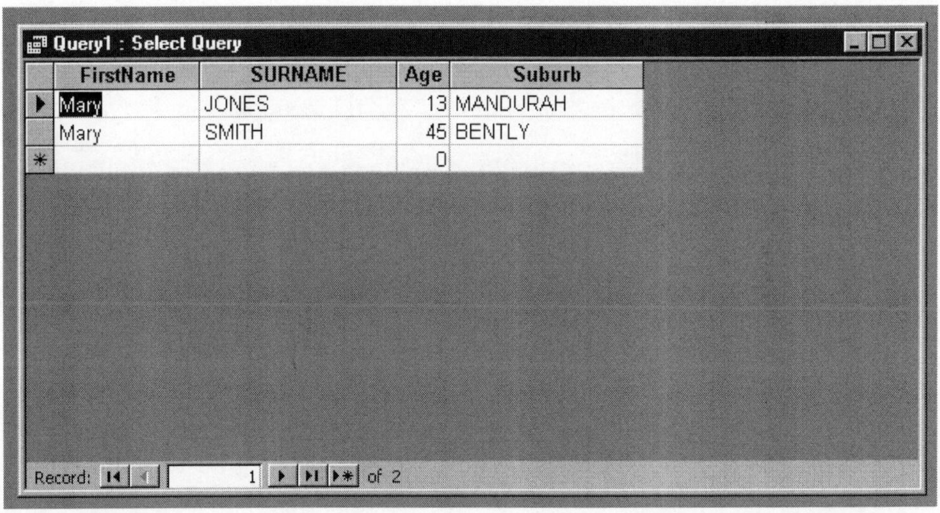

STEP 5 Experiment with other search criteria including the use of the "or" condition. You should be able to use greater than (">") and less than ("<") criteria to extract different age groups and people from different States. eg Age < 35, Postcode > 6000, etc.

12

Introduction to MS-Powerpoint

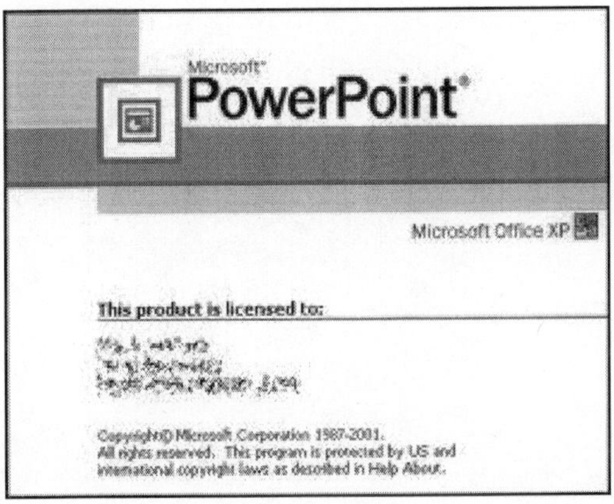

POWER POINT

PowerPoint presentations consist of a number of individual pages or "slides". The "slide" analogy is a reference to the slide projector. Slides may contain text, graphics, sound, movies, and other objects, which may be arranged freely. PowerPoint, however, facilitates the use of a consistent style in a presentation using a template or "Slide Master".

The presentation can be printed, displayed live on a computer, or navigated through at the command of the presenter. For larger audiences the computer display is often projected using a video projector. Slides can also form the basis of webcasts.

PowerPoint provides three types of movements:

1. Entrance, emphasis, and exit of elements on a slide itself are controlled by what PowerPoint calls Custom Animations
2. Transitions, on the other hand, are movements between slides. These can be animated in a variety of ways

CREATING OF POWER POINT

Open Power Point and you will be prompted by a dialog box with four choices. Each of these options is explained on this page. If Power Point is already open or this box does not appear, select **File | New** from the menu bar.

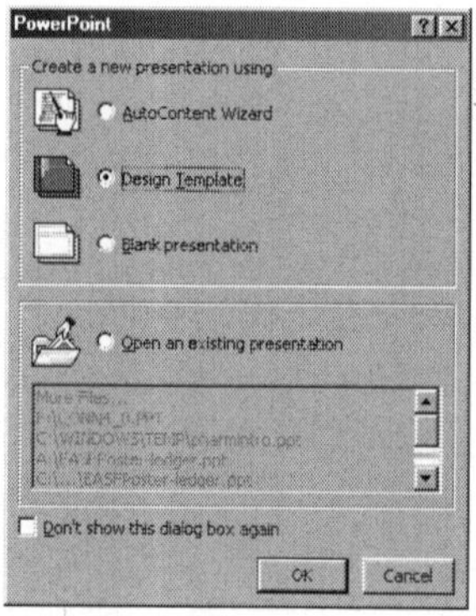

AutoContent Wizard

The AutoContent Wizard provides templates and ideas for a variety of presentation types. Page through the wizard by clicking the **Next** button on the bottom of each page after making necessary choices.

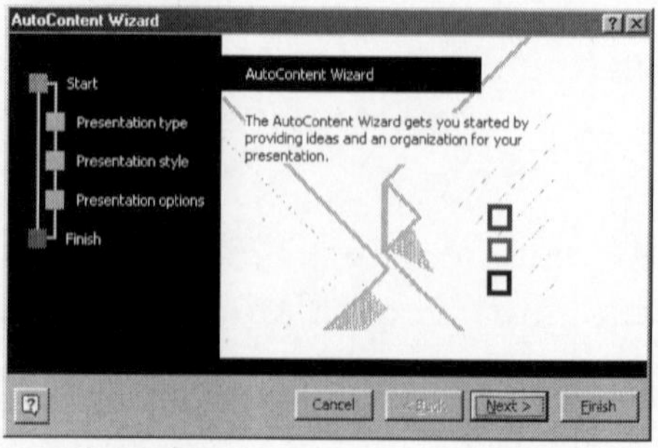

Design Template

Power Point provides many templates with different backgrounds and text formatting to begin your presentation. Preview each design by highlighting the template name on the list. Press **OK** after you have chosen the design.

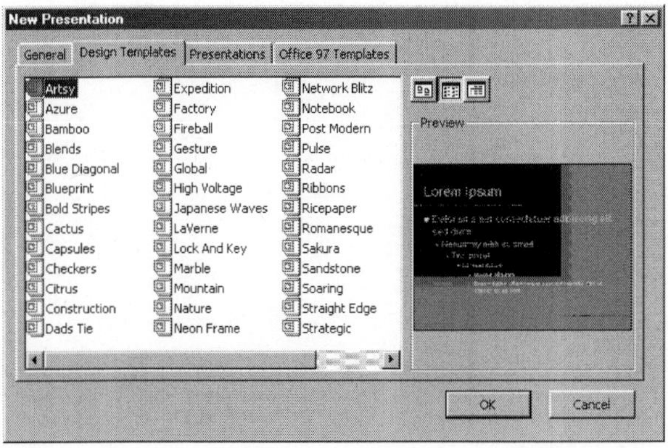

Blank Presentation

Select Blank Presentation to build the presentation from scratch with no preset graphics or formatting.

Open an Existing Presentation

Select this option to open a Power Point presentation that already exists. Select the folder the file is located in from the **Look in:** drop-down menu and highlight the file on the list. Click **Open** to open the presentation.

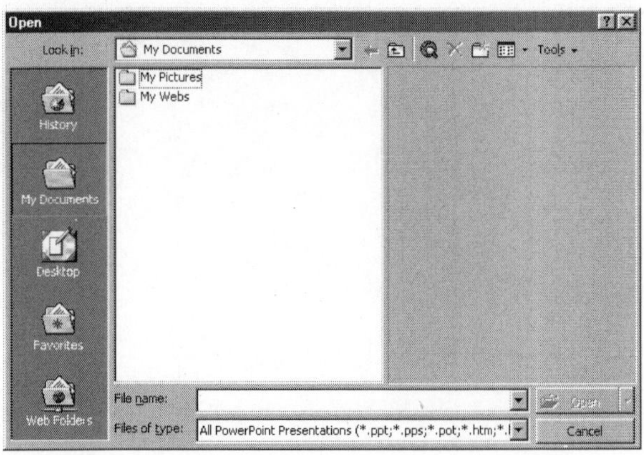

AutoLayout

After selecting the presentation type, you will be prompted to choose the layout of the new slide. These layouts include bulleted lists, graphs, and/or images. Click on each thumbnail image and a description will be printed in the message box. Highlight the layout you want and click **OK**.

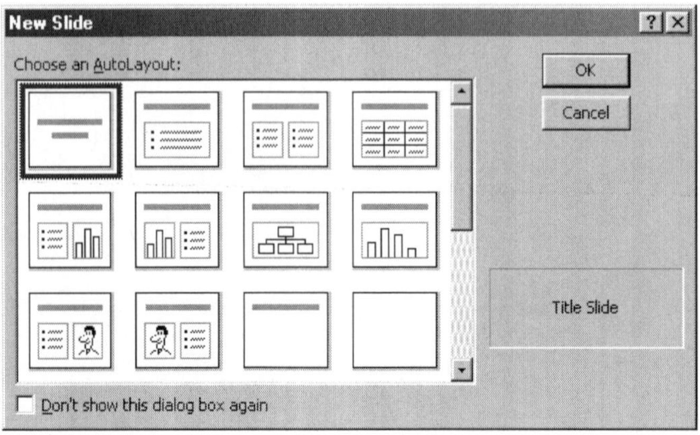

Screen Layout

The Power Point screen layout in **Normal View**:

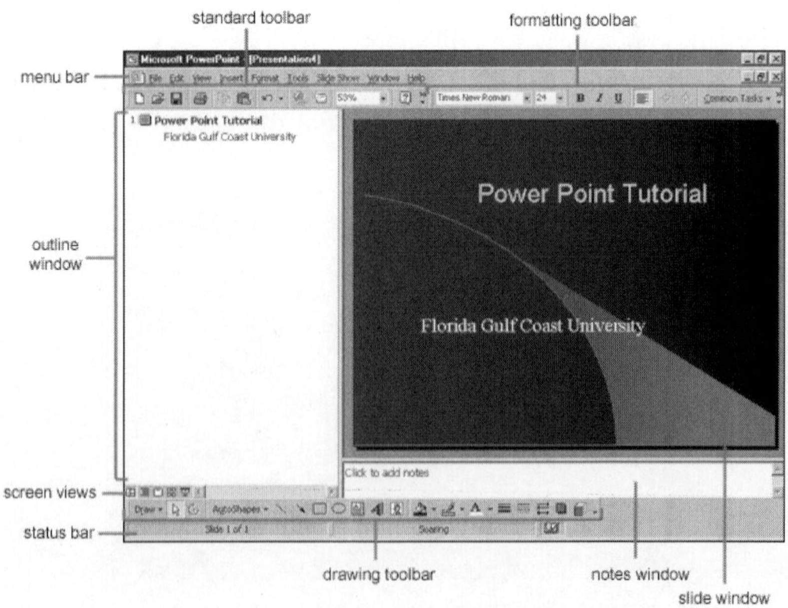

Views

Power Point gives you four screen layouts for constructing your presentation in addition to the Slide Show. You can select the page view by clicking the buttons just above the formatting toolbar and the bottom of the page.

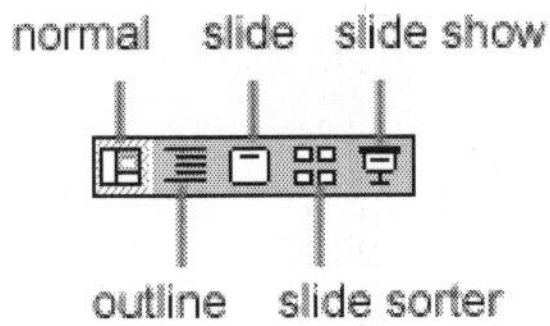

What is Power Point?

Power point is

- A tool.
- Presentation software package.
- Multimedia capable

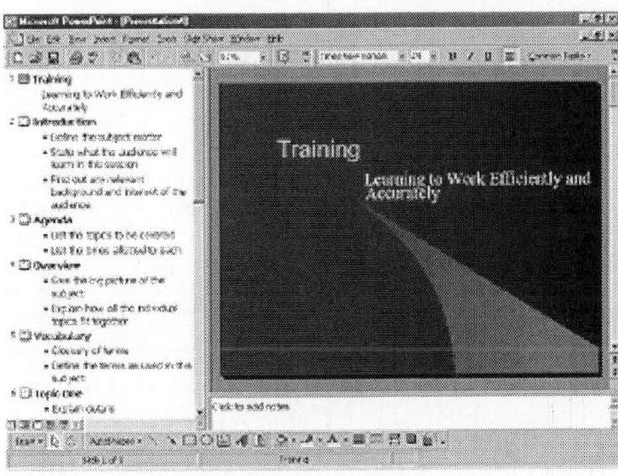

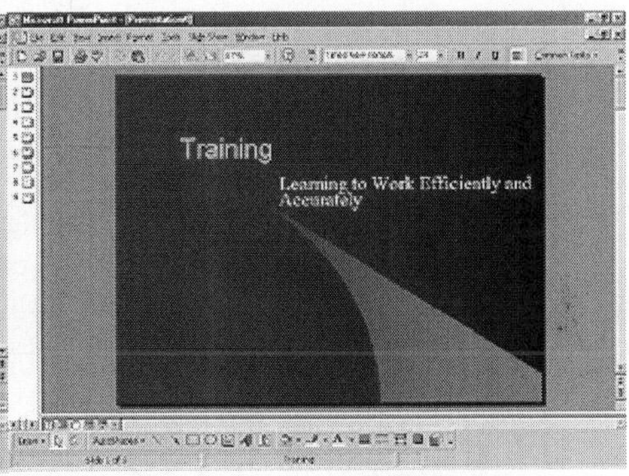

Normal View

This screen is split into three sections showing the presentation outline on the left, the slide in the main window, and notes at the bottom.

Slide View

The slide view displays each slide on the screen and is helpful for adding images, formatting text, and adding background styles.

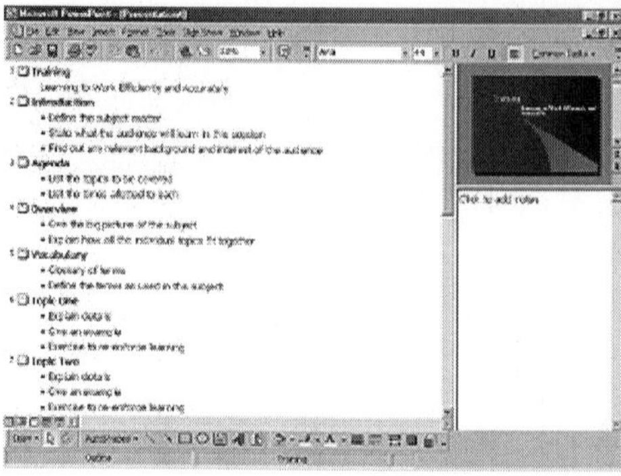

Outline View

The presentation outline is displayed on the majority of the screen with small windows for the slide and notes. This view is recommended for editing text.

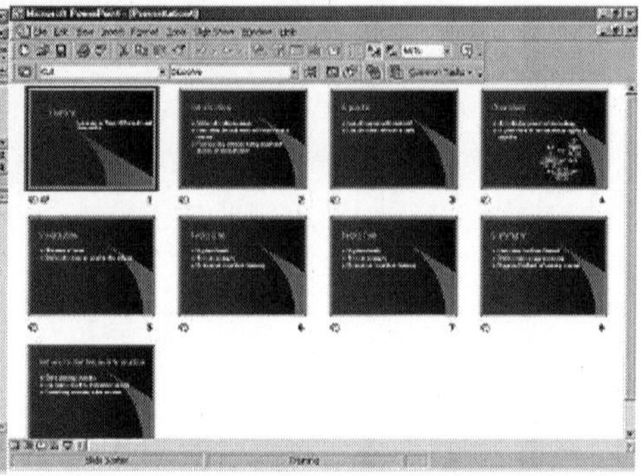

Slide Sorter View

A small image of each slide is displayed in Slide Sorter view. Slides can easily be ordered and sorted from this screen.

Click the **Slide Show** button to view the full-screen slide show.

USES OF POWER POINT

Power point in Education:

The "intelligent use" of educational technologies can be defined with three components (1) How do people learn (cognitive component)? (2) How can the learning experience be facilitated (instruction component)? (3) How can technology be used to improve instruction and learning (technology component)? Over the years there has been research to support the three components as individual entities and collectively as the cognitive theory of multimedia learning. The third component has received much attention as researchers try to evaluate the effectiveness of new educational technologies, particularly PowerPoint.

PowerPoint is best used when students are expected to retain complex graphics, animation, and figures.

PowerPoint is an excellent tool for educators, providing a method that can attract the students in an entertaining way, yet still getting across the information effectively. However, many educators use the PowerPoint ineffectively, either from inexperience or from simply not knowing how to implement it properly within their lectures. PowerPoint can be a useful tool to any educator, as long as they gain a better understanding of how to use the program.

TOP TEN USES OF POWERPOINT

Academic

1. Classroom Teaching: Power Point presentations help in improving the quality and impact of classroom teaching. The presentations can be made interesting and exhaustive, with supporting information to be accessed only if required.

2. Subject Tutorials: It is good for online and offline tutorials on wide range of subjects, user age groups and types.

3. Seminars: It is handy for students to make their presentations on assignments.

4. Meetings and Consultations: Decision makers can use Power Point for meetings and discussions to keep the focus on core issues.

5. Conferences: This is a popular use. Usually academicians use power point as it easy to present as well as print and distribute handouts or publish online, as per requirement.

Professionals & Business

6. Sales & Marketing: Power Point presentations are quick to prepare and can be structured for use such that the same presentation can be used for a specific target audience by selecting specific slides.

7. Events and Trade Shows: It is good to use in trade shows and events as it can be run by first timers or not so computer savvy exhibition support teams.

8. Corporate meetings: Ideal for the busy corporate for focused presentations with statistical information presented using graphics to facilitate easy comprehension and avoid monotony of too many numbers.

9. Corporate training and conferences: Widely used by trainers as well as corporate for conferences, workshops and training sessions.

Public

10. Information Kiosks: Power point is a good tool for presenting layout and other information at public places like museums, exhibitions, libraries, transit terminals etc. It can be made interactive for the public to view, learn and proceed.

Why to use Power Point?

- Provides ease of information organization.
- Easy to share, store, and modify information.
- Legibility.
- Makes use of multimedia.
- Can be interactive
- Multimedia shifting.
- Presenting Visual Information.
- Presenting pre-recorded audio information.
- Merging media
- Possible to Control the Flow of Information.

When to use power point?

- 2-way or multi-level learning/teaching.
- Divergent exercises.
- The standard lecture.
- To test student understanding.
- When the cost / benefit is not in your favor.

Presentations for Instruction

Use PowerPoint presentations to enhance the effectiveness of classroom instruction in many ways in every subject area.

- Main points can be emphasized and the presentation itself can be enhanced by using graphics, animation, or sound.
- Add flair to presentations with slide and bullet transitions and animated effects.

- Presentations can be used to make lessons more organized and flexible.
- Text on a PowerPoint presentation is much easier for students to read than trying to read notes that are written on an overhead projector or chalkboard.
- Student interest can be stimulated through the use of graphics and cartoons.
- Variety is the key to keeping the attention of students.
- Many tools are available for use with PowerPoint, so experiment to see what works best for you and your students.

Creative Presentation Ideas

- **Flash Cards** - Create Flashcard presentations for individual and group reinforcement. You can create a template and choose whether you or your students will insert the words or phrases. Topics may include: reinforcing math concepts; practicing parts of speech; practicing spelling; reinforcing story problems; and reinforcing numbers, letters, or colors.
- **Field Trip Slide Shows** - Develop field trip slide shows to review and apply knowledge learned on a field trip. Students can work together to make a slide show that presents what they saw, as well as what they learned.
- **Autobiographical Stories** - Students can create short autobiographical stories about themselves. Scanned photos can be inserted for interest. Once the slides are complete, you can put them together in a presentation to show an audience, such as an open house or parent night.
- **Interactive Book Reports** - Have students create a PowerPoint presentation about books they read.
- **Music Class Recitals** - For music teachers, PowerPoint is a useful tool for creating slide shows of student recitals. During a recital, take pictures of the students while they are performing and record a small portion of their music. On slides, include both each student's picture and music.
- **Group Slide Shows** - Give your students a topic (such as zoo animals) and tell them to choose parts of the topic to focus on (such as specific zoo animals). Have students research their

assigned portions of the topic and develop slides to serve as a part of a group presentation about the topic.

- **Poetry Readings** - Students can create slides exhibiting their personal poetry along with a voice recording.
- **Science Presentations** - Use PowerPoint to teach processes and how things work. Teachers or students can add additional items to a diagram to illustrate how a process grows and changes. Science principles work well using this format.
- **Student Portfolios** - PowerPoint can be used to create portfolios of student work.
- **Class Yearbook-Type Presentations** - Collect photos; information about special events; examples of class and student projects, etc. throughout the year and create a year-in-review presentation.

MENUS OF POWER POINT

FILE MENU

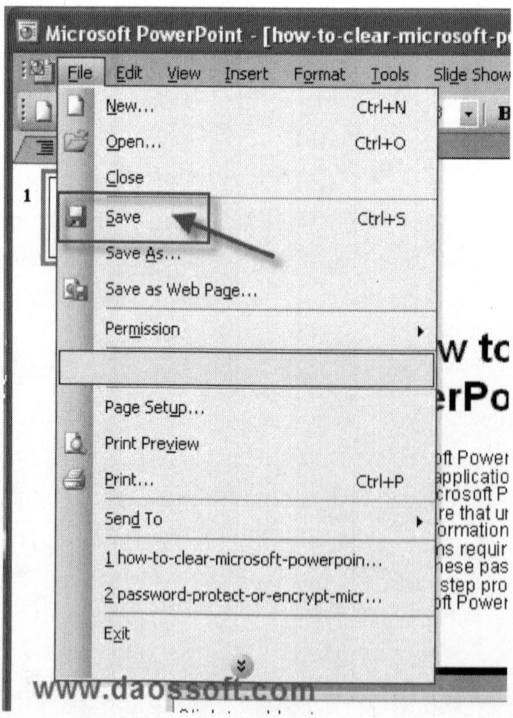

EDIT MENU

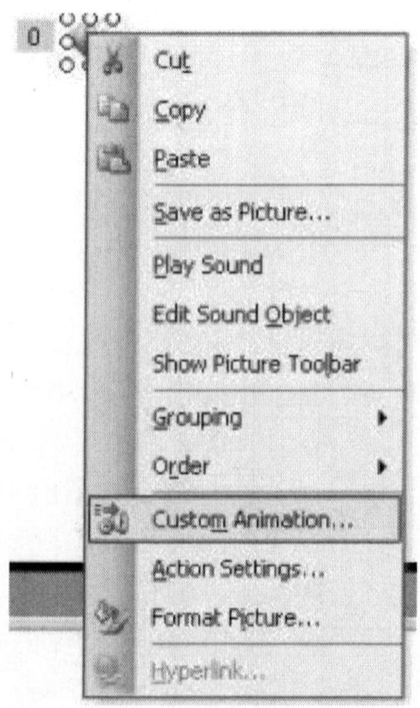

VIEW MENU

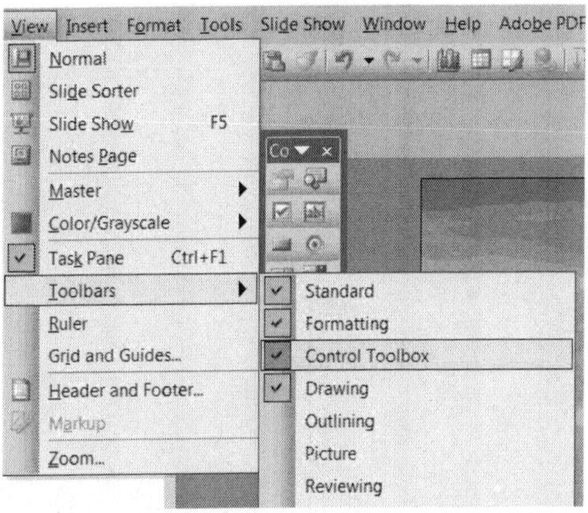

INSERT MENU

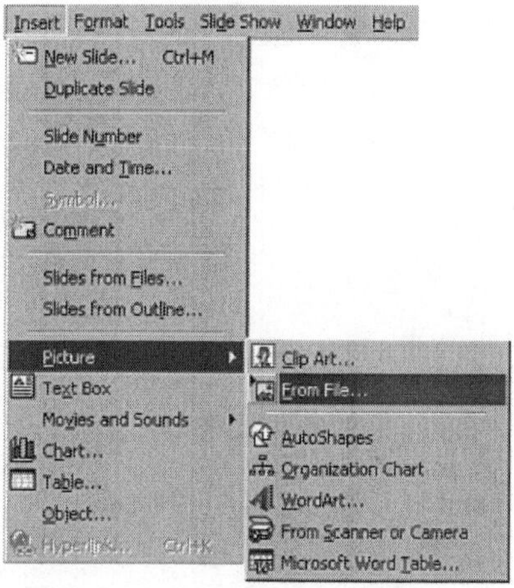

FORMAT MENU

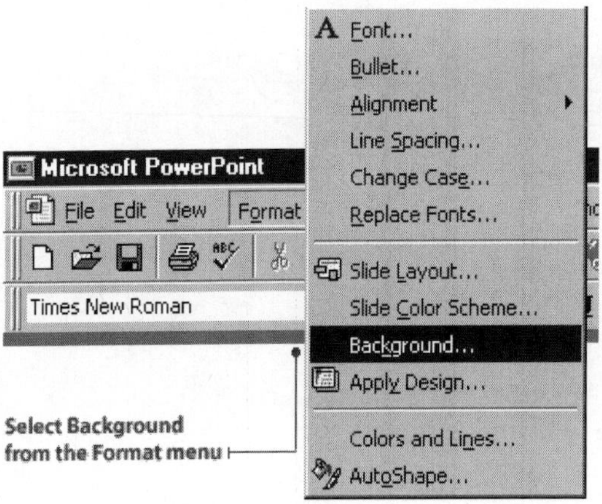

TOOLS MENU

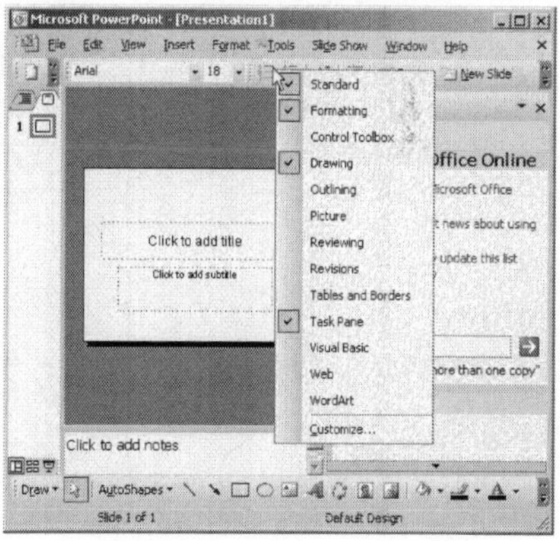

SLIDE MENU

WINDOW MENU

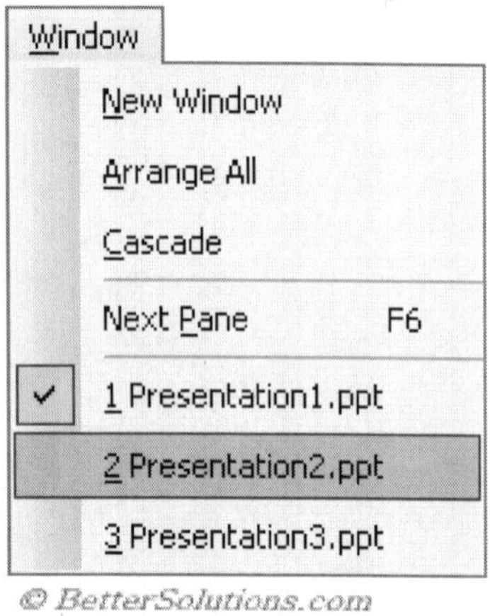

HELP MENU

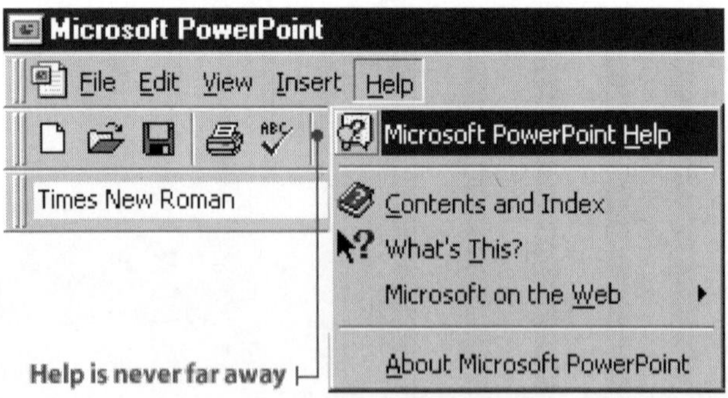

12

Introduction to the Internet

CONNECTING TO THE INTERNET

By connecting local, regional, national and international networks, the Internet forms the world's largest network of networks. Computers connected to the Internet work together to transfer information around the world using servers and clients. A server is a computer that manages the resources on a network and provides a centralized storage for programs and data. The server, also called a host, "serves" files and services out to clients, computers that access the contents of the server. The speed at which data can be transferred between the sender and receiver in a network is called the data transfer rate. Transfer rates are expressed in bits per second (bps). A bit, short for binary digit is the smallest unit of computerized data. A bit has a value of either 1 or 0 that the computer interprets as "on" or "off" respectively. When calculating Internet-access speeds, it is important to recognize the difference between bits and bytes. There are eight bits in a byte. The small "b" stands for bits, and the big "B" stands for bytes. Transfer speeds are often shown in kilobytes per second (KB/s), and connect speeds are usually quoted in kilobits per second (kbps). For example, if the Web browser is downloading a file at 100 KB/s over a cable modems connection, which is equal to a speed of 800 kbps. Bandwidth is the width of the communication channel, the total volume of traffic that can be transferred across a given transmission line in a given period of time, usually measured in bits per second.

There are four ways of connecting a client computer to the Internet: a dial-up connection using a telephone line or an Integrated Services Digital Network (ISDN), a Digital Subscriber Line (DSL), a cable TV connection and a satellite connection.

Dial-up Connection

A dial-up connection uses the analog telephone line for establishing a temporary communication. Computer's digital signals must be converted to analog signals before they are transmitted over standard telephone lines. This conversion is performed by a modem, a device that modulates (changes into an analog signal) and demodulates (converts an analog signal into a digital signal). Both the sending and receiving ends of a communication channel must have a modem for data transmission to occur. Using a dial-up line to transmit data is similar to using the telephone to make a call. The client computer modem dials the preprogrammed phone number for a user's Internet Service Provider (ISP) and connects to one of the ISP's modems. After the ISP has verified the user's account, a connection is established and data can be transmitted. When either modem hangs up, the communication ends. The advantage of a dial-up line is that it costs no more than a local telephone call. Computers at any two locations can establish a connection using modems and a telephone network, to include wireless modems and cellular telephone connections. The limitation of a connection using the ordinary telephone line is a low speed, 28 kbps. There are dedicated telephone lines that can transmit data at 56 kbps. Most 56 kbps modems connect at a speed less than 46 kbps because of the limitations of analog phone lines and Telephone Company switches.

ISDN

ISDNs are special digital telephone lines that can be used to dial into the Internet at speeds ranging from 64 to 128 kbps.

These types of connections are not available everywhere telephone companies have to install special ISDN digital switching equipment. ISDNs require use of a special "digital modem" that sends and receives digital signals over ISDN lines. With an ISDN, the telephone line is divided into three channels (BRI - Basic Rate Interface), two-64 kbps B (bearer) channels that send data and one 16 kbps D (data) channel that sends routing information. This type of access is commonly referred to as 2B+D. To use the ISDN access to the Internet, an ISP has to offer the ISDN access. ISDN lines cost more than normal phone lines, so the telephone rates are usually higher.

Cable TV Connection

Currently most households with cable TV have the option for cable modem Internet access. The cable modem offers a high-speed link at low cost for unlimited, "always connected" access. The connection speeds range from 128 kbps up to 10 mbps (megabits per second). A cable modem is a device that connects to the existing TV cable feed and to an Ethernet network card in the user's PC (also called an NIC - Network Interface Card). The cable network is designed to support the highest speeds in the "downstream" direction, which is from the Internet to the client computer. This downstream speed affects the performance of downloading Web pages and software. The "upstream" bandwidth for data sent from a user's computer to the Internet is typically less, in the range of 200 kbps to 2 mbps. The benefit of the cable modem for Internet access is that, unlike DSL, its performance doesn't depend on distance from the central cable office. However, with the cable TV network, the computer is put on a Local Area Network (LAN) with other users in the neighborhood and like with any LAN, the performance degrades as usage increases. A more disturbing issue is that of network security. One of the main purposes of a LAN is to allow file sharing among the computers on the LAN. This LAN feature doesn't work well with cable Internet access, as most users do not want neighbors accessing their files. Turning the sharing option off can prevent file sharing. Also, installing the firewall hardware or software may protect from hackers.

DSL (Digital Subscriber Line)

DSL service is a high-speed data service that works over POTS (Plain Old Telephone Service) copper telephone lines and is typically offered by telephone companies without costly installation of a higher-grade cable. DSL uses a different part of the frequency spectrum than analog voice signals, so it can work in conjunction with a standard analog telephone service, providing separate voice and data "channels" on the same line. ADSL (Asymmetric DSL) is the type of DSL that provides different bandwidths in the upstream and downstream directions, giving the user a much bigger "pipe" in the downstream direction. ADSL can support downstream bandwidths of up to 8 mbps and upstream bandwidths of 1.5 mbps. For comparison, a T-1 connection also provides 1.5 mbps. This scheme works well for the typical Internet user; upstream communication is usually small (link requests) compared to downstream communication (Web pages with graphics).

SDSL (Symmetric DSL) offers the same bandwidth capability in both directions. Besides higher bandwidth, some of the advantages of ADSL access from telephone companies are that there are no per-minute charges and the user gets an "always-on" connection for a monthly fee. Most modern computers can be easily equipped to connect to a DSL service. This is accomplished by connecting an ADSL modem to an Ethernet network card in the PC. The downside of DSL includes strict distance limitation that DSL circuits can operate within. As the connection's length increases, the signal quality decreases and the connection speed goes down. DSL services that provide greater that 1.5 mbps require shorter distances to the central office compared to a cable modem that can be located far away from the service provider.

The limit for ADSL service is 18,000 feet (5,460 meters), though for speed and quality of service reasons many ADSL providers place a lower limit on the distances for the service. At the extremes of the distance limits, ADSL customers may see speeds far below the promised maximums, while customers near the central office have the potential for very high speeds. Unlike cable modem technology, DSL provides a point-to-point connection to ISP. DSL proponents claim this technology is both more secure and less prone to local traffic fluctuations than its cable rival. By not sharing a LAN segment with other users, the systems are not as open to intrusion or susceptible to performance degradations related to local traffic.

Satellite Connection

Getting the Internet feed from a satellite is really not all that different from getting TV signals from one. In both cases data is being sent from the satellite to a user's equipment and then translated and decoded. One major limitation of satellite technology is that it can only send data from the satellite to a user's receiver—not the other way. To get around this problem, a separate ISP connection is needed to send data to the Internet, typically over an analog modem. This connection works in conjunction with the satellite feed. As information is requested via the modem line, data are sent back via the satellite. Since most Internet users need high bandwidth from the Web, downstream (typically Web pages and file downloads), and less bandwidth going to the Web, upstream (typically link requests), this scenario of sending upstream data over a standard modem line and downstream data over the high-bandwidth satellite feed has been effective. The newest satellite technology allows for two-way communications and higher upstream bandwidths. A satellite return channel can be added for traffic bound for the Internet. The upload speeds through this satellite return channel may peak at 128 kbps. Download speeds with this system are up to 400 kbps. Satellite technology has one strong advantage over cable modems and DSL: accessibility. For many it is today's only high-speed option. It can reach areas that are otherwise difficult to establish contact with. The infrastructure exists to provide 400 kbps downstream bandwidth to almost anyone with a 21" satellite dish. It is eight times faster than fastest analog telephone modems and three times faster than ISDN. However, it is not as fast as cable modems or DSL services, which both can provide more than megabits of bandwidth. Also, cable and DSL access methods are cheaper. Equipment required for satellite connection includes installation of a mini-dish satellite receiver and a satellite modem. Like cable modem systems, satellite provides a "shared bandwidth" pipe. This means that download performance may vary depending upon other users of the satellite transponder. Another potential problem can be associated with severe weather. In severe snowstorms and heavy rain, users may experience signal fade.

The general rule about the Internet connection is the faster, the better. The bandwidth and transfer rate determine how quickly pictures, sounds, animation and video clips will be downloaded. Since multimedia and interactivity make the Internet such an exciting tool for information sharing, the speed is the key. Dial-up access provides an easy and inexpensive way for users to connect to the Internet, however, it is a slow-speed technology and most users are no longer satisfied with dial-up or ISDN connections. Fortunately, the broadband access, we once dreamed of, is now possible with TV cable, DSL and satellite links.

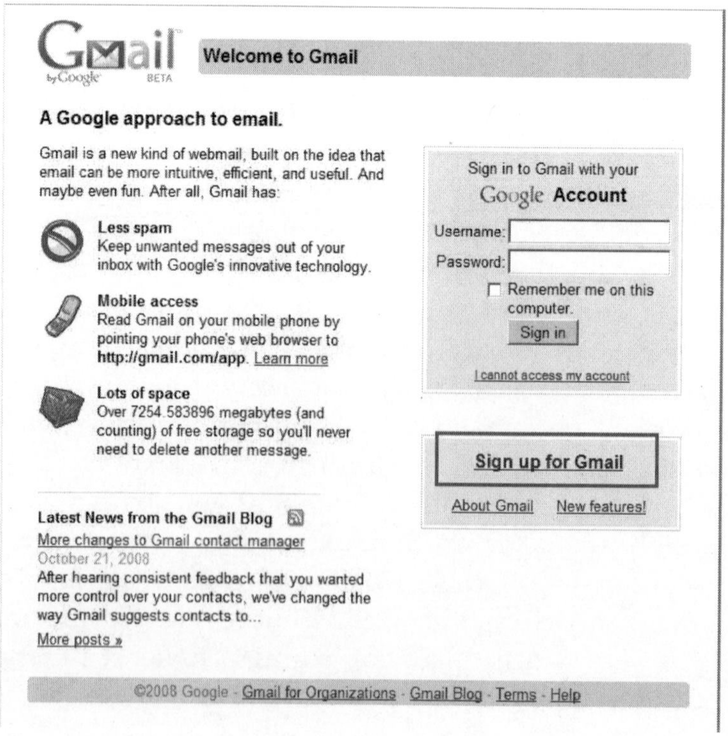

CREATING E-MAIL ACCOUNT

GMAIL

Open www.gmail.com. You will get the following window.

Create an Account

Get started with Gmail

First name: [ ]

Last name: [ ]

Desired Login Name: *@gmail.com*

[Choose a username ▾]

[ ]

Examples: JSmith, John.Smith

Choose a password: [ ] Password strength:

Minimum of 8 characters in length.

Re-enter password: [ ]

☑ Stay signed in

☑ Enable Web History Learn More

Default Homepage ☑ Set Google as my default homepage. Your default homepage in your browser is the first page that appears when you open your browser.

Security question: [ ]

[ ]

If you forget your password we will ask for the answer to your security question. Learn More

Answer: [ ]

Recovery email:

This address is used to authenticate your account should you ever encounter problems or forget your password. If you do not have another email address, you may leave this field blank. Learn More

Location:

Birthday:

MM/DD/YYYY (e.g. "11/22/2011")

Word Verification:

Type the two pieces of text: Type what you hear:

Get a new challenge Get an audio challenge "
Get a visual challenge Help

Terms of Service: Please check the Google Account information you've entered above (feel free to change anything you like), and review the Terms of Service below.

With Gmail, you won't see blinking banner ads. Instead, we display ads you might find useful that are relevant to the content of your messages. Learn more

Google Terms of Service

Welcome to Google!

1. Your relationship with Google

By clicking on 'I accept' below you are agreeing to the Terms of Service above and both the Program Policy and the Privacy Policy.

I accept. Create my account.

BROWSING A SITE & WWW

A web browser is a software application for retrieving, presenting, and traversing information resources on the World Wide Web. An information resource is identified by a Uniform Resource Identifier (URI) and may be a web page, image, video, or other piece of content. Hyperlinks present in resources enable users easily to navigate their browsers to related resources. A web browser can also be defined as an application software or program designed to enable users to access, retrieve and view documents and other resources on the Internet.

Although browsers are primarily intended to access the World Wide Web, they can also be used to access information provided by web servers in private networks or files in file systems.

The major web browsers are Internet Explorer, Firefox, Google Chrome, Safari, and Opera.

History of the Web Browser

The history of the web browser dates back to the late 1980s, when a variety of technologies laid the foundation for the first web browser, WorldWideWeb, by Tim Berners-Lee in 1991. That browser brought together a variety of existing and new software and hardware technologies.

The introduction of the NCSA Mosaic web browser in 1993 – one of the first graphical web browsers – led to an explosion in web use. Marc Andreessen, the leader of the Mosaic team at NCSA, soon started his own company, named Netscape, and released the Mosaic-influenced Netscape Navigator in 1994, which quickly became the world's most popular browser, accounting for 90% of all web use at its peak (see usage share of web browsers). Microsoft responded with its Internet Explorer in 1995 (also heavily influenced by Mosaic), initiating the industry's first browser war. Bundled with Windows, Internet Explorer gained dominance in the web browser market; Internet Explorer usage share peaked at over 95% by 2002.

Opera debuted in 1996; although it has never achieved widespread use, having less than 1% browser usage share as of February 2009 according to Net Applications, having grown to 2.14 in April 2011 its Opera-mini version has an additive share, in April 2011 amounting to 1.11 % of overall browser use, but focused on the fast-growing mobile phone web browser market, being preinstalled on over 40 million phones. It is also available on several other embedded systems, including Nintendo's Wii video game console.

In 1998, Netscape launched what was to become the Mozilla Foundation in an attempt to produce a competitive browser using the open source software model. That browser would eventually evolve into Firefox, which developed a respectable following while still in the beta stage of development; shortly after the release of Firefox 1.0 in late 2004, Firefox (all versions) accounted for 7.4% of browser use. As of August 2011, Firefox has a 27.7% usage share.

Apple's Safari had its first beta release in January 2003; as of April 2011, it has a dominant share of Apple-based web browsing, accounting for just over 7.15% of the entire browser market.

The most recent major entrant to the browser market is Google's Chrome, first released in September 2008. Chrome's take-up has increased significantly year on year, by doubling its usage share from 7.7 percent to 15.5 percent by August 2011. This increase seems largely to be at the expense of Internet Explorer, whose share has tended to decrease from month to month.

Function

The primary purpose of a web browser is to bring information resources to the user. This process begins when the user inputs a Uniform Resource Locator (URL), for example http://en.wikipedia.org/, into the browser. The prefix of the URL determines how the URL will be interpreted. The most commonly used kind of URI starts with http: and identifies a resource to be retrieved over the Hypertext Transfer Protocol (HTTP). Many browsers also support a variety of other prefixes, such as https: for HTTPS, ftp: for the File Transfer Protocol, and file: for local files. Prefixes that the web browser cannot directly handle are often handed off to another application entirely. For example, mailto: URIs is usually passed to the user's default e-mail application, and news: URIs is passed to the user's default newsgroup reader.

In the case of http, https, file, and others, once the resource has been retrieved the web browser will display it. HTML is passed to the browser's layout engine to be transformed from markup to an interactive document. Aside from HTML, web browsers can generally display any kind of content that can be part of a web page. Most browsers can display images, audio, video, and XML files, and often have plug-ins to support Flash applications and Java applets. Upon encountering a file of an unsupported type or a file that is set up to be downloaded rather than displayed, the browser prompts the user to save the file to disk.

Information resources may contain hyperlinks to other information resources. Each link contains the URI of a resource to go to. When a link is clicked, the browser navigates to the resource indicated by the link's target URI, and the process of bringing content to the user begins again.

User interface

Most major web browsers have these user interface elements in common:

- Back and forward buttons to go back to the previous resource and forward respectively.
- A refresh or reload button to reload the current resource.
- A stop button to cancel loading the resource. In some browsers, the stop button is merged with the reload button.
- A home button to return to the user's home page.
- An address bar to input the Uniform Resource Identifier (URI) of the desired resource and display it.
- A search bar to input terms into a search engine.
- A status bar to display progress in loading the resource and also the URI of links when the cursor hovers over them, and page zooming capability.

Major browsers also possess incremental find features to search within a web page.

BROWSING A SITE

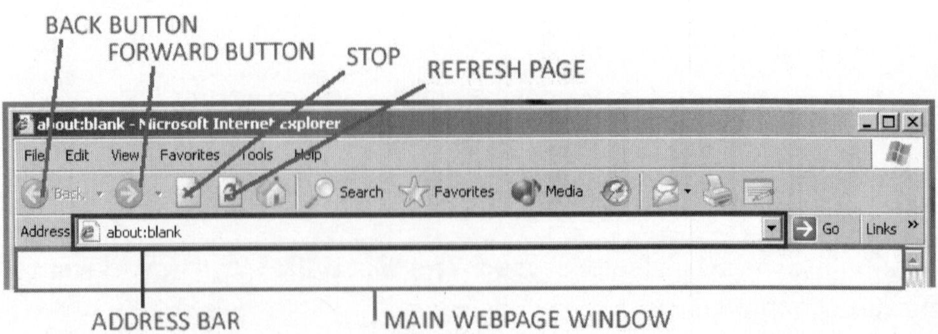

With the help of Internet Explorer we can browse any site easily by typing site name/address in the address bar.

STEPS TO BROWSE A SITE

1. Type the site address in the address bar.
2. Press the enter button to view the given site.
3. Window will be opened.4. Browse want you want.

Internet Explorer 9

Internet Explorer 9 was released in March 2011.

New features:

- **Revamped Interface** - Gives you the basic controls and puts the focus on site viewing
- **Breezing Fast Speed** - IE9 is much faster than its previous IE versions. Hardware-accelerated text, video and graphics speed up performance that makes websites perform like programs installed on your computer. Also, IE9 uses video card to make everything faster
- **Pin Websites To Windows 7 Taskbar** - Microsoft have partnership with sites like Facebook, Twitter and Pandora which allows you to see own taskbar complete with jumplist support
- **Unified Address Bar** - The address bar is a unified box for navigating the site or start a search
- **Redesigned New Tab Page** - Gives a quick access to the sites you visit often. You can also reopen closed tabs, or your last browsing session, or start a new InPrivate browsing session
- **Improved Add-on Management** - A new feature called Add-on Performance Adviser gives you an idea about which add-on is slowing down your browsers and allows you to remove it
- **Better Privacy Features** - The tracking protection feature enables you to limit the sites that can track your information
- **HTML5 Support** - IE9 now supports HTML5. IE9 also supports SVG and Canvas graphics
- **New Download Manager** - Allows you to view files that are downloading through your browser, and notifies when a file is malicious or contains viruses. It also helps you to pause any of the download and resume it later.

- **Enhanced Tab Management** - You can easily move tabs between windows by tearing them from one window to another. After placing your tab in new windows it won't reload the page.

WWW (WORDWIDEWEB)

The World Wide Web (or the proper World-Wide Web; abbreviated as WWW or W3 and commonly known as the Web) is a system of interlinked hypertext documents accessed via the Internet. With a web browser, one can view web pages that may contain text, images, videos, and other multimedia and navigate between them via hyperlinks.

Using concepts from earlier hypertext systems, British engineer and computer scientist Sir Tim Berners-Lee, now Director of the World Wide Web Consortium (W3C), wrote a proposal in March 1989 for what would eventually become the World Wide Web. At CERN in Geneva, Switzerland, Berners-Lee and Belgian computer scientist Robert Cailliau proposed in 1990 to use hypertext "... to link and access information of various kinds as a web of nodes in which the user can browse at will", and they publicly introduced the project in December.

"The World-Wide Web was developed to be a pool of human knowledge, and human culture, which would allow collaborators in remote sites to share their ideas and all aspects of a common project."

Functions

The terms Internet and World Wide Web are often used in every-day speech without much distinction. However, the Internet and the World Wide Web are not one and the same. The Internet is a global system of interconnected computer networks. In contrast, the Web is one of the services that run on the Internet. It is a collection of textual documents and other resources, linked by hyperlinks and URLs, transmitted by web browsers and web servers. In short, the Web can be thought of as an application "running" on the Internet.

Viewing a web page on the World Wide Web normally begins either by typing the URL of the page into a web browser or by following a hyperlink to that page or resource. The web browser then initiates a series of communication messages, behind the scenes, in order to fetch and display it. As an example, consider the Wikipedia page for this article with the URL http://en.wikipedia.org/wiki/WorldWideWeb.

First, the browser resolves the server-name portion of the URL (en.wikipedia.org) into an Internet Protocol address using the globally distributed database known as the Domain Name System (DNS); this lookup returns an IP address such as 208.80.152.2. The browser then requests the resource by sending an HTTP request across the Internet to the computer at that particular address. It makes the request to a particular application port in the underlying Internet Protocol Suite so that the computer receiving the request can distinguish an HTTP request from other network protocols it may be servicing such as e-mail delivery; the HTTP protocol normally uses port 80. The content of the HTTP request can be as simple as the two lines of text.

Some characteristics of the Internet:

(1) Immediacy: right now, 24 hours a day
(2) Ubiquity: Wherever you are
(3) Transparency: everything is available
(4) Relevancy: Directly relates to you, not to a mass market.

USES OF INTERNET

Search Engines

A search engine is designed to search for information on the internet. Search engine presents the search results in the form of a search results list. The search results can be web pages, images, videos, and other type of files.

To gather and present the searched information, each search engines has their own algorithm, or combination of algorithmic and human input.

Google.com is currently the most popular and frequently used search engine.

Web Browsers / Internet Browsers

A Web Browser is a type of software that retrieves and presents information resources on the internet. The information resource can be text, image, sound, video, or other type of content.

In a simple way, we can describe a web browser as a type of software that we use to 'surf' the internet.

These are some examples of web browsers, each with their own plus and minuses:

- Microsoft Internet Explorer
- Firefox
- Opera
- Safari
- Google Chrome

MOST USES

Since the internet has become popular, it is being used for many purposes. Through the help of the World Wide Web and websites, the internet has become very useful in many ways for the common man. Today internet has brought a globe in a single room. Right from news across the corner of the world, wealth of knowledge to shopping, purchasing the tickets of your favorite movie-everything is at your finger tips.

Here is the list of some common uses of internet

1) Email: By using internet now we can communicate in a fraction of seconds with a person who is sitting in the other part of the world. Today for better communication, we can avail the facilities of e-mail. We can chat for hours with our loved ones. There are plenty messenger services and email services offering this service for free. With help of such services, it has become very easy to establish a kind of global friendship where you can share your thoughts, can explore other cultures of different ethnicity.

2) Information: The biggest advantage that internet offering is information. The internet and the World Wide Web has made it easy for anyone to access information, and it can be of any type, as the internet is flooded with information. The internet and the World Wide

Web have made it easy for anyone to access information, and it can be of any type. Any kind of information on any topic is available on the Internet.

3) Business: World trade has seen a big boom with the help of the internet, as it has become easier for buyers and sellers to communicate and also to advertise their sites. Nowadays most of the people are using online classified sites to buy or sell or advertising their products or services. Classified sites saves you lot of money and time so this is chosen as medium by most of people to advertise their products. We have many classified sites on the web like craigslist, Adsglobe.com, Kijiji etc.

4) Social Networking: Today social networking sites have become an important part of the online community. Almost all users are members use it for personal and business purposes. It is an awesome place to network with many entrepreneurs who come here to begin building their own personal and business brand.

5) Shopping: In today's busy life most of us are interested to shop online. Nowadays almost anything can be bought with the use of the internet. In countries like USA most of consumers prefer to shop from home. We have many shopping sites on internet like amazon.com, Dealsglobe.com etc. People also use the internet to auction goods. There are many auction sites online, where anything can be sold.

6) Entertainment: On internet we can find all forms of entertainment from watching films to playing games online. Almost anyone can find the right kind of entertainment for themselves. When people surf the Web, there are numerous things that can be found. Music, hobbies, news and more can be found and shared on the Internet. There are numerous games that may be downloaded from the Internet for free.

7) E-Commerce: Ecommerce is the concept used for any type of commercial maneuvering, or business deals that involves the transfer of information across the globe via internet. It has become a phenomenon associated with any kind of shopping, almost anything. It has got a real amazing and range of products from household needs, technology to entertainment.

8) Services: Many services are now provided on the internet such as online banking, job seeking, purchasing tickets for your favorite movies, and guidance services on array of topics in the every aspect of life, and hotel reservations and bills paying. Often these services are not available off-line and can cost you more.

9) Job Search: Internet makes life easy for both employers and job seekers as there are plenty of job sites which connect employers and job seekers.

10) Dating/Personals: People are connecting with others though internet and finding their life partners. Internet not only helps to find the right person but also to continue the relationship.

14

Visual Basic

Introduction

Visual Basic (VB) is the third-generation event-driven programming language and integrated development environment (IDE) from Microsoft for its COM programming model. Visual Basic is designed to be relatively easy to learn and use.

Visual Basic was derived from BASIC and enables the rapid application development (RAD) of graphical user interface (GUI) applications, access to databases using Data Access Objects, Remote Data Objects, or ActiveX Data Objects, and creation of ActiveX controls and objects. Scripting languages such as VBA and VBScript are syntactically similar to Visual Basic, but perform differently.

A programmer can put together an application using the components provided with Visual Basic itself. Programs written in Visual Basic can also use the Windows API, but doing so requires external function declarations.

The final release was version 6 in 1998. Microsoft's extended support ended in March 2008 and the designated successor was Visual Basic .NET (now known simply as Visual Basic).

VISUAL BASIC

The "visual" part refers to the method used to create the graphical user interface. Rather than writing numerous lines of codes to describe the appearance and location of interface elements you simply drag and drop free built objects into place on screen. The "basic" part refers to the BASIC (Beginners All Purpose Symbolic Code) language. Visual basic has evolved from the original basic language and now contains several hundred statements, functions and keyboards; many of which relate directly to the windows GUI.

Visual basic is not only a programming language, but also a complete Graphical development environment. These environments allow users with little programming experience to quickly develop useful Microsoft windows applications.

Event Driven Programming

Event driven programming is a particular type of paradigm that functions as a result of some form of input. This input can be from somebody operating the human computer interface or it can also be influenced by messages and orders that are received from another computer program.

When you are using a computer, you are constantly provoking events that will lead to actions being performed by the computer. For example, when you are moving the computer mouse, the sensory input on the bottom of the device is telling the cursor on the screen to move. Likewise, if you were to click an icon on the screen, the clicking event is initiated as a result of that action.

This sort of programming is very common in computer operating systems and graphical user interfaces. This means you are likely to come across event driven programming when you are playing a computer game or navigating your computer's user interface. It makes use of input devices such as a mouse or a joystick, as well as giving users the ability to move around and interact with a system with relative ease.

In the past, computers could only be operated solely by entering the precise code required to initiate an action. This meant that a considerable amount of training was needed if you were to operate a computer correctly. However, thanks to the technological developments over time, event driven programming has made computers far easier to operate.

Event driven programming is greatly beneficial because of how user friendly it makes computer applications. It means that almost everyone can operate these systems without the need for expert knowledge on computer programming code such as Visual Basic and SQL.

Integrated Development Environment (IDE)

Like any other Windows application, VB consists of multiple windows which appear at startup. The windows that are displayed when you start VB are collectively known as the Visual Basic Integrated Development Environment (IDE).

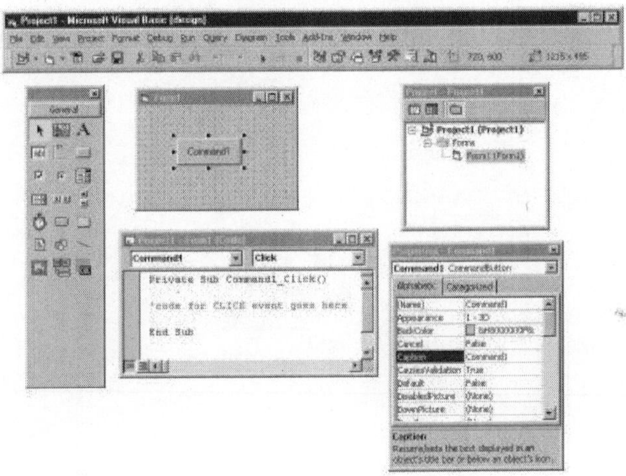

In particular, VB has the following windows:

- **Menu / Toolbar**

This is the only element of the IDE which is always visible. You use it to select which other IDE elements to view and to add forms or controls to your project. There are many other features which we will discuss later. (click to enlarge)·

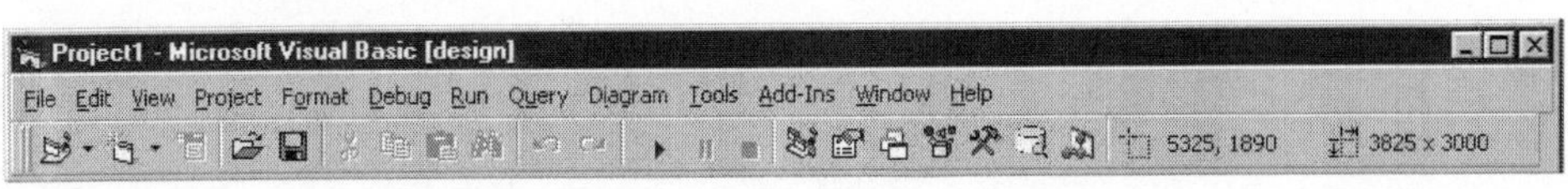

- **Toolbox**

The toolbox is simply a library of controls which you can place on your application. Once you've placed all the controls you need onto your applications forms, you can hide the toolbox to make room for working in the other elements of the IDE. ·

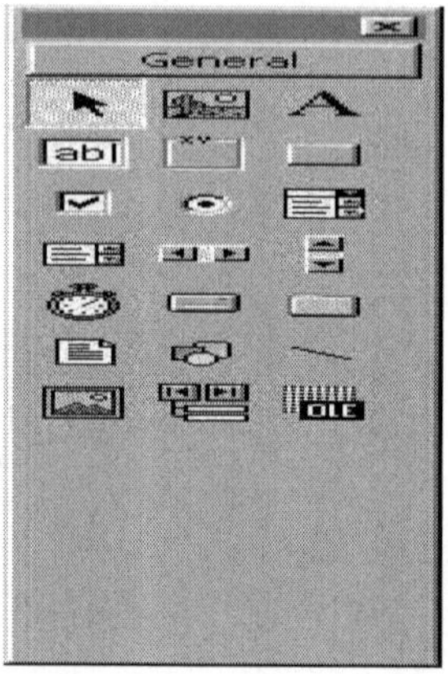

- **Project Window**

This is simply a list of all the forms which make up your VB project. There are several kinds of forms which we'll talk about later.

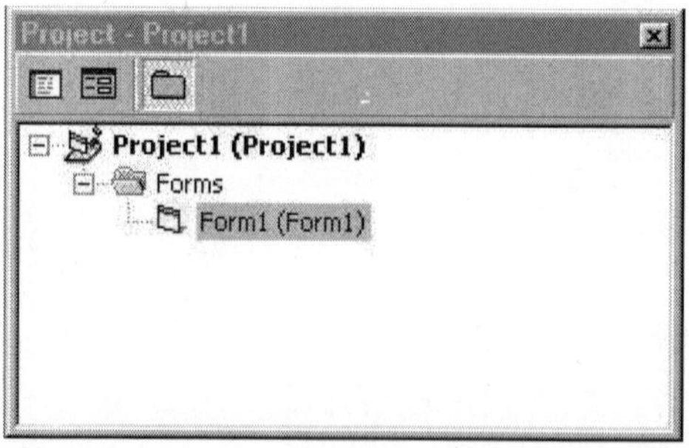

- **Property Window**

We'll talk about controls later, but such things as push-buttons, scrolling text boxes, pictures boxes and other features of most VB applications allow you to enter parameters which define how these controls work. In VB, these parameters are called properties. Some properties can be entered at design time within the IDE, while others must be entered with code while the program is running. ·

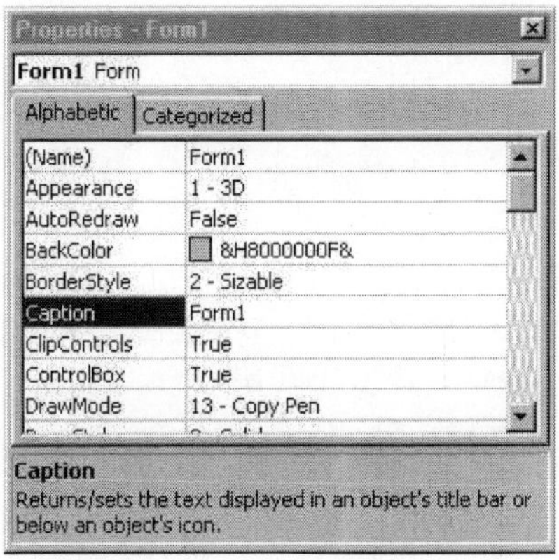

- **Forms**

You add these to your VB application as they are needed. They are the windows which hold the various controls (buttons, text boxes, etc.) which make up your application. ·

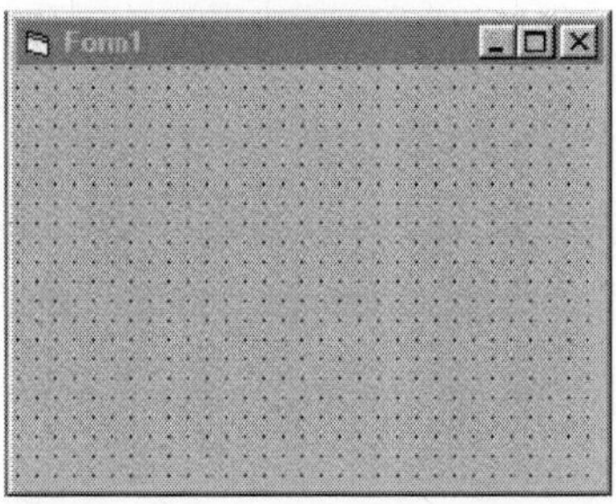

- **Code Window**

Like it's name implies, this is where you type in the code that VB executes. Notice that the heading of the window indicates with which event the code is associated.

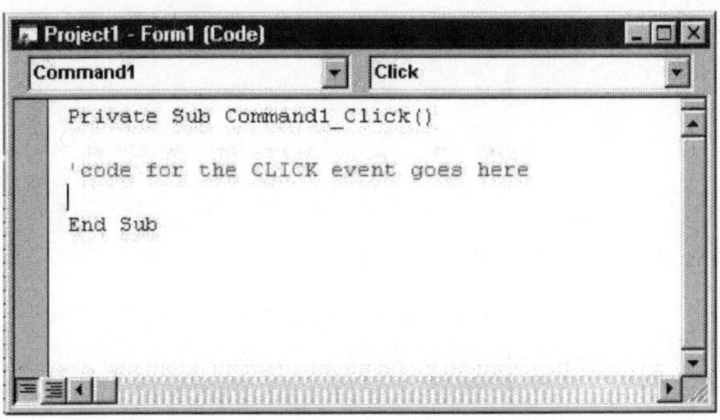

Visual Basic Standard Control

1. **Label control**: It is used to identify objects on a form. Label controls are used to display texts and can't be edited by the user.
2. **Text box control**: The text box control is used to display information entered by the user at one time or assign to the text property of the control at run time.
3. **Command button**: The command button control is used to begin, interrupt or end a process when clicked it invokes a command that has been written into its click event procedure.
4. **Fixture box**: It draws a box to display graphics.
5. **Option button or Radio button**: This control is used on a form if we want to select an only one option from a list of option button group.
6. **Check box**: This command is used for selecting a list of items from a list group.
7. **List box**: This control is used for minimizing user data entry.
8. **Combo box**: This control is used on a form when we want to add a new element that is not available in a list.

When you write a visual basic program you first have to design the user interface. If VB user interface consists of objects that you place on the screen and arrange them in an attractive manner.

The common elements of a visual basic interface are:

1. Forms (also known as windows)
2. Buttons (such as command & radio)3. Boxes (such as text and check boxes)
4. Label
5. Fixtures (icons & graphics)

Variable

Variable is temporary storage space for numbers, text, and objects. Variables are constantly being created and destroyed and will not hold any values after your program have ended. If you want to save the values of variables or other data. Before allocating storage space for a variable, decide what the variable's lifetime will be, or in other words, which procedures and which modules should have access to the variable's value.

- Procedure-level variables are created with a Dim statement placed right in the procedure where it's going to be used. The value of a procedure level variable cannot be accessed outside it's procedure. When the procedure finishes (End Sub or End Function), the variable is destroyed and memory allocated to the variable is released.
- Module-level variables are created with a Private statement in the general declarations section of a Form or code module. The value of the module level variable is available to every procedure in that module. Memory allocated to the module-level variable is not destroyed until the module is Unloaded. o Global variables are created with a Public statement in the general declarations section of a Form or code module. The value of a Global variable is available to any procedure, in any Form or code module. Memory allocated to a Global variable is not released until your program shuts down.

Arrays (collection, selection, display)

An array is a lot like a CD rack. You know: one of those rectangular boxes with slots to slide CDs in, each above another. There are two types of Visual Basic arrays: fixed-size and dynamic.

Fixed-Size Arrays

A fixed-size array most closely matches our CD rack analogy. There are a limited number of slots you can slide CDs into. Pretend you have three CDs - one by the Deftones, another by Tool, and a third by Disturbed. To fit all of these in your rack, the rack must contain at least three slots. So you declare your CD rack as having three slots: Dim strCDRack(0 to 2) As String

Dynamic Arrays

The new Charlotte Church CD came out but your rack only has three slots. You don't want to throw away any of your CDs to make room for the new one so you decide to use your ultimate building skills to attach another slot. You start building:

Dim strCDRack() As String

String (cord, series or thread)

Data structures composed of a sequence of alphanumeric characters, strings are basic in concept, but getting the information you require from them can be a different story.

The process of combining two strings together to form one string is called concatenation.

Boolean Variables

When Visual Basic converts numeric data type values to **Boolean**, 0 becomes **False** and all other values become **True**. When Visual Basic converts **Boolean** values to numeric types, **False** becomes 0 and **True** becomes -1.

Operator — Operation:

1. Not — negation
2. And — conjunction
3. Or — disjunction
4. Xor — exclusive disjunction
5. Eqv — equivalent
6. Imp — implies

Object Oriented Programming

Object Oriented Programming allows developers to mimic real world items and concepts. In an OOP world, each object knows what information describes it and what actions it can perform with that information. OOP allows developers to create reusable objects that interact with each other to form complex entities.

Definition of Classes

A "Class" is a template which defines the attributes (properties in VB) and the actions or methods which can be performed upon those attributes for a given type of entity. The class definition is used to create "Instances" of the class, which are the actual objects used within your application.

A Class is generally considered to be a "Black Box". That is, you can use the object created from a Class without knowing how the internal code works. All the developer needs to know is which methods to call to perform certain functions. How those functions perform their tasks is hidden.

Programmers generally create a Class for each separate entity used within their application. Classes allow developers to write modifiable, readable, reusable code.

Objects = Attributes + Actions

An object is an "Instance" of a Class. In Visual Basic you can create any number of "Object Variables" from a single Class Definition. Each object knows what data describes it and how to manipulate that data.

Each data item is called an "Attribute" in OOP. Visual Basic implements these attributes as "Properties". Properties are exposed through the Public Interface of an object. Each object can have internal variables, not seen by users, which are used to store information the object requires to perform its task(s).

Inheritance

A key feature of OOP is reusability. It's always time saving and useful if we can reuse something that already exists rather than trying to create the same thing again and again. Reusing the class that is tested, debugged and used many times can save us time and effort of developing and testing it again. Once a class has been written and tested, it can be used by other programs to suit the program's requirement. This is done by creating a new class from an existing class. The process of deriving a new class from an existing class is called Inheritance. The old class is called the base class and the new class is called derived class. The derived class inherits some or everything of the base class. In Visual Basic we use the Inherits keyword to inherit one class from other.

Using Inheritance we can use the variables, methods, properties, etc, from the base class and add more functionality to it in the derived class.

Polymorphism

Polymorphism provides for multiple implementations of the same method. For example, different objects can have a **Save** method, each of which perform different processing.

Data type in VB

Data type	Description
Integer	Numeric, Integer
Long	Numeric, Integer
String	Text
Currency	Numeric, Fixed decimal
Single	Numeric, Real
Double	Numeric, Real
Data/Time	Date & Time
Byte	Numeric, Integer
Boolean	True/False
Variant	Any of the above

15

Evaluation Technique of E-leaning in Tamil Language

Introduction

Web-Based Teaching Learning Process (WBTLP) is a rapidly growing area in Education. Traditional forms of teacher education are transformed, as the Internet becomes a new medium for communication. Traditionally teachers have fulfilled dual roles as presenters of structured information and social agents in the educational process. Students are in need of good interactive resources with learning tools and techniques. Hence, there is a need for training in WBTLP so as to enable the teacher to provide good resources in the web. The web-based learner resources can improve the quality of teacher education by availing various tools and techniques of evaluation. The evaluation of web-based learning resources helps to provide quality web resources in teacher education. It is also used to help teacher to have better resources and environment in which teaching takes place. The environment includes the organization, the learning materials, use of media, delivery methodology and various approaches in details.

Evaluation is a judgment regarding the worth or value of something. Typically the evaluation process is divided into two parts. The first is a teacher evaluation, which relates to interaction and guidance of a teacher with students and the second is a learning resources evaluation, which relates to quality of materials and resources of a course. However, the primary function of the evaluation is to help teacher to improve the total quality of education in web teaching learning environment.

The rise of e-learning and web-based training in Teaching Learning Process in Tamil Language (TLPTL) has lead to a growth in the use of web based learning evaluation, which will increase as the use of elearning becomes more widespread. Designing web-based tools, making resources and quality evaluation of the learning resources is a challenging task for educators, curriculum designers, computer programmer and evaluator of the resources in the Web-Based Teaching Learning Process (WBTLP). The teacher in online should take special effort for implementation and development of the instructional resources which is clear, accessible support, simplicity, transparency of the educational materials, and likelihood of the students' misconceptions as a result of interacting with materials. The teacher or trainer evaluation is also very important to learners' motivation, self-regulated learning, continues education, knowledge improvement, people with disability and poor social background. This paper presents an overview of web based learning evaluation cycle in two different aspect viz. Web Based Learning Teacher Evaluation Cycle (WBLTAC) and Web Based Learning Resources Evaluation Cycle (WBLRAC).

Web Based Learning Teacher Evaluation Cycle

An online teacher/trainer plays a key role in developing and maintaining an effective online learning environment and possesses a unique set of skills to success of a student. A quality of online teacher is very important than any resources in online. The role of online teacher is not just respect their need; they need to be involved in proper guidance, formative and summative evaluation, counseling, administration and learners' motivation.

They should also support their feelings, and make facilitate to communicate with the learners with different media and methods. This means that the online teacher should make their time efficiently with their students. Hence, the quality of teacher/ trainer can assess in six major categories viz.:

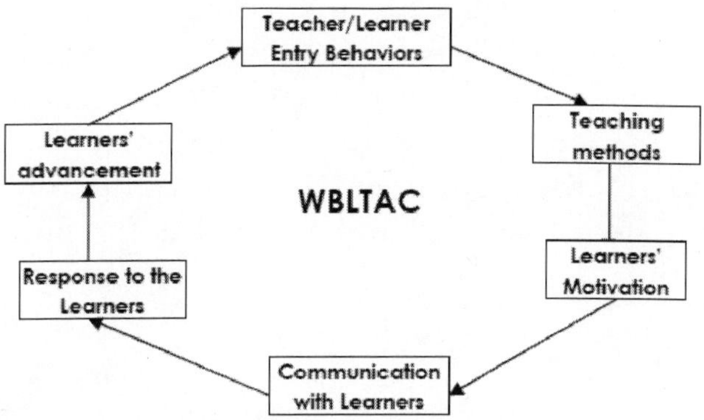

Teacher/Trainer Entry Behaviors

Once you have identified a person as an online teacher/trainer for a specific task or target groups the organizer determine what kind of knowledge, skill, and experience need to be taken into account for the specific training process. The entry behavior may be determined by three major areas viz.:

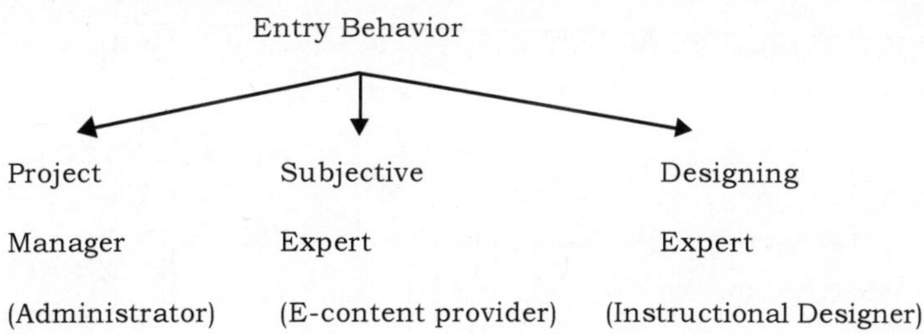

Project Manager

Project manager is an achievement of academic qualification, administrative power, attitude level, communicative ability, leadership quality, involvement in students' achievement, investigative technique of students' problems; task oriented training activities, cooperation with student on assignment, equal treatment made to each student, responsibility, freedom, and support by giving opportunity to express their opinion and relationship with students, teacher and designer.

Subjective Expert

Subjective Expert is based on theoretical and experimental experience in a different content area. The e-content provider should have knowledge of content development, material editing and method of teaching. E-content development is essential for learner, multimedia producer, Instructional designer and distributors. These are the quality needed for bearing on the delivering of the training product/event.

Designing Expert

Designing expert should have knowledge of expectation of an online learner. The e-content material designer have different roles in a web based learning materials developing a project viz. instructional designer, multimedia designer, graphics artist, internet based application developer, media producer, and web administrator.

Teaching Methods

Web based trainer use different methods to deliver an instructional material. The structure of an online teaching method consists of following three components.

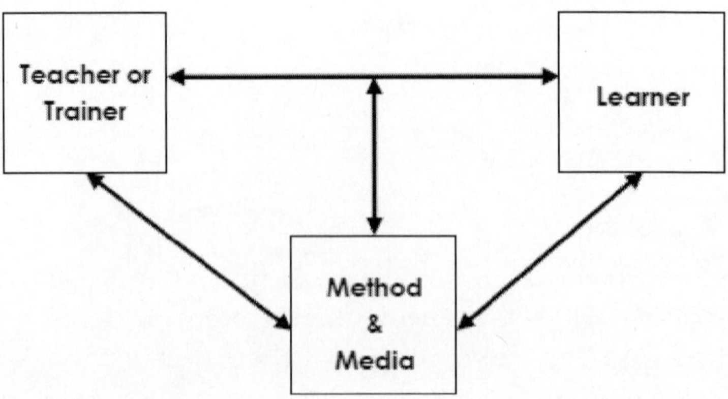

The trainer provides content in different media viz. text, pictures, audio, video, animation, and simulation which helps student to understand the concept easily. It implies that the learner has freedom to choose his choice by the way of his interest and preference of his learning materials.

Learners' Motivation

Encourage learners to solve their problems by interaction with facilitator, peer group discussion, and expert in their chosen subject. The models of achievement motivation most often attribute students' academic motivation to cognitive processes (Bandura, 1986; Weiner, 1992) which regulate students' Teacher or Trainer Learner Method & Media learning behaviour. There is a growing body of evidence (Wentzel, 1991, 1994, 1996), however, that a consideration of social motivation of classrooms should not be excluded from the model of achievement motivation. Three aspect of learners' motivation is important in web based teaching process viz.:

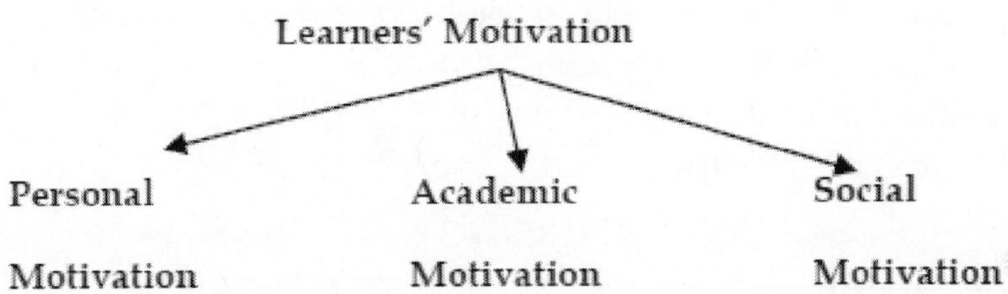

Success at online teaching learning process requires students to achieve three outcomes of education: individual power, academic achievement, and social adjustment. Judgments on levels of motivation were made using the following criteria: teacher interaction with learners and individual pupils, time keeping, teaching style, and observed enthusiasm in different aspect.

Communication with Learner

Continues communication with learner helps to overcome the isolation problems. Web based teacher have many channel to communicate with their learner viz.

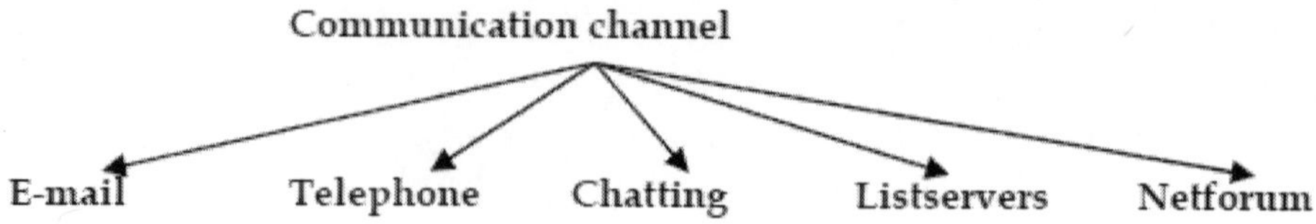

Electronic mail (E-mail) can be used by the facilitator and learners-to-learners communication. E-mail is cost-efficient, fast and convenient. Group e-mail can also be used to contact all learners simultaneously.

The telephone has used as a synchronous method of supporting the learners. The telephone allows learners to communicate with their teacher/trainer. Learners can discuss instructional and non-instructional problems with their facilitator.

Chatting helps to learner to communicate with his facilitator and his peer groups. Two types of chatting methods are available viz. video chatting and audio chatting. Video chatting is like a face-to-face communication and the audio chatting is like a telephone communication.

List servers is an e-mail list that allows any of the users registered on the list to e-mail a specific list serve address, after which the e-mail is forwarded to everyone on the list. It is useful for the learner to discuss of topics relevant to the learning event.

Net forum allow the facilitator to post learning event information or announcements, changes to the learning event or deadlines for assignments. It is also used by learner to post questions about the learning event which the facilitator and other learner can answer. Learners and researchers are encouraged to discuss and reply in discussion forum.

Response to the Learner

It is the quality of awareness that is evoked in collaborative meaning-making with students that defines the quality of a teacher's response to the teaching situation. Immediate feedback, which makes encourage, interest on further and continuing education, helps the learner to achieve their goal. A variety of possibilities exists. The teacher may have a word or phrase of affirmation:

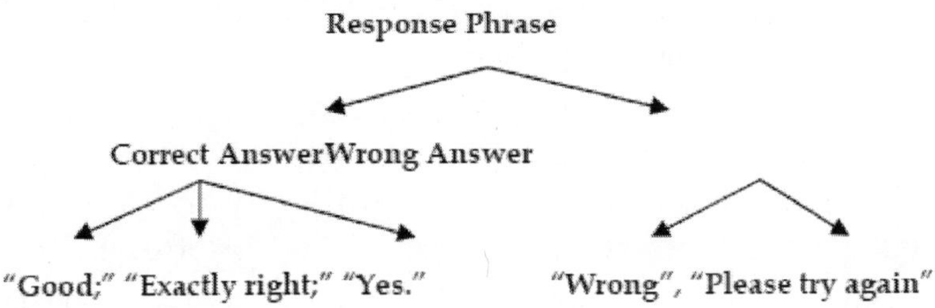

Learners' Advancement

Learners' record shows the quality of teacher/facilitator in web based teaching learning process. Ensuring the achievement of learners in different aspects viz. academic achievement, personal improvement, social behaviors, communication development, self-awareness, self-motivation, etc.

Web Based Learning Resources Evaluation Cycle

Instructional resources are plays an important role to deliver the learning materials through online. Using these resources, the learner can contact their facilitator at any time or in a fixed time when they are having problems. A quality resources make quality learning product and provide quality learner in web based training process. The quality resources can be assessed by six major categorize viz.

Instructional Objectives

Objectives are useful in content development, material designing and implementation of the web based learning process and evaluation of the learner. The instructional objective describes a kind of performance expected by learners at the end of a learning event. The objective helps learner to plan the learning opportunity in their interested area. The development of instructional objectives is a task whose importance should not be overlooked. The instructional objectives can be divided into two major categories.

Instructional Objectives

Educational Objectives (Knowledge domains)	Environmental Objectives (Resources domains)

Educational Objectives (EdO)

Educational objectives help learners know where they are going and how they are going to achieve their goal. EdO is designed based on learners' interest and involvement. In this domain the facilitator investigate the learners' interest to achieve their goal.

Environmental Objectives (EnO)

This environment helps learner to achieve their goal at their own location. In virtual learning environment the learner gets freedom to choose their interest subject with establish guidelines for including graphics, videos, audios, animations, pictures, and various presentation media. This environment makes more benefits to a learner to achieve their goal without any strain and pain.

Content Analysis

The content review team might include the client, instructional designer, subject-expert(s) and programmer. Developing new

Learning Materials (LM) is a major task involving their design, development, delivery and evaluation to ensure their effectiveness. Check the existing materials before providing a new one. If there is large number of subject matter and other information relevant to the learners' achievement goal on the web, then it is probably suitable for web-based delivery. The LM should provide more opportunity to the learner to choose their specific content area. The learning event needs to be updated regularly. In content analysis the following points need to consider for analyzing to provide a better learning materials.

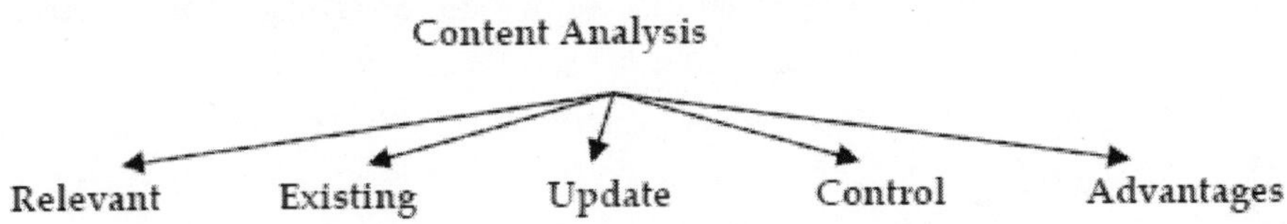

Analyze, how well the content and material presented in the way that was both interesting and stimulating. The evaluation of these materials should include gathering data regarding the relevance of various assignments and the quality of the various evaluations.

Instructional Media Evaluation

In an online environment, media are used to provide variety to what is essentially a text-based methodology. Such media may include video, although this is limited unless learners have access to a broadband network, graphics, simulation, other visual effects and synchronous and asynchronous communication. Instructional media makes learner with self-learning, self-confident and self-control.

Evaluation of Learners

This evaluation of reaction is based on measurement of learners' feelings and opinions about the course after completed. The facilitator can get the information here relates to methods of instruction, course content, learning methods and materials. Behavioral changes of learners are a measurement of the behavioral changes occurring as a result of the learning event after completed.

Delivery Methodology

The learning materials should be downloaded easily at learners place. The instructional media delivered with minimum space and maximum speed at learners' center. The material and media should flexible to the learners' environment.

Revising Resources

The facilitator can determine the ability of the web system to support the learner, the effectiveness of the learning environment, the effectiveness of the support offered to the learner, how web based learning benefits when compared with the traditional methods. Based on the above findings of the evaluation changes may be needed to the learning methods and materials to support the learner.

Conclusion

Methods and media play a major role in the success of a web-based learning process. Hence we need to assess the material and media to provide a better learning event. A web-based learning process cannot be successful without well-designing learning material, good facility support and evaluation. Web-based learning is a self-based leaning and places the responsibility for study directly on the learners themselves. They need to know how to use the web based learning environment to be successful.

References

1. Bandura, A. (1986). Social foundations of thought and action: A social cognitive theory, Englewood Cliffs, NJ; Prentice Hall.
2. Weiner, B. (1992). Human motivation: Metaphors, theories and research. Newbury Park, CA: Sage.
3. Wentzel, K. R. (1991). Relations between social competence and academic achievement in early adolescence. Child Development, 62, 1066-1078.
4. Wentzel, K. R. (1994). Relations of social goal pursuit to social acceptance, classroom behaviour and perceived social support. Journal of Educational Psychology, 86, 173-182.

5. Wentzel, K. R. (1996). Social goals and social relationships as motivators of school adjustment. In J.Juvonen, & K. R. Wentzel (Eds.), Social motivation: understanding children's school adjustment (pp. 226-247). New York: Cambridge University Press.

16

Role of Information Technology in Teacher Education

Now we are living in the modern world. A lot of change is occurring in every day. With the help of science and technology we have developed in all the fields. With the help of technology now it is easy to know any type of information with in seconds through out the world.

Radio, Television, Phone, Mobile, Computer and Internet have changed the human life. Through education we can learn any thing easily with the help of these instruments. According to Mahatma Gandhi, the father of Indian Nation, by giving good education to each and every one we can remove poverty and develop good character. India is a developing country. Now we have very much demand in the IT filed. The development of IT is a wonder. Now lacks of student are entering in to the IT filed. Our central and state governments are also giving more importance for Information Technology. There is a separate department for Information Technology under the Ministry of Communication and Information Technology.

Definition of Information Technology

Information technology (IT): The science and activity of using computers and other electronic equipment to store and send information. Information Technology is also defined as, "The technology involved with the transmission and storage of information, especially the development, installation, implementation, and management of computer systems within companies, universities" and other organizations".

Goals and Objectives

1. To provide in-service training to teachers and teacher educators on computers and IT.
2. To incorporate all the IT facilities into teacher education model.
3. To extend internet, e-mail facilities to all teachers and students in teacher education.
4. To provide network how to operate computers and internet to all the student teachers.
5. To provide network to teacher education centres all over India.
6. To extend distance mode of teacher education online and also include a live interactive practical teaching.
7. To restructure teacher education curriculum.
8. To incorporate use of IT in special education.
9. To use IT in teacher education research.
10. To create a virtual teacher education centre.
11. To incorporate good hidden curriculum strategies to restore the humanistic tendencies required for a teacher.
12. Ensure the protection and security of data.
13. Minimize duplication of effort, services and resources.
14. Eliminate inefficient and costly redundancies.
15. Define what services, if any, should be restructured or eliminated.
16. Eliminate non-compatible standards and architectures.
17. Identify obstacles for departments wanting to move computing operations to the Division of Information Technology.
18. Recommend a strategy for evaluating the university-wide

impacts of major information technology purchases including analysis of total cost of ownership.

19. Evaluate the complexity and risks of managing a complex distributed computing environment, including system security, exposure to data loss and virus protection.
20. Identify issues and trends in technology that may affect the university's technology infrastructure and long-term architecture.
21. Recommend the most effective balance of central and distributed technology services, staffing and resources. Detail any logical alternatives. Recommendations will include background, advice and alternatives that address the following:
    - Create a cost efficient blend of centralization and decentralization of information technology resources - properly aligning the university's information technology infrastructure to best meet the needs of its teaching, research and outreach missions.
    - Create a coherent campus-wide information technology computing architecture and a solid foundation for the university's information technology infrastructure.
    - Develop a long-term organizational process and structure to ensure the best utilization of the university's information technology resources for the future.
    - Estimate the costs of infrastructure and support, including personnel and training, in the current distributed environment and to estimate the same costs for the alternatives proposed.

Need of Information Technology in Teacher Education

It is well known fact that IT and Cyber age have brought a revolutionary transformation and drifted the whole life style of people. No area left untouched with it. We have arrived at global village concept with all virtual realities on our desktops. But is it the teacher education, which has remained untouched in this direction.

We have a lot of educational institutions in the filed of Information Technology like 'Indian Institute of Information

Technology (IIIT), 'International Institute of Information Technology, 'Tata Institute of Information Technolgoy' and 'Deerubai Ambani Institute of Information Technology'. There are so many Information Technology departments in the universities at both state and central level. The effect of Information Technology in our daily life is very much. It is very necessary to take Information Technology help for teacher education. There is a separate subject for trainee teacher 'Educational Technology'. With the help of Information Technology it is possible to give quality and effective education for trainee teachers.

A nation's development potential depends upon its ability to continuously educate its population and its ability to create armies of skilled manpower. In particular, use of Information Technology (IT) in acquiring knowledge and skill has become an essential element in education and training. These IT elements in the educational process have magical effects.

Higher education without the support of IT makes the lives of learner and teachers equally difficult. A nation's intellectual strength depends on IT support. The use of computing and communication technology to enhance the efficacy of transaction and productivity is the driving force in this new era of social and economic transformation in the new society called Information Society.

A strong IT infrastructure can give an institution a competitive advantage for the best students and faculty and an advantage in competition for absorbing external research grants to execute studies, research etc. in a short time and with great resolution. The quality of an institution's environment for digital information storage and retrieval has, for any disciplines, become more important than the institution's conventional, library resources in print media.

Virtually every economic sector that is labour intensive has managed to improve productivity through the use of technology except education. Faculty/student ratios in higher education have changed significantly in more than 50 years. The most advanced technology in common use in the classroom today in our country is the overhead projector, and it took nearly three decades to migrate from the national level training institute to the classroom. Institutions like UGC, IGNOU, and CIET have begun to transact curriculum on DD 1 but the ETV programmes are mostly of enrichment type and not as per the demand of the students. It is unlikely that IT will have a major impact on teaching and learning if the current paradigm for instruction changes.

Generally majority trainee teachers have no knowledge about usage of technology. Because their lower classes curriculum is separate. It is necessary to change curriculum at school level and implement Information Technology at school level also. 'Today's children are tomorrow's citizens', so it is necessary to take care about school curriculum. It is government duty to provide Information Technology labs for all type of Educational Institutions in the country.

Uses of Information Technology

Now we are using Information Technology in all the fields like education agriculture, banking, transport, medicine, research and manufacturing and in social service mode.

Specific Uses of Information Technology

1. Animation for simulation of urban environments and video for assembling and disseminating results of the analysis and design work.
2. Graphic Information System (GIS) for the study of housing and development patterns.
3. Computer Aided Design (CAD) for geometric modeling: Digital image archival systems for compiling data about the built environment.

Role of Information Technology in Teacher Education

In-service Training

There is a need to provide in-service training to all the teachers and teacher educators with updated computer operation skills and provide with IT know how. To utilize the facilities to access updated information and solutions to their problems in their areas of specialization, it can be provide on-line.

Teacher Education Training Programmes through IT facilities

A virtual teacher education centre can be created. All the necessary skills and training can be provided in different modes on the network. It should incorporate all the available facilities like, tele-education, teleconferencing, floppy diskettes and CD-ROMs in teacher education. Networks like ERNET, INTERNET and futuristic concept of bringing satellite channels directly to homes by DTS (Direct to Home) service and expert talks through virtual classrooms can also be made available.

Distance Mode of Education

The present practice of TV and other media in distance mode of education can be substituted by multimedia systems which have an extra advantage of intractability through GUI (Graphics User Interface) which controls the response of information transfer process according to the learners pace. It helps in using screen as an instructor for self-learning.

IT in special Education

IT is providing solutions for the education of physically challenged people as well. As reported by BBC web-site (web-site at BBC news, science), the Germans have developed a technology and associated software for which people, where computer will sense the signals from the head of a paralyzed person through two attached electrodes, and thereby, allow him to surf the net like a normal person. These facilities will transform the lives of the physically challenged and IT can be used even for diagnosing.

Research and INTERNET

Internet facilities should be made available to research students, teacher educators. All the departments should have internet connectivity. It helps in accessing information about the ongoing research in their respective fields and it also avoids overlapping.

Restructuring Curricula of Teacher Education

1. Teacher education curriculum needs drastic changes by incorporating all facilities available through IT. Primarily IT can be used to keep on par with the existing knowledge structure. It can be thoroughly incorporated into methodologies of teacher education.
2. There should not be exclusive theoretical orientation in curriculum. It shall have more practically demonstrable skill and strategies in the curriculum.
3. All possible attempts should be made to train teachers apart from virtual classrooms, to incorporate the necessary live interactive experiences to understand the significance of physical interaction with the child in the classroom.
4. Humanistic and affective hidden curriculum and an effective training to acquire all traits and qualities required in teacher to handle human society should also be included in the curriculum.

Conclusion

Information Technology has a prominent role in the filed of teacher education. With the help of information technology it is easy to know any type of information with in seconds through out the world. The advanced knowledge of information technology is much helpful for research in all the fields of education. With the help of Information Technology it is easy to educate trainee teachers. By knowing the usage of technology they have a change to share their opinions with other teacher through out the world. Information Technology motivates the teacher to learn lot of things in their subject area.

Now we are happy that our State and Central Governments have taking good steps to introduce online education in the educational institutions. There are separate subjects in D.Ed., and B.Ed., like Computer Education and Educational Technology. Now teachers are using computers and internet in the educational institutions. But the percentage is very less. It is more important to give equal importance to theory and practical in the computer education and educational technology subjects. It is the duty of the Government to provide Computer and Educational technology labs for each and every teacher education institution in the country.

Now NCTE, CIET, NIEPA, NCERT, SCERT and other educational departments have recognized the advantages of Information Technology in the field of education. They motivate the students to use IT. They are conducting national seminars, workshops, and conferences about Information Technology. Teachers must be given excellent training in setting, grading papers and preparing assignment, etc. These can be used in teacher training network. Excellent stimulated models can be made available to access on network.

References

1. Promotion of Quality of Teacher Education for 21st Century, Dr. N. Ramanath Kishan, Editor, Ashoka Krishna Offset Printers, Warangal.
2. http://www.ciet.nic.in/
3. http://www.aponline.gov.in/

17

The Role of Information and Communication Technologies (ICTS) in Distance Education

Introduction

Education is the backbone of a nation. Despite knowing this, a huge number of people of least developed countries are far beyond the reach of higher education. One of the key reasons may be the poor economic condition of those countries. Perhaps this is the crucial challenge to be addressed by those nations for overall development where education may be on the top list. Information, Knowledge, and Communication Technology also play vital role in the growth as well as producing and offering goods and services at relatively reduced costs. Smart use of ICTs can process information, create knowledgebase and make them available wherever and whenever necessary. But despite having relatively poor economic condition, Information and Communication. Technologies (ICTs) in most cases have tremendous success in providing services at reduced costs to the people's door steps. ICTs have the same to do for making the higher education available to all classes of people throughout the country at a lower cost. As a result, on one hand people will have the access right on higher education and on the other hand will gain the necessary knowledge, skills, and experiences to serve the nation and prosper accordingly.

In 21st century, one can hardly find a country where higher education through distance mode is not available. In fact it has been practiced since long before. But at present days, having revolution of ICTs, the higher education through distance mode has been more practical and well accepted by the all people around the globe. It is now being called Virtual learning. In developed country, people are getting more interested in learning through Virtual Campus than that of a Brick-and-Mortar Campus. Virtual Campus is nothing but ICT enabled campus, where students are attending their classes, discussing with teachers, accessing learning resources, seating exams, joining forums/clubs, submitting assignments etc virtually having the facility of real-time interactions between teacher and students.

Practically, from records and researches into it plans of last two decades (the mid 80s to the millennium), evolving rolling plans are consistently observed and reviewed to accommodate changes in the ambit of standardisation, upgradeability, compatibility and operate ability both cost effective synchronous and asynchronous systems of delivering education contents. Hence the ICT department is always faced a dynamic and rolling plan that will consistently and integrated rolled into the overall goal of the distance learning institution which is to provide and deliver quality education contents removing the distance barrier.

The planning process involves a conducted wide systems analysis and consultation with the various units on their operations in order to have a system design for the distance learning institution. Events such as admission and registration exercises that involve collation of forms, processing and the collaborations that evolved from such exercises will give the it department the necessary logic and defined procedures to adopt.

According to Everett Rogers (2003) the perceived attributes of innovations are:

- Relative advantage (how the innovation is perceived to be an improvement),
- compatibility (consistency with existing experience, values and needs),
- complexity (perceived difficulty in understanding and using an innovation),
- trialability (the degree to which an innovation can be experimented with),
- observability (how visible the results of an innovation are to others).

Each of these five very useful concepts can be seen to have an "external" dimension that can be measured and quantified, and an "internal" dimension, the perception, that is relative to the individual. In order to distinguish clearly between these two dimensions as well as to bring out the complexity of introducing ICT solutions in a learning environment, we have chosen to combine diffusion theory of analysis of the observability on how these new information technologies are effectively used by the end users.

Despite this new trend a very few research has been done on the impact this new change has brought in meeting student's learning needs and expectations, and learner's ability to use these technology effectively, during their study. This research will focus on the types of types of Physical learning environments or resources learners use for online studying. Here a physical learning environment is defined as the place or physical surroundings where a student can gain knowledge or skills either by themselves, or by interaction with a teacher or other students.

Objectives of the study

Following broad based objectives were derived for his study.

- To identify the types of physical learning environments and resources used by the students.

- To analyze the theory and practice on the use of online teaching and learning.
- To inform the course designers and teachers to apply appropriate teaching strategies and students support systems to meet the needs and demands of students.
- To inform the appropriateness of the physical learning environment as an important component in the design of course materials and support systems to meet the needs and demands of students.

Methodology

The main aim of the study is to assess the place or physical surroundings where a student can gain knowledge either by themselves or by interaction with teachers and fellow students. How the students use the internet resources for their learning purpose. The research is done by using a survey technique. The survey is divided into two sections.

- The first section asked the participant (Both distance education/Regular) questions relating to the types of information gathering techniques used for their study. How often they have participated in different learning environments? The types of resources they have used in their previous study. Responses are collected on a four point likert-type scale ranging from –Never, Sometimes, Often and Always.
- The second section sought students demographic information including the number of courses the participants had undertaken previously an online component and their previous level of education etc. These were used as variables such gender, age, income, education, occupation, personal access, frequency of computer use were included in the questionnaires

Components of survey questionnaires

Questions relating to the types of information gathering techniques used

1. How often they have participated in different physical learning environments

2. Types of resources they have used in their learning process.

Student demographic information

The course the participant is undergoing, e.g. Distance mode or regular mode.

Study sample

A particular cohort of participants were selected who were pursuing various courses offered in distance mode where online component is mandatory and students who where doing their course in regular mode. The data is collected from the students who have online component mandatory for their study. The study sample is collected from selected students who have some prior knowledge of ICTs and computer literacy.

The study was conducted in Chennai on Distance Education Students of Symbiosis, GNIIT, and IGNOU Students for whom Online Component is Mandatory. Majority of the course materials used by these students are online or web based. As the questionnaires were send to the mailboxes of the respondents we were able to get only 17 participants.

The samples were also selected from some of the Regular College students who were pursuing there higher studies in college for whom the necessity of using online resource is more for their study. This is also done by sending the questionnaires online. Of this we were able to get 18 participants of the expected 83.

The variables used in this study were gender, age and mode of study. Data from the spread sheet were analyzed using Microsoft excel. The Table I shows the participants breakdown of the sample. We had 35 respondents of the total sample of 100. Of the 35 respondent 17 students were students for whom the online study component is mandatory.

Learning Environment: The usual assumption with distance education students is that they learn at home with material provided with their educational institution. In this study 90% of the respondents indicated that they often or always study at home.

Students have also indicated that they do study at their place of work, in the library, or in computer Lab.

Online Communication: The main components of online communication are text based, E-mail, bulletin boards and Chat rooms. This table shows the usage of online communication by students as percentage.

The results shows that most of the students use E-mail often for their study, most of them hardly prefer chat, sizeable proportions are using bulletin board. 50% of the students have never used chat rooms for their study.

Use of paper based resources by Online Distance education students Most of the online distance education provide following course materials for the study of the students, Textbooks, Printed Study Guide, Handout provided by lecturer and study resources. This table shows the frequency of use of paper-based materials by online students.

The results of survey indicate that more than 90% of the respondents preferred Text books always. Majority of respondents were not interested in the Handouts provided by the lecturers.

Usage of ICT resources by students: The results indicate that all respondents at some stages of their learning have used online grade checking, at some stages of their learning. When using online course materials over 90% have indicated that they often and always use online search tools. Electronic Library access is however not used as frequently with only 15.0% indicating that they always use this resource. This survey indicates that ICTs were very well used by the students.

Interactive components such as quizzes and online tests are widely used by the students. Nearly 70% of the respondents preferred using online quizzes.

Also around 75% of the respondents were using internet for submitting the assignements. Also around 65% of the students always used URL links for their study purpose. The access to electronic library is very poor as the data indicates nearly fifty percentages of the students hardly use these resources.

Preferred learning environment: The preferred learning environment of the regular students and the online students can be compared in this table

Both regular as well as distance education students prefer to study among themselves, similarly most of them prefer using tutorials.

Preferred physical learning environment are quite same for both distance learning students and regular campus based students. None of the regular students preferred to study using videoconferencing session.

Use of ICT Components-Comparison between regular and distance education students:

This table shows the comparison chart of the regular and distance education students More than 50% of the students don't prefer using online chat for their studying purpose. Online search tools were often used by both regular and distance education students.

CONCLUSION

IT has been shown that the physical learning environments of distance students are not all that different from those used by regular on-campus students. Unexpected results from this study are that distances students' needs are apparently appear similar to that of the on-campus students. This is both in relation to resources and communication needs. Both distance and on-campus students in this study made a made selective use of online resources. Both group indicated that most of their study was done at home using paper based or web based materials. Students are able to use ICT's; there is need by course designer's and developers to maximize its potential for learning purpose. The results from the study suggests that more research needs to be done to more fully understand the environments students use for their study to make online course maximize student study needs and demands.

The most used part of the new ICTs in universities is the Internet as a delivery tool for academic content and for student support. Distance learning platforms have been developed by almost every higher education institution, as panacea for issues like the increasing number of students, lack of appropriate and enough study space, standardisation, quality assurance and control of the information delivered, increasing costs of higher education and so on.

As a result, there is now a need for support concerning the methodology of development good distance courses, the quality level of tuition offered, pedagogical and technical standards, development of pedagogical basis, operative legislative regulations, a frame for distance programmes evaluation etc.

18

ICT in Education

Introduction

Globalization and technological change-processes that have accelerated in tandem over the past fifteen years-have created a new global economy "powered by technology, fueled by information and driven by knowledge." The emergence of this new global economy has serious implications for the nature and purpose of educational institutions. As the half-life of information continues to shrink and access to information continues to grow exponentially, schools cannot remain mere venues for the transmission of a prescribed set of information from teacher to student over a fixed period of time. Rather, schools must promote "learning to learn,": i.e., the acquisition of knowledge and skills that make possible continuous learning over the lifetime. "The illiterate of the 21st century," according to futurist Alvin Toffler, "will not be those who cannot read and write, but those who cannot learn, unlearn, and relearn."

Concerns over educational relevance and quality coexist with the imperative of expanding educational opportunities to those made most vulnerable by globalization-developing countries in general; low-income groups, girls and women, and low-skilled workers in particular. Global changes also put pressure on all groups to constantly acquire and apply new skills. The International Labour Organization defines the requirements for education and training in the new global economy simply as "Basic Education for All"," Core Work Skills for All" and "Lifelong Learning for All". Information and communication technologies (ICTs) which include radio and television, as well as newer digital technologies such as computers and the Internet-have been touted as potentially powerful enabling tools for educational change and reform. When used appropriately, different ICTs are said to help expand access to education, strengthen the relevance of education to the increasingly digital workplace, and raise educational quality by, among others, helping make teaching and learning into an engaging, active process connected to real life.

However, the experience of introducing different ICTs in the classroom and other educational settings all over the world over the past several decades suggests that the full realization of the potential educational benefits of ICTs is not automatic. The effective integration of ICTs into the educational system is a complex, multifaceted process that involves not just technology-indeed, given enough initial capital, getting the technology is the easiest part!-but also curriculum and pedagogy, institutional readiness, teacher competencies, and long-term financing, among others.

This primer is intended to help policymakers in developing countries define a framework for the appropriate and effective use of ICTs in their educational systems by first providing a brief overview of the potential benefits of ICT use in education and the ways by which different ICTs have been used in education thus far. Second, it addresses the four broad issues in the use of ICTs in education-effectiveness, cost, equity, and sustainability. The primer concludes with a discussion of five key challenges that policymakers in developing countries must reckon with when making decisions about the integration of ICTs in education, namely, educational policy and planning, infrastructure, capacity building, language and content, and financing.

(1) Definition of Terms

What are ICTs and what types of ICTs are commonly used in education?

ICTs stand for *information and communication technologies* and are defined, for the purposes of this primer, as a "diverse set of technological tools and resources used to communicate, and to create, disseminate, store, and manage information." These technologies include *computers, the Internet, broadcasting technologies (radio and television), and telephony.*

In recent years there has been a groundswell of interest in how computers and the Internet can best be harnessed to improve the efficiency and effectiveness of education at all levels and in both formal and non-formal settings. But ICTs are more than just these technologies; older technologies such as the telephone, radio and television, although now given less attention, have a longer and richer history as instructional tools. For instance, radio and television have for over forty years been used for open and distance learning, although print remains the cheapest, most accessible and therefore most dominant delivery mechanism in both developed and developing countries· The use of computers and the Internet is still in its infancy in developing countries, if these are used at all, due to limited infrastructure and the attendant high costs of access.

Moreover, different technologies are typically used in combination rather than as the sole delivery mechanism. For instance, the Kothmale Community Radio Internet uses both radio broadcasts and computer and Internet technologies to facilitate the sharing of information and provide educational opportunities in a rural community in Sri Lanka. The Open University of the United Kingdom (UKOU), established in 1969 as the first educational institution in the world wholly dedicated to open and distance learning, still relies heavily on print-based materials supplemented by radio, television and, in recent years, online programming. Similarly, the Indira Gandhi National Open University in India combines the use of print, recorded audio and video, broadcast radio and television, and audio conferencing technologies.

What is e-learning?

Although most commonly associated with higher education and corporate training, e-learning encompasses learning at all levels, both formal and non-formal, that uses an information network-the Internet, an intranet (LAN) or extranet (WAN)-whether wholly or in part, for course delivery, interaction and/or facilitation. Others prefer the term *online learning. Web-based learning* is a subset of e-learning and refers to learning using an Internet browser (such as Netscape or Internet Explorer).

What is blended learning?

Another term that is gaining currency is blended learning. This refers to learning models that combine traditional classroom practice with e-learning solutions. For example, students in a traditional class can be assigned both print-based and online materials, have online mentoring sessions with their teacher through chat, and are subscribed to a class email list. Or a Web-based training course can be enhanced by periodic face-to-face instruction. "Blending"was prompted by the recognition that not all learning is best achieved in an electronically-mediated environment, particularly one that dispenses with a live instructor altogether. Instead, consideration must be given to the subject matter, the learning objectives and outcomes, the characteristics of the learners, and the learning context in order to arrive at the optimum mix of instructional and delivery methods.

What is open and distance learning?

Open and distance learning is defined by the Commonwealth of Learning as "a way of providing learning opportunities that is characterized by the separation of teacher and learner in time or place, or both time and place; learning that is certified in some way by an institution or agency; the use of a variety of media, including print and electronic; two-way communications that allow learners and tutors to interact; the possibility of occasional face-to-face meetings; and a specialized division of labour in the production and delivery of courses."

What is meant by a learner-centered environment?

The National Research Council of the U.S. defines learner-centered environments as those that "pay careful attention to the knowledge, skills, attitudes, and beliefs that learners bring with them to the classroom." The impetus for learner-centeredness derives from a theory of learning called constructivism, which views learning as a process in which individuals "construct" meaning based on prior knowledge and experience. Experience enables individuals to build mental models or schemas, which in turn provide meaning and organization to subsequent experience. Thus knowledge is not "out there", independent of the learner and which the learner passively receives; rather, knowledge is created through an active process in which the learner transforms information, constructs hypothesis, and makes decisions using his/her mental models. A form of constructivism called social constructivism also emphasizes the role of the teacher, parents, peers and other community members in helping learners to master concepts that they would not be able to understand on their own. For social constructivists, learning must be active, contextual and social. It is best done in a group setting with the teacher as facilitator or guide.

(2) The Promise of ICTs in Education

For developing countries ICTs have the potential for increasing access to and improving the relevance and quality of education. It thus represents a potentially equalizing strategy for developing countries.

However, the reality of the Digital Divide-the gap between those who have access to and control of technology and those who do not-means that the introduction and integration of ICTs at different levels and in various types of education will be a most challenging undertaking. Failure to meet the challenge would mean a further widening of the knowledge gap and the deepening of existing economic and social inequalities.

How can ICTs help expand access to education?

ICTs are a potentially powerful tool for extending educational opportunities, both formal and non-formal, to previously underserved constituencies-scattered and rural populations, groups traditionally excluded from education due to cultural or social reasons such as ethnic minorities, girls and women, persons with disabilities, and the elderly, as well as all others who for reasons of cost or because of time constraints are unable to enroll on campus.

- **Anytime, anywhere.** One defining feature of ICTs is their ability to transcend time and space. ICTs make possible asynchronous learning, or learning characterized by a time lag between the delivery of instruction and its reception by learners. Online course materials, for example, may be accessed 24 hours a day, 7 days a week. ICT-based educational delivery (e.g., educational programming broadcast over radio or television) also dispenses with the need for all learners and the instructor to be in one physical location. Additionally, certain types of ICTs, such as teleconferencing technologies, enable instruction to be received simultaneously by multiple, geographically dispersed learners (i.e., synchronous learning).

Access to remote learning resources

Teachers and learners no longer have to rely solely on printed books and other materials in physical media housed in libraries (and available in limited quantities) for their educational needs. With the Internet and the World Wide Web, a wealth of learning materials in almost every subject and in a variety of media can now be accessed from anywhere at anytime of the day and by an unlimited number of people. This is particularly significant for many schools in developing countries, and even some in developed countries, that have limited and outdated library resources. ICTs also facilitate access to resource persons- mentors, experts, researchers, professionals, business leaders, and peers-all over the world.

How does the use of ICTs help prepare individuals for the workplace?

One of the most commonly cited reasons for using ICTs in the classroom has been to better prepare the current generation of students for a workplace where ICTs, particularly computers, the Internet and related technologies, are becoming more and more ubiquitous. Technological literacy, or the ability to use ICTs effectively and efficiently, is thus seen as representing a competitive edge in an increasingly globalizing job market. Technological literacy, however, are not the only skill well-paying jobs in the new global economy will require? EnGauge of the North Central Regional Educational Laboratory (U.S.) has identified what it calls "21st Century Skills," which includes digital age literacy (consisting of functional literacy, visual literacy, scientific literacy, technological literacy, information literacy, cultural literacy, and global awareness), inventive thinking, higher-order thinking and sound reasoning, effective communication, and high productivity.

The potential of ICTs to promote the acquisition of these skills is tied to its use as a tool for raising educational quality, including promoting the shift to a learner-centered environment.

How can the use of ICTs help improve the quality of education?

Improving the quality of education and training is a critical issue, particularly at a time of educational expansion. ICTs can enhance the quality of education in several ways: by increasing learner motivation and engagement, by facilitating the acquisition of basic skills, and by enhancing teacher training. ICTs are also transformational tools which, when used appropriately, can promote the shift to a learner-centered environment.

Motivating to learn

ICTs such as videos, television and multimedia computer software that combine text, sound, and colorful, moving images can be used to provide challenging and authentic content that will engage the student in the learning process. Interactive radio likewise makes use of sound effects, songs, dramatizations, comic skits, and other performance conventions to compel the students to listen and become involved in the lessons being delivered. More so than any other type of ICT, networked computers with Internet connectivity can increase learner motivation as it combines the media richness and interactivity of other ICTs with the opportunity to connect with real people and to participate in real world events.

Facilitating the acquisition of basic skills

The transmission of basic skills and concepts that are the foundation of higher order thinking skills and creativity can be facilitated by ICTs through drill and practice. Educational television programs such as *Sesame Street* use repetition and reinforcement to teach the alphabet, numbers, colors, shapes and other basic concepts. Most of the early uses of computers were for computer-based learning (also called computer-assisted instruction) that focused on mastery of skills and content through repetition and reinforcement. *(See section below on Computer-Based Learning.)*

Enhancing teacher training

ICTs have also been used to improve access to and the quality of teacher training. For example, institutions like the Cyber Teacher Training Center (CTTC) in South Korea are taking advantage of the Internet to provide better teacher professional development opportunities to in-service teachers. The government-funded CTTC, established in 1997, offers self-directed, self-paced Web-based courses for primary and secondary school teachers. Courses include "Computers in the Information Society," Education Reform," and "Future Society and Education." Online tutorials are also offered, with some courses requiring occasional face-to-face meetings. In China, large-scale radio and television-based teacher education has for many years been conducted by the China Central Radio and TV University, the Shanghai Radio and TV University and many other RTVUs in the country. At Indira Gandhi National Open University, satellite-based one-way video- and two-way audio-conferencing was held in 1996, supplemented by print-materials and recorded video, to train 910 primary school teachers and facilitators from 20 district training institutes in Karnataka State. The teachers interacted with remote lecturers by telephone and fax.

Electronic Tutorials to Enhance Learner Support at Universities Terbuka, Indonesia

Since its establishment in 1984 as the first distance and open learning institution in Indonesia, the Universitas Terbuka (Indonesian Open Learning University) has made great strides in making higher education available to Indonesians, having served more than 400,000 students nationwide in its 14 years of existence. The mandate of Universitas

Terbuka, however, is not only to expand educational opportunity but also to "improve[e] the quality of education and make it more relevant to national development needs." In its effort to address issues of quality in instruction, it has recently introduced the use of the Internet and a combination of facsimile and Internet technologies for student tutorials in 40 of its more than 700 courses on offer. These electronic tutorials are a supplement to more traditional tutorial models-including face-to-face, regular mail, radio and television-already employed by the university.

Two electronic tutorial models are being used: tutorials via email lists, and tutorials via a combination of email and fax messages. In the latter, tutors send email messages to a "fax gateway" which are then received by students as fax messages while student's messages are sent by fax and then converted to email messages to the tutors. While both models allow tutor-student and student-student interaction, the fax/Internet model is the more accessible of the two since fax services in Indonesia are cheaper than Internet access, and do not require students to have basic computing and emailing skills.

These two models were initially piloted over a two-semester period and results revealed low participation rates for both students and tutors. This was due partly to the lack of familiarity and comfort with using the technology and partly to more basic confusion over the purpose of the tutorials. Tutors also claimed that the limited availability of computers, lack of time and low student participation dampened their initial interest in electronic tutorials.

Thus, while Internet and fax technologies have the potential to enhance learning support at Universities Terbuka, practical steps must be taken to improve tutor-to-computer ratios, upgrade the computing and emailing skills of both academic staff and students, more aggressively promote the electronic tutorial model, and not least, collaborate with external institutions to create more Internet access points throughout Indonesia.

Source: *Tian Belawati, et al. Electronic Tutorials: Indonesian Experience; available from http://www.irrodl.org/content/v3.1/belawati_rn.html; Internet; accessed 7 August 2002.*

How can ICTs help transform the learning environment into one that is learner-centered?

Research has shown that the appropriate use of ICTs can catalyze the paradigmatic shift in both content and pedagogy that is at the heart of education reform in the 21st century. If designed and implemented properly, ICT-supported education can promote the acquisition of the knowledge and skills that will empower students for lifelong learning.

When used appropriately, ICTs-especially computers and Internet technologies- enable new ways of teaching and learning rather than simply allow teachers and students to do what they have done before in a better way. These new ways of teaching and learning are underpinned by constructivist theories of learning and constitute a shift from a teacher-centered pedagogy-in its worst form characterized by memorization and rote learning-to one that is learner-centered. *(See Table 2 for a comparison of a traditional pedagogy and an emerging pedagogy enabled by ICTs.)*

- **Active learning.** ICT-enhanced learning mobilizes tools for examination, calculation and analysis of information, thus providing a platform for student inquiry, analysis and construction of new information. Learners therefore learn as they do and, whenever appropriate, work on real-life problems in-depth, making learning less abstract and more relevant to the learner's life situation. In this way, and in contrast to memorization-based or rote learning, ICT-enhanced learning promotes increased learner engagement. ICT-enhanced learning is also "just-in-time" learning in which learners can choose what to learn when they need to learn it.

- **Collaborative learning.** ICT-supported learning encourages interaction and cooperation among students, teachers, and experts regardless of where they are. Apart from modeling real-world interactions, ICT-supported learning provides learners the opportunity to work with people from different cultures, thereby helping to enhance learners' teaming and communicative skills as well as their global awareness.
- **Creative Learning.** ICT-supported learning promotes the manipulation of existing information and the creation of real-world products rather than the regurgitation of received information.
- **Integrative learning**. ICT-enhanced learning promotes a thematic, integrative approach to teaching and learning. This approach eliminates the artificial separation between the different disciplines and between theory and practice that characterizes the traditional classroom approach.
- **Evaluative learning.** ICT-enhanced learning is student-directed and diagnostic. Unlike static, text- or print-based educational technologies, ICT-enhanced learning recognizes that there are many different learning pathways and many different articulations of knowledge. ICTs allow learners to explore and discover rather than merely listen and remember.

(3) The Uses of ICTs in Education

Education policymakers and planners must first of all be clear about what educational outcomes (as discussed above) are being targeted. These broad goals should guide the choice of technologies to be used and their modalities of use. The potential of each technology varies according to how it is used. Haddad and Draxler identify at least five levels of technology use in education:

presentation, demonstration, drill and practice, interaction, and collaboration.

Each of the different ICTs-print, audio/video cassettes, radio and TV broadcasts, computers or the Internet-may is used for presentation and demonstration, the most basic of the five levels. Except for video technologies, drill and practice may likewise be performed using the whole range of technologies. On the other hand, networked computers and the Internet are the ICTs that enable interactive and collaborative learning best; their full potential as educational tools will remain unrealized if they are used merely for presentation or demonstration.

How have radio and TV broadcasting been used in education?

Radio and television have been used widely as educational tools since the 1920s and the 1950s, respectively. There are three general approaches to the use of radio and TV broadcasting in education:

1) **Direct class teaching,** where broadcast programming substitutes for teachers on a temporary basis;
2) **School broadcasting,** where broadcast programming provides complementary teaching and learning resources not otherwise available; and
3) **General educational programming over community,** national and international stations which provide general and informal educational opportunities.

The most notable and best documented example of the *direct class teaching* approach is Interactive Radio Instruction (IRI).This consists of "ready-made 20-30 minute direct teaching and learning exercises to the classroom on a daily basis. The radio lessons, developed around specific learning objectives at particular levels of maths, science, health and languages in national curricula, are intended to improve the quality of classroom teaching and to act as a regular, structured aid to poorly trained classroom teachers in under-resourced schools." IRI projects have been implemented in Latin America and Africa. In Asia, IRI was first implemented in Thailand in 1980; Indonesia, Pakistan,

Bangladesh and Nepal rolled out their own IRI projects in the 1990s. What differentiates IRI from most other distance education programs is that its primary objective is to raise the quality of learning-and not merely to expand educational access-and it has had much success in both formal and non-formal settings. Extensive research around the world has shown that many IRI projects have had a positive impact on learning outcomes and on educational equity. And with its economies of scale, it has proven to be a cost-effective strategy relative to other interventions.

Mexico's *Telesecundaria* is another notable example of direct class teaching, this time using broadcast television. The programme was launched in Mexico in 1968 as a cost-effective strategy for expanding lower secondary schooling in small and remote communities.Perraton describes the programme thus:

Centrally produced television programs are beamed via satellite throughout the country on a scheduled basis (8 am to 2 pm and 2 pm to 8 pm) to Telesecundaria schools, covering the same secondary curriculum as that offered in ordinary schools. Each hour focuses on a different subject area and typically follows the same routine-15 minutes of television, then book-led and teacher-led activities. Students are exposed to a variety of teachers on television but have one home teacher at the school for all disciplines in each grade.

The design of the programme has undergone many changes through the years, shifting from a "talking heads" approach to more interactive and dynamic programming that "link[s] the community to the programme around the teaching method. The strategy meant combining community issues into the programs, offering children an integrated education, involving the community at large in the organization and management of the school and stimulating students to carry out community activities."

Assessments of Telesecundaria have been encouraging: drop out rates are slightly better than those of general secondary schools and significantly better than in technical schools. In Asia, the 44 radio and TV universities in China (including the China Central Radio and Television University), Universitas Terbuka in

Indonesia, and Indira Ghandi National Open University have made extensive use of radio and television, both for direct class teaching and for school broadcasting, to reach more of their respective large populations. For these institutions, broadcasts are often accompanied by printed materials and audio cassettes.

Japan's University of the Air was broadcasting 160 television and 160 radio courses in 2000. Each course consists of 15 45-minute lectures broadcast nationwide once a week for 15 weeks. Courses are aired over University-owned stations from 6 am to 12 noon. Students are also given supplemental print materials, face-to-face instruction, and online tutorials.

Often deployed with print materials, cassettes and CD-ROMS, school broadcasting, like *direct class teaching*, is geared to national curricula and developed for a range of subject areas. But unlike direct class instruction, school broadcasting is not intended to substitute for the teacher but merely as an enrichment of traditional classroom instruction. School broadcasting is more flexible than IRI since teachers decide how they will integrate the broadcast materials into their classes. Large broadcasting corporations that provide school broadcasts include the British Broadcasting Corporation Education Radio TV in the United Kingdom and the NHK Japanese Broadcasting Station. In developing countries, school broadcasts are often a result of a partnership between the Ministry of Education and the Ministry of Information.

General educational programming consists of a broad range of programme types-news programs, documentary programs, quiz shows, educational cartoons, etc.-that afford non-formal educational opportunities for all types of learners. In a sense, any radio or TV programming with informational and educational value can be considered under this type. Some notable examples that have a global reach are the United States-based television show *Sesame Street*, the all-information television channels *National Geographic* and *Discovery*, and the radio programme *Voice of America*. The *Farm Radio Forum*, which began in Canada in the 1940s and which has since served as a model for radio discussion programs worldwide, is another example of non-formal educational programming.

What is teleconferencing and what have been its educational uses?

Teleconferencing refers to "interactive electronic communication among people located at two or more different places." There are four types of teleconferencing based on the nature and extent of interactivity and the sophistication of the technology: 1) audio conferencing; 2) audio-graphic conferencing, 3) videoconferencing; and 4) Web-based conferencing.

Audio conferencing involves the live (real-time) exchange of voice messages over a telephone network. When low-bandwidth text and still images such as graphs, diagrams or pictures can also be exchanged along with voice messages, then this type of conferencing is called audio graphic. Non-moving visuals are added using a computer keyboard or by drawing/writing on a graphics tablet or whiteboard. *Videoconferencing* allows the exchange not just of voice and graphics but also of moving images. Videoconferencing technology does not use telephone lines but either a satellite link or television network (broadcast/cable). *Web-based conferencing*, as the name implies, involves the transmission of text, and graphic, audio and visual media via the Internet; it requires the use of a computer with a browser and communication can be both synchronous and asynchronous.

Teleconferencing is used in both formal and non-formal learning contexts to facilitate teacher-learner and learner-learner discussions, as well as to access experts and other resource persons remotely. In open and distance learning, teleconferencing is a useful tool for providing direct instruction and learner support, minimizing learner isolation. For instance, an audio graphic teleconferencing network between Tianjin Medical University in China and four outlying Tianjin municipalities was piloted in 1999 as part of a multi-year collaboration between Tianjin Medical University and the University of Ottawa School of Nursing funded by the Canadian International Development Agency. The audio graphic teleconferencing network aims to provide continuing education and academic upgrading to nurses in parts of Tianjin municipality where access to nursing education has been extremely limited. Other higher education institutions using teleconferencing in their online learning programs include the Open University of the United Kingdom, Unitar (University Tun Abdul Ruzak) in Malaysia, Open University of Hong Kong, and Indira Gandhi National Open University.

Promoting Learner-Centered Pedagogy through Computers

Project CHILD (Computers Helping Instruction and Learning Development) is a computer-integrated instruction programme developed in 1988 by the University of Florida for grades K-5 (pre-school and primary school).The programme focuses on three subject areas-reading, writing and mathematics. Each Project CHILD classroom has a learning station with between three to six computers. Butzin describes a typical Project CHILD classroom scenario thus:

- A class period begins with the teacher conducting a whole group lesson-let's says an introduction to fractions. After about 10 minutes of direct instruction, the students fan out to their first assigned learning station. Each station will have an activity related to fractions. Some stations will focus on skill practice, while others will focus on concept development. The station activities encompass kinesthetic (hands-on) learning as well as auditory and visual modalities. The teacher assigns instructional software at each computer station to tie in with the lesson objectives.
- As student groups work at their stations, the teacher circulates to help, probe, assess, and encourage students as they work on their assigned tasks. When a student finishes an activity...[s/he] moves on [to the next station] as needed. At the end of the period, the teacher gathers the class together for reflection and discussion on the day's activities.
- Teachers form cross grade subject-specific clusters (K-2 or 3-5) and work with children over three years, the better to judge

what software is appropriate for the subject and to allow students to learn at their own pace.

- Teachers are also given one year training on integration and are provided with research-based materials for lesson planning and technology integration.

Over a decade's worth of research on Project CHILD students have shown that they have scored consistently higher on standardized tests than their counterparts in traditional classrooms, and that the positive effects of the programme have increased over time. Project CHILD students also exhibited better attitudes toward school and learning, and better discipline as well. Project CHILD has been recognized as an effective programme by the U.S. Department of Education's National Diffusion Network and has received funding for nationwide expansion.

Source: *Butzin, S.,"Project CHILD: A Decade of Success for Young Children". Available Online http://www.thejournal.com/magazine/vault/A2882.cfm Accessed 22 June 2002.*

How have computers and the Internet been used for teaching and learning?

There are three general approaches to the instructional use of computers and the Internet, namely:

1. Learning about computers and the Internet, in which technological literacy is the end goal;
2. Learning with computers and the Internet, in which the technology facilitates learning across the curriculum; and
3. Learning through computers and the Internet, integrating technological skills development with curriculum applications.

What does it mean to learn about computers and the Internet?

Learning about computers and the Internet focuses on developing technological literacy. It typically includes:

- Fundamentals: basic terms, concepts and operations
- Use of the keyboard and mouse
- Use of productivity tools such as word processing, spreadsheets, data base and graphics programs

- Use of research and collaboration tools such as search engines and email
- Basic skills in using programming and authoring applications such as Logo or HyperStudio
- Developing an awareness of the social impact of technological change.

South Korean Universities Go Virtual

South Korea has one of the most advanced ICT infrastructures in the world-computer penetration is extensive, and broadband Internet access is one of the best globally. The pervasiveness of ICT use in South Korean society has spilled over to the higher educational system.

South Korea currently has 15 single-mode virtual universities that offer only ICT-based courses. Among these are the Korea Cyber University, the Korea Digital University, and the Open Cyber University. These universities specialize in lifelong learning and vocational education-a deliberate strategy to prevent unnecessary competition with more established campus-based universities- and have a combined projected enrolment of 17,200 in 2002. Courses offered cover a wide range of fields, including technology, management, law, languages, social sciences, education, and theology.

Online courses are also offered by over 100 of South Korea's dual-mode universities. Ewha Woman's University, for instance, offers Internet-based courses in language, e-learning, drug prevention, in-service teacher training, and Korean and Women's studies for local and foreign students as well as working adults.

The accelerated adoption of virtual education in South Korea was a result of deliberate planning by government.

It began in 1998 with the launch of the Virtual University Trial Project (VUTP).With 65 universities and five companies participating, the VUTP was designed to:

1) create a cost-effective virtual education system without diminishing quality;

2) develop and implement Web-based or other types of distance education courses;

3) identify appropriate policies and standards for running a virtual university; and

4) share experiences during the trial period.

Participating institutions experimented with various technologies: satellite broadcasting, videoconferencing, video-on-demand, intranets, and the Internet. Based on the VUTP experience, detailed criteria for establishing virtual universities in South Korea were added to the Lifelong Education Law.

Two years after the VUTP, however, policymakers and educators in South Korea continue to grapple with issues of quality management, capacity building, cost-savings, open access, and the appropriateness of the instructional model for adult learners.

Source: *Jung, In Sung," Virtual Education at the Tertiary Level: The Experience of Korea". Available Online http://www.TechKnow-Logia.org... Accessed 4 July 2002.*

What about learning with computers and the Internet?

Learning with the technology means focusing on how the technology can be the means to learning ends across the curriculum. It includes:

- Presentation, demonstration, and the manipulation of data using productivity tools
- Use of curriculum-specific applications types such as educational games, drill and practice, simulations, tutorials, virtual laboratories, visualizations and graphical representations of abstract concepts, musical composition, and expert systems
- Use of information and resources on CD-ROM or online such as encyclopedia, interactive maps and atlases, electronic journals and other references.

Technological literacy is required for learning with technologies to be possible, implying a two-step process in which students learn about the technologies before they can actually use them to learn. However, there have been attempts to integrate the two approaches.

What does learning through computers and the Internet mean?

Learning through computers and the Internet combines learning about them with learning with them. It involves learning the technological skills "just-in-time" or when the learner needs to learn them as he or she engages in a curriculum-related activity. For example, secondary school students who must present a report on the impact on their community of an increase in the price of oil for an Economics class may start doing research online, using spreadsheet and database programs to help organize and analyze the data they have collected, as well using a word processing application to prepare their written report.

How are computers and the Internet used in distance education?

Many higher educational institutions offering distance education courses have started to leverage the Internet to improve their programmer's reach and quality. The Virtual University of the Monterrey Institute of Technology in Mexico uses a combination of print, live and recorded broadcasts, and the Internet to deliver courses to students throughout Mexico and in several Latin American countries. Similarly, the African Virtual University, initiated in 1997 with funding support from the World Bank, uses satellite and Internet technologies to provide distance learning opportunities to individuals in various English-speaking and French-speaking countries throughout Africa.

At the University of the Philippines Open University, course materials are still predominantly printbased but online tutorials are becoming a convenient alternative to face-to-face tutorials especially for students unwilling or unable to go to UPOU's various physical learning centers. About 70-90% of UPOU's degree courses offer online tutorials as an option, while in several of its non-degree courses tutorials are conducted only online.

But even in Korea, where infrastructure is among the best in the world, and government has put considerable financial and other resources behind an ambitious ICT-based re-tooling of its educational system, challenges to online education persist. *(See Box 3.)*

Internet- and Web-based initiatives have also been developed at the secondary education level. The Virtual High School is a result of efforts of a nationwide consortium of school districts in the United States to promote the development and sharing of Web-based courses. In Canada, Open School offers a wide range of courses and resources to grades K-12 teachers and students that meet the requirements of the British Columbia curriculum. Course delivery is done through a mix of broadcast and video, while some courses are delivered totally online.

The biggest movers in e-learning, however, are not found within academe but in the private sector. John Chambers, CEO of Cisco, famously predicted that e-learning would be the next big killer application, and corporations are moving aggressively to fulfill this prediction. Merrill Lynch estimates that the combined higher education and corporate e-learning markets in the US will grow from $US2.3 billion in 2000 to US$18 billion in 2003, with corporate training accounting for almost two thirds of that growth. Indeed, the number of corporate universities has grown from 400 to 1,800 over the last 13 years. Corporate universities are primarily in-house organizations in large multinational companies that make use of videoconferencing and the Internet for employee training. If this rate of growth continues, the number of corporate universities will exceed the number of traditional universities by 2010. A parallel development in business is the growth of a new breed of companies that offer online training services to small- and medium-sized enterprises.

What is telecollaboration?

Online learning involving students logging in to formal courses online is perhaps the most commonly thought of application of the Internet in education. However, it is by no means the only application. Web-based collaboration tools, such as email, listservs,message boards, real-time chat, and Web-based conferencing, connect learners to other learners, teachers, educators, scholars and researchers, scientists and artists, industry leaders and politicians-in short, to any individual with access to the Internet who can enrich the learning process.

The organized use of Web resources and collaboration tools for curriculum appropriate purposes is called telecollaboration. Judi Harris defines *telecollaboration* as "an educational endeavor that involves people in different locations using Internet tools and resources to work together. Much educational telecollaboration is curriculum-based, teacher-designed, and teacher-coordinated. Most use e-mail to help participants communicate with each other. Many telecollaborative activities and projects have Web sites to support them." The best telecollaborative projects are those that are fully integrated into the curriculum and not just extra-curricular activities, those in which technology use enables activities that would not have been possible without it, and those that empower students to become active, collaborative, creative, integrative, and evaluative learners (see Table 1).There are currently hundreds of telecollaborative projects being implemented worldwide and many more that have either been completed or are in development.

One example is the Voices of Youth project developed by UNICEF. It encourages students to share their views on global issues, such as HIV/AIDS and child labour, with other youth and adults around the world through an electronic discussion forum. The Voices of Youth website also provides background information on the different discussion topics as well as resource materials to help teachers integrate the Voice of Youth discussions in their other classroom activities.

The International Telementor Program (ITP) links students with mentor-experts through email and discussion forums. Founded in 1995 with support from Hewlett Packard, ITP provides project-based online mentoring support to 5th to 12th grade and university students, especially from at-risk communities. The ITP telementor typically meets online with the student at least once every two weeks to answer questions, discuss key issues, recommend useful resources, and comment on student output. The teacher's role, on the other hand, is to provide support to both student and telementor, monitor the telementoring process, and track the student's progress.

Perhaps the most widely cited telecollaborative project is the Global Learning and Observations to Benefit the Environment (GLOBE) Program. GLOBE is a U.S. Government-sponsored programme launched in 1994 that links primary and secondary students and teachers from over 10,000 schools in more than 95 countries to the scientific research community. GLOBE gives students the opportunity to collaborate with scientists in conducting earth science research. Participating students periodically take measurements of the atmosphere, water, soils, and land cover at or near their schools, following strict protocols designed by GLOBE scientists. They then enter this data to a central Web-based database. The database may be accessed by scientists, researchers and the general public. GLOBE also provides teachers with guidelines and materials for structured learning activities that take off from the students' hands-on experience. Students can also go to the GLOBE website for visualizations of the data they and other students have collected.

(4) Issues in the Use of ICTs in Education

Effectiveness, cost, equity, and sustainability are four broad intertwined issues which must be addressed when considering the overall impact of the use of ICTs in education.

Does ICT-enhanced learning really work?

The educational effectiveness of ICTs depends on how they are used and for what purpose. And like any other educational tool or mode of educational delivery, ICTs do not work for everyone, everywhere in the same way.

Enhancing access

It is difficult to quantify the degree to which ICTs have helped expand access to basic education since most of the interventions for this purpose have been small-scale and under-reported. One exception is the television-based project Telesecundaria (discussed in a previous section), which in 1997-98 was serving over 750,000 junior secondary students in 12,000 centers in Mexico. In Asia and Africa, assessments of distance learning projects at the junior secondary level using a combination of print, taped, and broadcast technologies have been less conclusive, while at the primary level there is little evidence that ICT-based models have thrived. In higher education and adult training, there is some evidence that educational opportunities are being opened to individuals and groups who are constrained from attending traditional universities. Each of the 11 so-called mega-universities, the biggest and most well-established open and distance institutions in the world (which include the Open University of the United Kingdom, the Indira Gandhi National Open University of India, the China TV University System, the Universitas Terbuka of Indonesia, and the University of South Africa, among others) has an annual enrollment of more than 100,000, and together they serve approximately 2.8 million. Compare that with the 14 million combined enrollments of the 3,500 colleges and universities in the United States.

Raising quality

The impact of educational radio and television broadcasts on the quality of basic education remains an under-researched area, but what little research there is suggests that these interventions are as effective as traditional classroom instruction. Of the many educational broadcast projects, the Interactive Radio Instruction project has been the most comprehensively analyzed. Findings provide strong evidence of the project's effectiveness in raising the quality of education as demonstrated by increased scores on standardized tests as well as improved attendance.

In contrast, assessments of the use of computers, the Internet and related technologies for distance learning have been equivocal. Russell, in his comprehensive review of research, claims that there is "non significant difference" between the test scores of learners taking ICT-based distance learning courses and those receiving face-to-face instruction. However, others claim that such generalizations are inconclusive; pointing out that the large number of articles on ICT-based distance learning does not include original experimental research or case studies. Other critics argue that dropout rates are much higher when instruction is delivered at a distance via ICTs.

There have also been many studies that seem to support the claim that the use of computers enhances and amplifies existing curricula, as measured through standardized testing. Specifically, research shows that the use of computers as tutors, for drill and practice, and for instructional delivery, combined with traditional instruction, results in increases in learning in the traditional curriculum and basic skills areas, as well as higher test scores in some subjects compared to traditional instruction alone.

Students also learn more quickly, demonstrate greater retention, and are better motivated to learn when they work with computers. But there are those who claim that these represent modest gains and, in any case, much of the researches on which these claims are based are methodologically flawed. Research likewise suggests that the use of computers, the Internet, and related technologies, given adequate teacher training and support, can indeed facilitate the transformation of the learning environment into a learner-centered one. But these studies are criticized for being mostly exploratory and descriptive in nature and lacking in empirical rigor. There is as yet no strong evidence that this new learning environment fosters improved learning outcomes. What does exist are qualitative data based on observations and analysis of student and teacher perceptions that suggest a positive impact on learning.

One of the most critical problems in trying to assess the effectiveness of computers and the Internet as transformational tools is that standardized tests cannot capture the kinds of benefits that are expected to be gained in a learner-centered environment. Moreover, since technology use is fully integrated into the larger learning system, it is very difficult to isolate the technology variable and determine whether any observed gains are due to technology use or to some other factor or combination of factors.

How much does it cost?

Broadly speaking, educational television broadcasts and computer-based and online learning are more expensive than radio broadcasts. There is disagreement, however, over whether television broadcasts are cheaper than computer-based and online learning. That said, categorical assessments of cost-effectiveness are difficult to make because of lack of data, differences in programs, problems of generalization, and problems of quantification of educational outcomes and opportunity costs.

Speaking specifically of computers and the Internet, Blurton argues that "[w]hen considering whether ICT is "cost-effective" in educational settings, a definitive conclusion may not be possible for a variety of reasons. However, when considering the alternative of building more physical infrastructure, the cost savings to be realized from sharing resources, and the societal price of not providing access, ICT as a means of enabling teaching and learning appears to be an attractive and necessary alternative."

A common mistake in estimating the cost of a particular ICT educational application is to focus too much on initial fixed costs-purchase of equipment, construction or retrofitting of physical facilities, initial materials production, and the like. But studies of the use of computers in classrooms, for example, show that installation of hardware and retrofitting of physical facilities account for only between 40% to 60% of the full cost of using the computers over their lifetime, or its *total cost of ownership*. In fact, while at first glance it may seem that the initial purchase of hardware and software is the costliest part of the process, the bulk of the total cost of ownership is spread out over time, with annual maintenance and support costs (known as variable or recurrent costs) constituting between 30% to 50% of the total cost of hardware and software. The cost of professional development, another variable cost, also accumulates over time. For computer-based approaches the total cost of ownership therefore includes:

FIXED COSTS

- Retrofitting of physical facilities
- Hardware and networking
- Software
- Upgrades and replacement (in about five years)

VARIABLE OR RECURRENT COSTS

- Professional development
- Connectivity, including Internet access and telephone time
- Maintenance and support, including utilities and supplies

In order to determine cost efficiencies, fixed costs must be distinguished from variable costs, and the balance between the two understood. If the fixed costs of a technology project are high and its variable costs are low, then there will be cost advantages to scaling up. This is the case with general educational radio and television broadcasting. Programs such as Sesame Street and Discovery are more cost-efficient the larger their audience since the high cost of production is distributed over a larger viewer base while no staff expenditures are made for learner support.

On the other hand, the case of Telesecundaria in Mexico demonstrates that the impact of higher variable costs related to learner support may be offset if the scale of the project is sufficiently large to the point where per student costs compare favorably with those of traditional schools. Similarly, with the Interactive Radio Instruction project annual cost per student is estimated to fall from US$8.25 with 100,000 students to US$3.12 with 1,000,000. Obviously, these economies of scale may be achieved only in countries with large populations. Open and distance learning institutions have also achieved cost-effectiveness through economies of scale. Per student costs of the 11 mega-universities range from only 5% to 50% of the average of the traditional universities in their respective countries.

The introduction of computers represents additional costs for schools but without short-term cost advantages. Data on cost of computer use per student in both primary and secondary schools in fact suggest cost-ineffectiveness. In Chile, for example, cost per primary school student is between US$22 and US$83, with expenditures for computer use requiring 10% to 37% of the national primary school budget. In the U.S., computer investments accounted for 1.3% of total expenditure on schools, with annual cost per student at US$70.

Perraton and Creed suggest that these levels of cost support the argument against putting computers in every classroom, particularly in primary schools where there are no strong curricular arguments for investment in computers. In secondary schools, spending money on computers may be justified by the curriculum but this will come with significant increases in total school expenditure.

Another dimension of cost is location, or who will pay for what. In projects that involve computers connected to the Internet, either the school or student or both bear the variable costs related to operations such as maintenance, Internet service charges, and telephone line charges. In contrast, with radio programming the learner has to pay only for a radio and a set of batteries.

Is there equity of access to ICTs in education?

Given the wide disparities in access to ICTs between rich and poor countries and between different groups within countries, there are serious concerns that the use of ICTs in education will widen existing divisions drawn along economic, social, cultural, geographic, and gender lines. Ideally, one wishes for equal opportunity to participate. But access for different actors-both as users and producers-is weighted by their resources. Hence, initial differences are often reproduced, reinforced, and even magnified....A formidable challenge, therefore, continues to face planners of international education: how to define the problem and provide assistance for development.

The introduction of ICTs in education, when done without careful deliberation, can result in the further marginalization of those who are already underserved and/or disadvantaged. For example, women have less access to ICTs and fewer opportunities for ICT-related training compared to men because of illiteracy and lack of education, lack of time, lack of mobility, and poverty. Boys are more likely than girls to have access to computers in school and at home. Not surprisingly, boys tend to enjoy working with computers more than girls. As the American Association of University Women reports, "Girls have narrowed some significant gender gaps, but technology is now the new 'boys' club' in our nation's public schools. While boys programme and problem solve with computers, girls use computers for word processing..."

In an evaluation of its programme in four African countries, World links, an organization that promotes project-based, international telecollaboration activities among secondary school teachers and students from developing countries, it was found that despite efforts to make the programme gender neutral, gender inequalities in access persist in Uganda and Ghana. Furthermore, while girls benefited more from the programme in terms of improved academic performance and communication skills, boys were able to hone their technological skills more. A complex of economic, organizational, and sociocultural factors account for these differences: "High student-to-computer ratios and first comefirst serve policies do not favour girls (typically heavily outnumbered by boys at the secondary level), girls have earlier curfew hours and domestic chore responsibilities which limit their access time, and local patriarchal beliefs tend to allow boys to dominate the computer lab environment." Measures proposed to address this gender bias include encouraging schools to develop "fair use" policies in computer labs, conducting gender sensitivity sessions, and advocating for reducing the after-school duties of girls to give them more time to use the computer lab. Girls also need to have female role models to inspire them to participate in technology-related activities.

Providing access to ICTs is only one facet of efforts to address equity issues. Equal attention must be paid to ensuring that the technology is actually being used by the target learners and in ways that truly serve their needs. An ICT-supported educational programme that illustrates this wholistic approach is the *Enlace*

Quiché: Bilingual Education in Guatemala through Teacher Training programme. The programme seeks to establish and maintain bilingual education technology centers for educators, students, teachers, parents, and community members in Quiché and neighboring areas. The technical teams for each centre are composed of three students, two teachers, and the centre administrator, with at least one female student and one female teacher. Another objective of *Enlace Quiché* is the creation of multimedia bilingual educational materials that are anchored on the Mayan culture and that reflect a constructivist approach to learning. As the project website notes, this "demonstrate[s] that the technology can be used to know, to conserve, to disclose and to value local knowledge." The project thus illustrates a model for bridging the digital divide arising from the monopoly in Internet content provision by Western and English-speaking groups and from uneven capacities to make purposeful, relevant and critical use of digital resources (see section on language and content below).

Another example of a wholistic approach to ICT integration in education is a radio instruction project in Mongolia called the Gobi Women's Project. It seeks to provide literacy and numeracy instruction built around lessons of interest to around 15,000 nomadic women, and to create income opportunities for them. Among the programme topics are livestock rearing techniques; family care (family planning, health, nutrition and hygiene); income generation using locally available raw materials; and basic business skills for a new market economy.

Are ICT-enhanced educational projects sustainable?

One aspect of development programs that is often neglected is sustainability. The long history of development aid has shown that too many projects and programs start with a bang but all too soon fade out with a whimper, to be quickly forgotten. This is true for many ICT-based educational projects as well. In many instances, these projects are initiated by third party donors-such as international aid agencies or corporations-and not enough attention is paid to establishing a mechanism by which the educational institution or community involved can pursue the project on its own or in partnership with other stakeholders after the initiating donor exits. But cost and financing are not the only barriers to sustainability. According to Cisler, the sustainability of ICT-enabled programs has four components: social, political, technological, and economic.

Economic sustainability refers to the ability of a school and community to finance an ICT-enabled programme over the long term. Cost-effectiveness is key, as technology investments typically run high and in many cases divert funds from other equally pressing needs. Planners should look to the total cost of ownership *(see preceding discussion on cost)* and build lucrative partnerships with the community to be able to defray all expenses over the long term. The need to develop multiple channels of financing through community participation ties economic sustainability closely to social and political sustainability.

Social sustainability is a function of community involvement. The school does not exist in a vacuum, and for an ICT-enabled project to succeed the buy-in of parents, political leaders, business leaders and other stakeholders is essential. Innovation can happen only when all those who will be affected by it, whether directly or indirectly, know exactly why such an innovation is being introduced, what the implications are on their lives, and what part they can play in ensuring its success. ICT-enabled programs must ultimately serve the needs of the community. Thus community-wide consultation and mobilization are processes critical to sustainability. In short, a sense of ownership for the project must be developed among all stakeholders for sustainability to be achieved.

Political sustainability refers to issues of policy and leadership. One of the biggest threats to ICTenabled projects is resistance to change. If, for instance, teachers refuse to use ICTs in their classrooms, then use of ICTs can hardly take off, much less be sustained over the long term. Because of the innovative nature of ICT-enabled projects, leaders must have a keen understanding of the innovation process, identify the corresponding requirements for successful adoption, and harmonize plans and actions accordingly.

Technological sustainability involves choosing technology that will be effective over the long term. In a rapidly changing technology environment, this becomes a particularly tricky issue as planners must contend with the threat of technological obsolescence. At the same time, there is the tendency to acquire only the latest technologies (which is understandable in part because these are the models which vendors are likely to push aggressively) generally, however, planners should go with tried and tested systems; stability issues plague many of the latest technologies. Again, the rule of thumb is to let the learning objectives drive the technology choice and not vice versa-the latest technologies may not be the most appropriate tools for achieving the desired educational goals. When making technology decisions, planners should also factor in not just costs but also the availability of spare parts and technical support.

(5) Key Challenges in Integrating ICTs in Education

Although valuable lessons may be learned from best practices around the world, there is no one formula for determining the optimal level of ICT integration in the educational system. Significant challenges that policymakers and planners, educators, education administrators, and other stakeholders need to consider include educational policy and planning, infrastructure, language and content, capacity building, and financing.

What are the implications of ICT-enhanced education for educational policy and planning?

Attempts to enhance and reform education through ICTs require clear and specific objectives, guidelines and time-bound targets, the mobilization of required resources, and the political commitment at all levels to see the initiative through. Some essential elements of planning for ICT are listed below.

a. A rigorous analysis of the present state of the educational system. ICT-based interventions must take into account current institutional practices and arrangements. Specifically, drivers and barriers to ICT use need to be identified, including those related to curriculum and pedagogy, infrastructure, capacity-building, language and content, and financing.

a) The specification of educational goals at different education and training levels as well as the different modalities of use of ICTs that can best is employed in pursuit of these goals. This requires of the policymaker an understanding of the potentials of different ICTs when applied in different contexts for different purposes, and an awareness of priority education needs and financial and human resource capacity and constraints within the country or locality, as well as best practices around the world and how these practices can be adapted for specific country requirements.
b) The identification of stakeholders and the harmonizing of efforts across different interest groups.
c) The piloting of the chosen ICT-based model. Even the best designed models or those that have already been proven to work in other contexts need to be tested on a small scale. Such pilots are essential to identify, and correct, potential glitches in instructional design, implement ability, effectiveness, and the like.
d) The specification of existing sources of financing and the development of strategies for generating financial resources to support ICT use over the long term.

What are the infrastructure-related challenges in ICT-enhanced education?

A country's educational technology infrastructure sits on top of the national telecommunications and information infrastructure. Before any ICT-based programme is launched, policymakers and planners must carefully consider the following:

- In the first place, are appropriate rooms or buildings available to house the technology? In countries where there are many old school buildings, extensive retrofitting to ensure proper electrical wiring, heating/cooling and ventilation, and safety and security would be needed.

- Another basic requirement is the availability of electricity and telephony. In developing countries large areas are still without a reliable supply of electricity and the nearest telephones are miles away. Experience in some countries in Africa point to wireless technologies (such as VSAT or Very Small Aperture Terminal) as possible levers for leapfrogging. Although this is currently an extremely costly approach, other developing countries with very poor telecommunications infrastructure should study this option.
- Policymakers should also look at the ubiquity of different types of ICT in the country in general, and in the educational system (at all levels) in particular. For instance, a basic requirement for computer-based or online learning is access to computers in schools, communities, and households, as well as affordable Internet service.

In general, ICT use in education should follow use in society, not lead it. Education programs that use cutting-edge technologies rarely achieve long term success: It is cheaper, and easier, to introduce a form of technology into education, and keep it working, where education is riding on the back of large-scale developments by governments or the private sector. Television works for education when it follows rather than precedes television for entertainment; computers in schools can be maintained once commercial and private use has expanded to the point where there is an established service industry.

What are the challenges with respect to capacity-building?

Various competencies must be developed throughout the educational system for ICT integration to be successful.

Teachers. Teacher professional development should have five foci: 1) skills with particular applications; 2) integration into existing curricula; 3) curricular changes related to the use of IT (including changes in instructional design); 4) changes in teacher role; and 5) underpinning educational theories.76 Ideally, these should be addressed in pre-service teacher training and built on and enhanced in-service. In some countries, like Singapore, Malaysia, and the United Kingdom, teaching accreditation requirements include training in ICT use. ICTs are swiftly evolving technologies, however, and so even the most ICT fluent teachers need to continuously upgrade their skills and keep abreast of the latest developments and best practices.

Will ICTs Replace the Teacher?

The answer is a resounding NO! In fact, with the introduction of ICTs in the classroom, the teacher's role in the learning process becomes even more critical. What can and should change is the kind of role that the teacher plays. The role of students, in turn, also expands. And since ICTs can open up the classroom to the outside world, the community can also play a new role in the classroom.

As learning shifts from the "teacher-centered model" to a "learner-centered model", the teacher becomes less the sole voice of authority and more the facilitator, mentor and coach-from "sage on stage" to "guide on the side". The teacher's primary task becomes to teach the students how to ask questions and pose problems, formulate hypotheses, locate information and then critically assess the information found in relation to the problems posed.

And since ICT-enhanced learning is a new experience even for the teachers, the teachers become co-learners and discover new things along with their students. Additionally, it is not uncommon to see students in an ICT-enabled classroom assume both formal and informal roles as teachers of their peers and younger students, sometimes even of their own teachers. Teachers and students from different schools, subject-matter experts, parents, community and business leaders, politicians, and other interested parties also become involved in the learning process-as resource persons, critics, mentors, and cheerleaders. They also comprise a public, and hopefully critical, audience for students' work published on the Web or through other media.

Yet many teachers are reluctant to use ICTs, especially computers and the Internet. Hannafin and Savenye identify some of the reasons for this reluctance: poor software design, skepticism about the effectiveness of computers in improving learning outcomes, lack of administrative support, increased time and effort needed to learn the technology and how to use it for teaching, and the fear of losing their authority in the classroom as it becomes more learner-centered. These are all issues that must be addressed by both pre-service teacher education and in-service teacher professional development programs if schools and other educational institutions are to fully exploit the potential of computers and the Internet as educational tools.

At the in-service level, ICT teacher professional development (TPD) should be long-term, teacher-directed, and as flexible as possible. For many under-qualified, overworked, and underpaid teachers in developing countries, effective adoption of ICTs hinges on being given continuous opportunities to learn what they need to learn based on their specific circumstances and experience, when they have the time to learn it. Institutionalized incentives and support for teachers to pursue ICT TPD are also critical. This may take the form of promotions for teachers who innovate with (as opposed to merely using) ICTs in the classroom or simply making sure those teachers have adequate access to technology after training.

While the first focus-skills with particular applications-is self-evident, the four other foci are of equal, if not ultimately greater, importance. Research on the use of ICTs in different educational settings over the years invariably identify as a barrier to success the inability of teachers to understand why they should use ICTs and how exactly they can use ICTs to help them teach better.Unfortunately, most teacher professional development in ICTs are heavy on "teaching the tools" and light on "using the tools to teach."

Teacher anxiety over being replaced by technology or losing their authority in the classroom as the learning process becomes more learner-centered-an acknowledged barrier to ICT adoption-can be alleviated only if teachers have a keen understanding and appreciation of their changing role.

Education administrators. Leadership plays a key role in ICT integration in education. Many teacher- or student-initiated ICT projects have been undermined by lack of support from above. For ICT integration programs to be effective and sustainable, administrators themselves must be competent in the use of the technology, and they must have a broad understanding of the technical, curricular, administrative, financial, and social dimensions of ICT use in education.

Technical support specialists. Whether provided by in-school staff or external service providers, or both, technical support specialists are essential to the continued viability of ICT use in a given school. While the technical support requirements of an institution depend ultimately on what and how technology is deployed and used, general competencies that are required would be in the installation, operation, and maintenance of technical equipment (including software), network administration, and network security. Without on-site technical support, much time and money may be lost due to technical breakdowns.

In the Philippines, for example, one of the major obstacles to optimizing computer use in high schools has been the lack of timely technical support. In some extreme cases involving schools in remote areas, disabled computers take months to be repaired since no technician is available in the immediate vicinity and so the computers have to be sent to the nearest city hundreds of kilometers away.

Content developers. Content development is a critical area that is too often overlooked. The bulk of existing ICT-based educational material is likely to be in English (see section on language and content below) or of little relevance to education in developing countries (especially at the primary and secondary levels). There is a need to develop original educational content (e.g., radio programs, interactive multimedia learning materials on CD-ROM or DVD, Web-based courses, etc.), adapt existing content, and convert print-based content to digital media. These are tasks for which content development specialists such as instructional designers, scriptwriters, audio and video production specialists, programmers, multimedia course authors, and web-developers are needed. Like technical support specialists, content developers are highly skilled professionals and are not, with the exception of instructional designers, historically employed by primary and secondary schools. Many universities with distance education programs, and those who otherwise make use of ICTs, have dedicated technical support and content development units.

What challenges need to be addressed in the areas of language and content?

English is the dominant language of the Internet. An estimated 80% of online content is in English. A large proportion of the educational software produced in the world market is in English. For developing countries in the Asia-Pacific where English language proficiency is not high, especially outside metropolitan areas, this represents a serious barrier to maximizing the educational benefits of the World Wide Web.

Even in countries where English is a second language (such as Singapore, Malaysia, the Philippines, and India) it is imperative that teaching and learning materials that match national curriculum requirements and have locally meaningful content, preferably in the local languages, be developed. *(See Box 6.)* This would ensure that the Web is a genuinely multicultural space and that peoples of different cultures have an equal stake and voice in the global communities of learning and practice online. Particularly vulnerable to exclusion of this sort are isolated, rural populations, cultural minorities, and women in general. Thus attention must be paid to their special needs.

One encouraging trend has been the emergence of national and regional school networks, or School Nets, that facilitate the sharing of content and information-curriculum guides, teaching and learning resources, telecollaborative project registries, school and teacher directories, training curricula and materials, research and policy papers, technology management guides, and start-up toolkits, among others. Countries like Australia, France, Finland,

Japan, Canada, Thailand, Ghana, South Africa, and Zimbabwe, to name a few, all have national SchoolNets.The Enlaces programme in Latin America has linked schools from Spanish-speaking countries like Chile, Paraguay, Costa Rica, Colombia, and Peru. In Southeast Asia, efforts are currently underway to pilot School Nets in the Philippines, Indonesia, Cambodia, Laos, Myanmar and Vietnam, and to link these to existing national School Nets to create a region-wide ASEAN School Net.

In Web-based learning, technical standardization of content has also become a pressing issue. Standardization allows different applications to share content and learning systems. Specifications in content, structure, and test formats are proposed so that interoperability may exist between different management systems, resulting in some cost-efficiencies. Standards must be general enough to support all kinds of learning systems and content. Worth mentioning are initiatives conducted by the Instructional Management System (IMS), the Advanced Distributed Learning / Shareable Courseware Object Reference Model (ADL/SCORM) initiative, the Aviation Industry Computer Based Training Committee (AICC), and the European ARIADNE project, since some of the standards they have proposed are already being widely applied.

The ease by which Web-based educational content can be stored, transmitted, duplicated, and modified has also raised concerns about the protection of intellectual property rights. For instance, is intellectual, property rights violated when lectures broadcast over the television or on the Web incorporate pre-existing materials, or when students record educational broadcast on tape for later viewing? While schools and universities may already have agreements that expressly authorize the use of certain materials for classroom purposes, these agreements may not be broad enough to accommodate telecommunications transmission, videotape recording, or the distribution of course-related materials beyond the classroom setting.

The United Nations International World Intellectual Property Organization is leading international efforts in setting global standards for the protection of intellectual property rights that would not at the same time unduly curtail the accessing and sharing of information. For teachers and students, each of whom are potential publishers of multimedia materials that incorporate the works of others, information and training about the ethical use of intellectual property should be an important component of ICT-based programs.

What are the challenges related to financing the cost of ICT use?

One of the greatest challenges in ICT use in education is balancing educational goals with economic realities. ICTs in education programs require large capital investments and developing countries need to be prudent in making decisions about what models of ICT use will be introduced and to be conscious of maintaining economies of scale. Ultimately it is an issue of whether the value added of ICT use offsets the cost, relative to the cost of alternatives. Put another way, is ICT-based learning the most effective strategy for achieving the desired educational goals, and if so what is the modality and scale of implementation that can be supported given existing financial, human and other resources?

Content is King: Lessons from Thailand

Three years after its inception in 1995, School Net Thailand, a joint project of the National Electronics and Computer Technology Center (NECTEC), the Telephone Organization of Thailand, the Communications Authority of Thailand, and the Ministry of Education, found itself facing a challenge it had not entirely expected. Having built a network infrastructure for education in Thailand that connected 152 local secondary schools to the Internet, it discovered that schools hardly used the Internet as a tool for teaching and learning. It soon became apparent that the lack of quality educational online resources in the local language, Thai, was discouraging Internet use among teachers and students. SchoolNetThailand thus had to expand what had largely been a "universal access" programme to include content development-complemented by training-in the Thai language.

In September 1998, School Net Thailand commissioned Kasetstart University and the Institute for the Promotion of Teaching Science and Technology to create Thai language websites on secondary school-level Mathematics, Physics, Chemistry, Biology, Engineering, the Environment, and Computer Science. Collectively called the "Digital Library", these websites were launched a little over a year later. School Net Thailand also developed an easy-to-use web authoring application called the "Digital Library Tool Kit" that allowed teachers to create Web-based lessons in Thai. Teachers and students were also given instruction on web page development. By May 2001, the Digital Library already contained 1,113 lessons, created mostly by classroom teachers. Complementing the "Digital Library" project was the production of multimedia professional development materials called "Thai Teacher 2000" which included a printed manual, a video tape, and a CD-ROM. School Net Thailand's content development efforts also benefited from a national documentation project spearheaded by the Office of the National Cultural Commission called "Thai Cultural Information System." This programme was intended to, among others, collect information on Thai culture and disseminate this information through CD-ROMs and the Internet.

At present, School Net Thailand boasts of approximately 4,000 schools in its network, with over 900 of these with their own web pages in Thai. It expects to extend Internet service provision to the estimated 34,000 schools nationwide in the coming years and to continue to lead in local content development in Thailand.

Source:*NECTEC. (July 2002). ICT for Poverty Reduction: Examples of Programmes/Projects in Thailand,pp. 6-13.*

The ease by which Web-based educational content can be stored, transmitted, duplicated, and modified has also raised concerns about the protection of intellectual property rights. For instance, is intellectual, property rights violated when lectures broadcast over the television or on the Web incorporate pre-existing materials, or when students record educational broadcast on tape for later viewing?

While schools and universities may already have agreements that expressly authorize the use of certain materials for classroom purposes, these agreements may not be broad enough to accommodate telecommunications transmission, videotape recording, or the distribution of course-related materials beyond the classroom setting.

The United Nations International World Intellectual Property Organization is leading international efforts in setting global standards for the protection of intellectual property rights that would not at the same time unduly curtail the accessing and sharing of information. For teachers and students, each of whom are potential publishers of multimedia materials that incorporate the works of others, information and training about the ethical use of intellectual property should be an important component of ICT-based programs.

What are the challenges related to financing the cost of ICT use?

One of the greatest challenges in ICT use in education is balancing educational goals with economic realities. ICTs in education programs require large capital investments and developing countries need to be prudent in making decisions about what models of ICT use will be introduced and to be conscious of maintaining economies of scale. Ultimately it is an issue of whether the value added of ICT use offsets the cost, relative to the cost of alternatives. Put another way, is ICT-based learning the most effective strategy for achieving the desired educational goals, and if so what is the modality and scale of implementation that can be supported given existing financial, human and other resources?

Whyte suggests the following potential sources of money and resources for ICT use programs:

1. Grants
2. Public subsidies
3. Private donations, fund-raising events
4. In-kind support (e.g., equipment, volunteers)
5. Community support (e.g. rent-free building)

6. Membership fees
7. Revenues earned from core business:
   - Connectivity (phone, fax, Internet, web pages)
   - Direct computer access to users
   - Office services (photocopying, scanning, audiovisual aids
8. Revenues earned from ancillary activities:
   - Business services (word-processing, spreadsheets, budget preparation, printing, reception services)
   - Educational services (distant education, training courses)
   - Community services (meeting rooms, social events, local information, remittances from migrant workers)
   - Telework and consulting
   - Specialized activities (telemedicine)
   - Sales (stationary, stamps, refreshments, etc.)

Private sector-public sector partnerships to either pilot or fast track ICT-based projects are a strategy that has gained currency among Ministries of Education in developing countries. These partnerships take many forms, including private sector grants with government counterpart contributions, donations of equipment and education-related content by corporations to state-run schools, and the provision of technical assistance for planning, management, and strengthening human resources at the grassroots level. Multilateral organizations and international aid agencies have also driven many of the most significant ICT in education efforts in the developing world.

But the financial litmus test of ICT-based programs is survival after donor money has run out. Many ICTbased education programs funded by aid agencies or by corporations could not be sustained because government failed to step in with the necessary financing; nor were the local communities in a position to generate the resources needed to continue these programs. This was the case with some of the Interactive Radio Instruction projects initiated by USAID. Therefore, a two-fold strategy is key: government support and local community mobilization.

Will ICT use be the silver bullet that will rid a developing country of all of its educational problems?

If there is one truism that has emerged in the relatively brief history of ICT use in education, it is this: It is not the technology but how you use it! Put another way: "How you use technology is more important than if you use it at all...[and] unless our thinking about schooling changes along with the continuing expansion of [ICTs] in the classroom then our technology investment will fail to live up to its potential."

Technology then should not drive education; rather, educational goals and needs, and careful economics, must drive technology use. Only in this way can educational institutions in developing countries effectively and equitably address the key needs of the population, to help the population as a whole respond to new challenges and opportunities created by an increasingly global economy. ICTs, therefore, cannot by themselves resolve educational problems in the developing world; as such problems are rooted in well entrenched issues of poverty, social inequality, and uneven development. What ICTs as educational tools can do, if they are used prudently, is enable developing countries to expand access to and raise the quality of education. Prudence requires careful consideration of the interacting issues that underpin ICT use in the school-policy and politics, infrastructure development, human capacity, language and content, culture, equity, cost, and not least, curriculum and pedagogy.

References

1. US Department of Labor (1999), *Futurework—Trends and Challenges for Work in the 21st Century. Quoted in EnGauge,*"21st Century Skills," North Central Regional Educational Laboratory; available from http://www.ncrel.org/engauge/skills/21skills.htm; accessed 31 May 2002.
2. For a convincing argument for the need to transform notions of "schooling" in light of technology driven social change see Thornburg, David (2000),"Technology in K-12 Education: Envisioning a New Future"; available from http://www.air-dc.org/forum/abthornburg.htm; accessed 3 July 2002.

3. International Labour Organization," Learning and Training for Work in the Knowledge Society;" available from http://www.Ilo.org/public/English/employment/skills/ recommit/report; accessed 31 May 2002, p. 5.
4. Blurton, C.,"New Directions of ICT-Use in Education". Available online http://www.unesco.org/education/ educprog/lwf/dl/edict.pdf; accessed 7 August 2002.
5. See for example Cuban, L. (1986), *Teachers and Machines: The Classroom Use of Technology Since 1920* (New York: Teachers College Press).
6. Potashnik,M.and J.Capper,"Distance Education: Growth and Diversity;" available from http://www.worldbank. org/fandd/english/pdfs/0398/0110398.pdf; accessed 14 August 2002.
7. See Taghioff, Daniel (April 2001),"Seeds of Consensus—The Potential Role for Information and Communication Technologies in Development: Empowerment, Appropriateness and Measuring if Needs Really Get Met;" available from http://www.btinternet.com/~daniel.taghioff/index.html; accessed 14 August 2002.
8. http://www.open.ac.uk
9. http://www.ignou.ac.in
10. The Commonwealth of Learning," An Introduction to Open and Distance Learning"; available from http://www.col.org/ODLIntro/introODL.htm; accessed 14 August 2002.
11. Quoted in Founts, Jeffrey T. (February 2000),"Research on Computers and Education: Past, Present and Future"; available from http://www.gatesfoundation.org/nr/dpwnloads/ ed/evaluation/Computer_Research_Summary.pdf; accessed 30 October 2002, p. 11.
12. World Bank (1998), *The World Development Report 1998/99. Quoted in Blurton, C., New Directions of ICT-Use in Education.*
13. EnGauge. North Central Regional Educational Laboratory; available from http://www.ncrel.org/engauge/skills/21skills.htm; accessed 31 May 2002.
14. Haddad,Wadi D. and Jurich, Sonia (2002),"ICT for Education: Potential and Potency", in Haddad,W. & Drexler, A. (eds),T*echnologies for Education: Potentials, Parameters, and Prospects* (Washington DC: Academy for Educational Development and Paris: UNESCO), pp. 34-37.
15. Jung, I.," Issues and Challenges of Providing Online In-service Teacher Training: Korea's Experience"; available from http://www.irrodl.org/content/v2.1/jung.pdf; accessed 4 August 2002.

16. Carnoy,Martin, et al. (June 2, 2001),"Distance Education in China: A Discussion of the History, Challenges and Implications for China in the 21st Century"; available from http://ldt.stanford.edu/~yokonaga/portfolio/ed236x/China.jjy.htm; accessed 4 August 2002.
17. http://www.ignou.ac.in. See also Asian Development Bank (1997), *Distance Education for Primary School Teachers: Papers and Proceedings of the Regional Seminar on Distance Education* (Manila: Asian Development Bank).
18. International Center for Distance Learning,"Universitas Terbuka/Indonesian Open Learning University"; available from http://www-icdl.open.ac.uk/ instResult.ihtml?inst_id=5777&p=1; accessed 14 August 2002.
19. See for example Bransford, J. (ed.) (1999), H*ow People Learn: Brain, Mind, Experience, and School* (Washington,DC: National Research Council).
20. Haddad,Wadi D. & Alexandra Drexler (2002),"The Dynamics of Technologies for Education", in Haddad,W. & Drexler, A. (eds.) *Technologies for Education: Potentials, Parameters, and Prospects* (Washington DC: Academy for Educational Development and Paris: UNESCO), p. 9.
21. Perraton, H. and C. Creed," Applying New Technologies and Cost-Effective Delivery Systems in Basic Education"; available from http://unesdoc.unesco.org/images/ 0012/001234/12348 2e.pdf; accessed 31 May 2002. Perraton and Creed use the term "general children's programming" to refer to the broad target audience of basic education. Although their discussion is limited to this level of education, the broadcasting approaches they identify may also be applied to other educational levels.
22. Ibid, p. 13.
23. TechnKnowLogia,"Are You Talkin' to Me?: Interactive Radio Instruction"; available from http://www.techknowlogia.org/TKL_active_pages2/CurrentArticles/main.asp? Issue Number=2& File Type=PDF&ArticleID=46; accessed 29 May 2002.
24. Bosch, A.," Interactive Radio Instruction for Mathematics: Applications and Adaptations from Around the World"; available from http://www.techknowlogia.org/TKL_active_pages2/CurrentArticles/main.asp?FileType=HTML&Arti cleID=255; accessed 15 August 2002, p. 45.
25. *Ibid*, pp. 46-49.
26. Perraton, H. and C. Creed," Applying New Technologies..."

27. UNESCO,"Telesecundaria,Mexico"; available from http://www.unesco.org/education/educprog/lwf/protfolio/abstract8.htm; accessed 15 August 2002, p. 2.
28. Perraton, H. and C. Creed," Applying New Technologies...
29. Iwanaga, M.,"The Present and the Future of Multimedia in Japan's Open Learning"; available from http://www.ouhk.edu.hk/cridal/gdenet/Technology/technology.html; accessed 11 January 2002.
30. Nwaerondu, N.G. and G.Thompson,"The Use of Educational Radio in Developing Countries: Lessons from the Past" ; available from http://www.clrec.org/nwaeronduthompson; accessed 3 May 2002, pp. 2-3.
31. Rao,V. Rama,"Audio Teleconferencing—A Technological Prescription for Interactive Learing"; available from http://www.clrec.org/rama; accessed 14 August 2002.
32. Edwards, N."Development and Integration of Web-based Technology in Distance Education for Nurses in China: A Pilot Study"; available from http://www.clerc.org/ edwardsn; accessed 9 June 2002.
33. Richmond, Ron. *Integration of Technology in the Classroom: An Instructional Perspective.* SSTA Research Centre Report #97-02; available from http://www.ssta.sk.ca/ research/technology/97-02.htm#BIBLIOGRAPHY; accessed 30 October 2002.
34. Ibid
35. Ibid.
36. Dirr, R.,"The Development of New Organizational Arrangements in Virtual Learning", in *The Changing Faces of Virtual Education*; available from http://www.col.org/virtualed/virtual2pdfs/Virtual2_complete.pdf; accessed 7 August 2002
37. Moe, M. and H. Blodget,"The Knowledge Web". Cited in A.Bates,"The Continuing Evolution of ICT Capacity: Implications for Education", in Glen M.Farrell (ed.), *The Changing Faces of Virtual Education; available from* http://www.col.org/virtualed/virtual2pdfs/Virtual2_complete.pdf; accessed 7 August 2002.
38. Bates, A." The Continuing Evolution of ICT Capacity: Implications for Education", in Glen M.Farrell (ed.), *The Changing Faces of Virtual Education*; available from http://www.col.org/virtualed/virtual2pdfs/Virtual2_complete.pdf; accessed 7 August 2002.
39. Web-based Education Commission," The Power of the Internet for Learning"; available from
40. http://www.ed.gov/offices/AC/WBEC/Final Report/WBEC Report.pdf; accessed 12 April 2002.
41. Ibid.

42. Harris, Judi," First Steps in Telecollaboration"; available from http://ccwf.cc.utexas.edu/~jbharris/Virtual-Architecture/Articles/First-Steps.pdf; accessed 6 March 2002, p. 1.
43. http://www.unicef.org/voy
44. http://www.telementor.org
45. http://www.globe.org
46. Perraton, H. and C. Creed," Applying New Technologies...", p. 38-39. Potashnik, M. and J. Capper. (1998)."Distance Education...", p. 42, 44.
47. Hannafin, R.D., & Savenye, S. (1993).Technology in the classroom...
48. Perraton, H. and C. Creed," Applying New Technologies...", p. 38-39.
49. Russel,T.L (1999). *The no significant difference phenomenon* (5th ed.). Raleigh NC: North Carolina State University.
50. Merisotis, Jamie P. and Ronald A. Phipps (1999,May/June),What's the Difference? Outcomes of Distance vs. Traditional Classroom-Based Learning, in *Change*, pp. 13-17.
51. Fouts, J. (February 2002). Research on Computers and Education: Past, Present and Future; available from http://www.gatesfoundation.org/nr/downloads/ed/evaluation/ Computer_Research_Summary.pdf; accessed 30 October 2002.
52. Ibid.
53. Blurton, C.,"New Directions of ICT-Use in Education", p. 21.
54. See for example, Blurton, C.,"New Directions of ICT-Use in Education" and Perraton, H. and C. Creed, "Applying New Technologies..."
55. Blurton, C.,"New Directions of ICT-Use in Education", p. 20.
56. Ibid., p. 24.
57. Consortium for School Networking," Taking TCO to the Classroom: A School Administrator's Guide to Planning for the Total Cost of New Technology"; available from http://ctap.fcoe.k12.ca.us/ctap/dhs3.4/tco2class.pdf; accessed 3 February 2002, p. 10.
58. Adkins,D. (1999),"Cost and Finance," in Dock, A. and Helwig, J. (eds.), *Interactive Radio Instruction: Impact, Sustainability, and Future Directions* (Washington DC:World Bank Human Development Network Education Group, Education and Technology Team/USAID Advancing Basic Education and Literacy Project, Education Development Center). Cited in Perraton, H. and C. Creed," Applying New Technologies...,"p. 40.
59. Potashnik, M. and J. Capper. (1998)."Distance Education...", p. 44.
60. Perraton, H. and C. Creed," Applying New Technologies...,"pp. 40-41.

61. Orivel, F. (2000),"Finance, Costs and Economics", in J.Bradley and C.Yates (eds.), *Basic Education at a Distance: World Review of Distance Education and Learning,* Vol. 2 (London: Routledge).
62. Ibid, p. 41.
63. Hernes,G. (2002),"Emerging Trends in ICT and Challenges to Educational Planning," in Haddad,W. and A. Drexler (eds.), *Technologies for Education: Potentials, Parameters, and Prospects* (Washington DC: Academy for Educational Development and Paris:UNESCO),p. 25.
64. Tandon,N. (November 1998),"Distance Education in the Commonwealth Countries of Asia," Appendix to Commonwealth of Learning, *Barriers to Information and Communication Technologies Encountered by Women: Summary Report*; available from http://www.col.org/wdd/BarriersICT_Asia_Report.pdf; accessed 14 September 2002, p. 44.
65. Mark, J."Beyond Equal Access: Gender Equity in Learning with Computers"; available from http://www.edc.org/WomensEquity/pubs/digests/digest-beyond.html; accessed 23 October 2002.
66. AAUW Education Foundation (14 October 1998),"Technology Gender Gap Develops While Gaps in Math and Science Narrow, AAUW Foundation Report Shows" [Press Release]; available from http://www.auuw.org/2000/ggpr.html.Quoted in Blurton, C.,"New Directions of ICT-Use in Education", p.44.
67. http://www.world-links.org
68. Gadio, C.M. (November 2001),"Exploring the Gender Impact of the World Links Program: Summary of the Findings of an Independent Study Conducted in Four African Countries"; available from http://www.world-links.org/english/assets/ gender_study_summary.pdf; accessed 6 December 2002, p. 1.
69. Ibid., p. 2.
70. Haddad,W. and S. Jurich (2002)."ICT for Education: Potential and Potency", p. 52.
71. http://www.enlacequiche.org.gt/english/vision.htm
72. "The Gobi Women's Project of Mongolia: Portfolio"; available from http://www.unesco.org/education/ educprog/lwf/doc/portfolio/case1.htm; accessed 16 January 2003.
73. S. Cisler,"Planning for Sustainability: How to Keep Your ICT Project Running"; available from http://www2.ctcnet.org/ctc/Cisler/sustain.doc; accessed 4 August 2002.
74. Hawkins, R.,"Ten Lessons for ICT and Education in the Developing

World"; available from http://www.cid.harvard.edu/cr/pdf/gitrr2002_ch04.pdf; accessed 7 August 2002, p. 40.
75. Perraton, H. and C. Creed," Applying New Technologies...", p. 41.
76. MacDougall, A. and D. Squires (1997),"A framework for reviewing teacher professional development programmes in information technology". Cited in Blurton, C.,"New Directions of ICT-Use in Education", p.29.
77. World Links for Development. Phase II: Telecollaborative Learning Projects. Training Manual, June 2001,
78. Ibid.
79. Hannafin, R.D., and S. Savenye. (1993),"Technology in the Classroom: The Teacher's New Role and Resistance to It, in *Educational Technology*, 33 (6), 26-31.
80. Tinio,V. (2002),"Survey of ICT Utilization in Philippine Public High Schools: Preliminary Findings" [Unpublished Manuscript].
81. Anzalone, Stephen,"ICTs to Support Learning in Classrooms in SEAMEO Countries: At What Costs?". Paper prepared for SEAMEO conf. In Bangkok, March 26-9, 2001.
82. Salomon, K.,"A Primer on Distance Learning and Intellectual Property Issues"; available from http://www.teletrain.com/copyrigh.htm#3.student%20Waivers; accessed 4 August 2002, p.5.
83. Blurton, C.,"New Directions of ICT-Use in Education", p. 35.
84. Whyte, A.," Assessing Community Telecentres. Guidelines for Researchers". cited in S. Cisler, "Planning for Sustainability..."
85. Thornburg,D.,"Technology in K-12 Education...", p. 1.

For Further Reading

1. Bates, A.W. 2000. *Managing Technological Change: Strategies for University and College Leaders.* San Francisco: Jossey Bass.
2. Brown, J.S. and P.Duguid. 2000. *The Social Life of Information.* Boston MA:Harvard Business School Press.
3. Carlson, S. and C. T. Gadio. 2002. "Teacher Professional Development in the Use of Technology", in Haddad, W. and A. Drexler (eds). *Technologies for Education: Potentials, Parameters, and Prospects.* Washington DC: Academy for Educational Development and Paris: UNESCO.
4. Cuban, L. 2002. *Oversold and Underused: Computers in the Classroom.* Cambridge MA: Harvard University Press.
5. Daniel, J. 1996. *Mega Universities and Knowledge Media: Technology Strategies for Higher Education.* London: Kogan Page.
6. Haddad,W. 1994. *The Dynamics of Education Policymaking: Case*

Studies of Burkina Faso, Jordan, Peru, and Thailand. EDI Development Policy Case Series, Analytical Case Studies No. 10.Washington DC:The World Bank.

7. Steffe, L. P. and J.Gale.1995. *Constructivism in Education.* Hillsdale, NJ: Lawrence Erlbaum.
8. Rusten, E. and H. Hudson. 2002. "Infrastructure: Hardware, Networking, Software, and Connectivity", in Haddad, W. and A. Drexler (eds). *Technologies for Education: Potentials, Parameters, and Prospects.* Washington DC: Academy for Educational Development and Paris: UNESCO.

Index

Z